D1558592

PURCHASING MANAGEMENT

Guide to

SELECTING SUPPLIERS

William Obie Ford

PRENTICE HALL
Englewood Cliffs, New Jersey 07632

Prentice-Hall International (UK) Limited, *London*
Prentice-Hall of Australia Pty. Limited, *Sydney*
Prentice-Hall Canada, Inc., *Toronto*
Prentice-Hall Hispanoamericana, S.A., *Mexico*
Prentice-Hall of India Private Limited, *New Delhi*
Prentice-Hall of Japan, Inc., *Tokyo*
Simon & Schuster Asia Pte. Ltd., *Singapore*
Editora Prentice-Hall do Brasil, Ltda., *Rio de Janeiro*

10 9 8 7 6 5 4 3 2 1

Library of Congress Cataloging-in-Publication Data

Ford, William Obie.
Purchasing management guide to selecting suppliers / William Obie Ford.
p. cm.
Includes index.
ISBN 0-13-742594-5
1. Purchasing—Management. 2. Industrial procurement. I. Title.
HF5437.F59 1993
658.7'22—dc20 93-29644
CIP

The author and publisher are grateful for permission to use the following material: To Zachary R. Chaky, Jr., for permission to reprint his letter, dated March 5, 1992, on Pilot Vendor Programs; to Reacond Associates for Robinair's "No Hassle" policy and for the Information sheet on C&R; to Aubrey Fulford for permission to quote from a letter dated May 5, 1984, on Supplier Selection and Evaluation Programs; and to Malco Products, Inc., for Malco Products, Inc., Policy Statements.

ISBN 0-13-742594-5

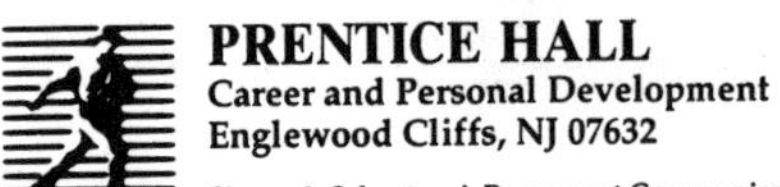

Printed in the United States of America

About the Author

WILLIAM O. FORD is an independent specialist in forecasting, purchasing, and inventory control, with a diverse background of academic and practical experience in aerospace, manufacturing, and distribution. His practical experience includes purchasing management, inventory control management, market research analysis, production forecasting, shipping, receiving, warehouse management, regional management, and lecturing, entry level to advanced theory. Mr. Ford holds an MBA degree from the University of Houston and taught Operations Management at the university level. His practical experience includes design and implementation of customized, automated forecasting and purchasing systems, automatic replenishment systems for branch inventories, and computer systems for cycle counting inventory. Mr. Ford has been affiliated with Ling-Temco-Vought, Rockwell International, Dresser Industries, Mark Controls, Thermal Supply, and Pameco.

Mr. Ford was the first to pioneer and implement a successful supplier evaluation and selection program.

His professional certifications are with the American Production and Inventory Control Society (CPIM) and the National Association of Purchasing Managers (C.P.M.)

WHAT THIS GUIDE WILL DO FOR YOU

Millions of dollars are wasted each year because of poor matches between buyer and seller. Supplier performance affects every person in the manufacturer's distribution chain and your company's profits.

Distributors and manufacturers that are striving to achieve and maintain quality images can no longer accept below-par performance from suppliers.

This book describes in detail how to achieve performance excellence in every phase of your business, whether you are in distribution or manufacturing, by establishing a proven supplier evaluation and selection program. The integrity of a working program such as this will pay dividends if you are willing to meet the challenge.

This book is the most current and authoritative guide on supplier evaluation and selection. It is written to help you understand the importance of developing and maintaining supplier/manufacturer/distributor/end-user communication in today's competitive marketplace. This book will show you:

- How to identify and document the need for a supplier evaluation and selection program (Chapter 1)
- How to audit manufacturing facilities (Chapter 2)
- How to reconcile end users' perceived product value to manufacturers' idea of product quality (Chapter 3)
- How to establish sales representation needs by measuring the performance of supplier representatives (Chapter 4)
- How to measure the effectiveness of product pricing (Chapter 5)
- How to monitor key technical issues that affect overall supplier performance (Chapter 6)
- How to set and use standards for measuring supplier performance (Chapter 7)
- How to select suppliers for evaluation (Chapter 8)
- How to select an evaluation team for grading supplier performance (Chapter 9)
- How to establish data documentation and collection
- How to grade suppliers (Chapter 10)
- How to handle supplier challenges (Chapter 11)
- How to recognize top performers (Chapter 12)

Throughout the book, information is reinforced by actual case examples, charts, and graphs. This book is an indispensable guide to an effective method for continual, controlled, constructive change in supplier/manufacturer/distributor/end-user relationships.

W.O. Ford

ABOUT THE SUPPLIER EVALUATION AND SELECTION PILOT PROGRAM

This book is based on a pilot program that was designed and implemented more than twelve years ago in Houston, Texas. It has many of the author's experiences and actual results of the original program throughout the text.

The original program was actually a control program. However, it didn't take long for those involved to recognize the potential the program had as a method to establish the 4 Cs—*continual, controlled, constructive change*—by improving partnerships with suppliers.

The program was continually updated and improved during 1980 through 1992, to reach the status of being the best Supplier Evaluation and Selection Program for the manufacturing and distribution industries.

The Supplier Evaluation and Selection Program was tried and proved to be a very effective means to performance improvement with outstanding results. The implementation of such a program will actually make an investment in your suppliers by helping them strive for performance excellence. There will be very tangible results in this investment—your suppliers will begin investing in you!

Acknowledgments

I would like to express my sincere appreciation to all the manufacturers, distributors, and their reps who met the challenge for performance excellence during the Pilot Program. The partnerships we developed were outstanding, and I still consider them among my greatest assets.

I also want to especially thank Joyce, my encourager.

CONTENTS

PART ONE

Supplier Evaluation Criteria

How Do Your Suppliers Rate in Terms of Total Reliability?

CHAPTER 1

PARTNERING: IMPROVING COMMUNICATION WITH SUPPLIERS AND LOWERING THE TOTAL COST OF PRODUCTS AND SERVICES

The art of communication, the personal relationship between the supplier and customer and the manufacturer and distributor, has disintegrated until it has become almost nonexistent. Thirty-five years ago it was not uncommon for businesses to be in entrepreneurial hands where the boss was on a first-name basis with employees, customers, and suppliers. It was not unusual for a distributor to call the president of a supplying company to get problems solved. The expansion of business, the increasing demands of a global economy, the speed with which these events took place, and the changes in technology have strenuously tested management. As a result, a constant decline in responsiveness to market needs has become apparent. The competitive edge companies had by using computers to assist them in forecasting, production, other types of material control, and accounting is disappearing because computers have become standard in business operations. These depersonalization and technical trends have been major factors in the loss of meaningful two-way communication—the key ingredient to successful business relationships or partnering.

The loss of communication goes even deeper than supplier/customer relations. Many industries are changing rapidly as new managers move into areas they know very little about. Takeover specialists are moving into companies without insight into supplier/customer relationships and without the people skills to manage long-term business relationships and continual, controlled, constructive changes.

For example, the wholesale distribution industry—a highly concentrated industry with strong personal ties among companies and people within companies—has been changing rapidly in the past few years.

A well-known wholesale distribution company that I had the privilege of doing business with spent several years establishing sound partnerships with suppliers. This company had a team of people on its staff who were unmatched in their abilities to manage company assets.

The owner of this company decided to retire and put the company up for sale.

A holding company purchased the firm. Not only was its knowledge about this particular industry limited, it did not bring in new management from the wholesale distribution industry. The results were devastating.

Management style went from asset management to cash flow management. Communication and partnership relations with suppliers were abandoned as depersonalization began to take place.

Within three years, long-established relationships were ruined, and serious problems within the organization began to surface. Cash flow became tighter, suppliers became alienated, and long-time employees became dissatisfied and began to leave the company. Within five years, the wholesale distribution company was on the brink of bankruptcy.

Once again, the company experienced management change, and the depersonalization process continued. Employee ranks continued to be diminished, sales continued to set new all-time lows, and market share was severely decreased.

This company, which once was one of the top 50 wholesale distributors in the nation, not only lost its reputation as a quality wholesale distributor focused on performance excellence, it had been run into the ground by a management that was not interested in cultivating manufacturer/supplier/distributor/end-user relationships.

The keys to the success of this company—people and relationships within and without—were completely overlooked with the new management takeover. The company could not survive without continually developing quality partnerships with open communication.

Unfortunately, this is not an isolated case. Many other companies and industries are experiencing the same kind of takeover and depersonalization with the same deadly outcome.

It is imperative in today's global marketplace for companies to reestablish manufacturer/supplier/distributor/end-user communication. It is the backbone of success. Communication can be achieved by establishing new commitments to performance excellence and by sharing common goals for performance improvement.

DEFINING THE SUPPLIER AND THE CUSTOMER

A supplier is one who provides or furnishes goods or services to meet a want or need. Everyone has a supplier. The end user obtains product supplies from the retailer or contractor. The retailer or contractor uses a wholesale distribution company to supply it with products to sell. In turn, the wholesale distribution company purchases products from a supplier. This supplier can either be an independent company acting as the agent for a manufacturing company or a manufacturing company itself. The manufacturing company has suppliers to furnish raw goods, component parts, and other types of industrial material. The chart in Figure 1-1 illustrates this chain of suppliers. You can see that each supplier in the chain is also a customer whose expectations have to be satisfied.

When you open the door for communication to build better business relationships, a chain reaction with far-reaching effects begins to takes place. Every person and every company in this chain of suppliers and customers become involved in continual, controlled, constructive change. The ultimate benefit is survival in a marketplace that demands performance excellence.

SURVIVING IN A MARKETPLACE THAT DEMANDS EXCELLENCE

The market is far less tolerant of inefficiency today than it was five years ago. Large industrial end users are demanding that their suppliers, including wholesale distributors, achieve excellence according to a detailed list of performance criteria. Distributors, in turn, are supposed to demand the same

Figure 1-1: Supplier and Customer Relationships in the Total Distribution Chain

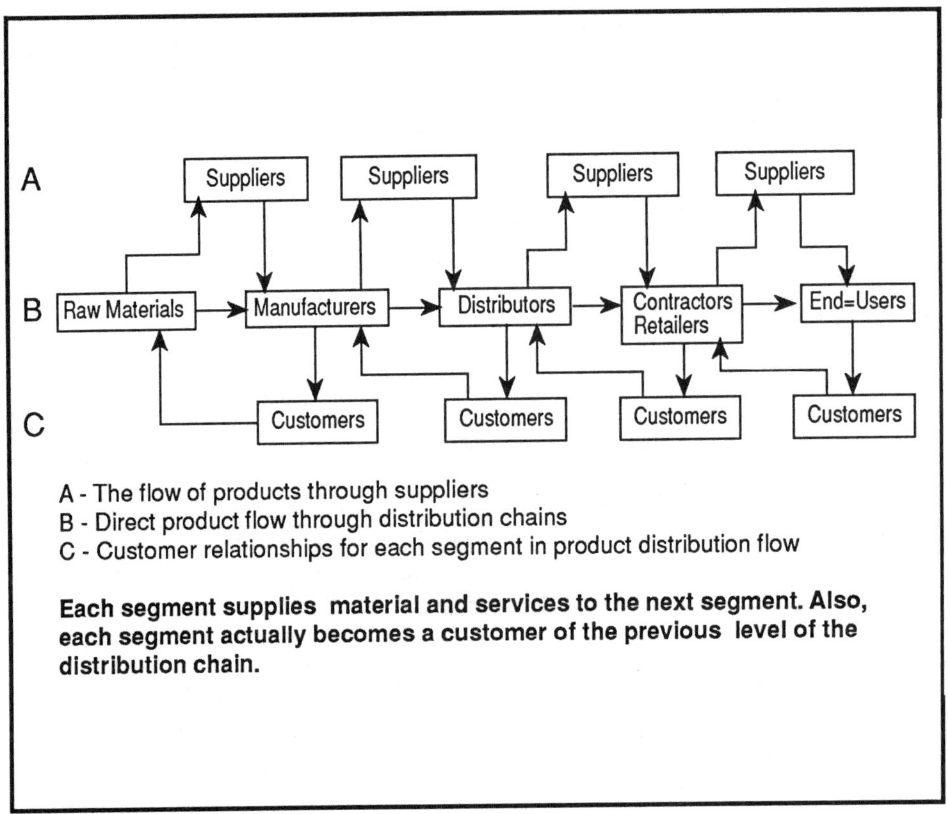

sort of excellence from their suppliers, and they are beginning to grade their suppliers on deliveries and fill rate of orders. However, these efforts barely touch the real potential for suppliers and distributors to actually achieve performance excellence in providing goods and services to their customers.

Customer and end-user needs are areas where suppliers and distributors alike are groping for more information. While customers and end users have become much more sophisticated and demanding in their expectations of a company's performance, quality performance will not necessarily earn their commendation—*They Expect Quality Performance All The Time!* On the other hand, if a company's performance in any area is unacceptable to its customers or end users, it will definitely begin to earn a negative image very quickly. The same is true of all suppliers.

Dave Howard, president of R.D. Harwood, Inc., Atlanta, Georgia, and also a specialist in education and consulting for manufacturing companies, stated on page 38 of the October 1990 issue of *P & IM Review,*

> As the marketplace becomes more global, the customers are shouting a clear message... 'Get better or get out!' We are already seeing that product quality, once a key difference in the 1980's, will likely become a commodity in the 1990's. Defect-free products will only get you a uniform and a chance to compete.

What a statement! Imagine—areas thought to be of prime importance by companies are only a starting point for further competition!

Only those suppliers capable of performing to set standards for performance excellence in all the categories defined in this book will become quality leaders. Suppliers at every level of the distribution chain not only need but also must start demanding this type of information from their customers, whether that customer is a manufacturing company or distributor.

Suppliers cannot reach your level of performance excellence until they know what your expectations of quality suppliers are!

It is vitally important to be able to communicate this information to them in a concrete and specific manner if your company wants to maintain the competitive edge in today's global market.

OPENING SUPPLIER/DISTRIBUTOR/ END-USER COMMUNICATION

Be assured, partnering is not a casual relationship. It is an in-depth, two-way communication of details between suppliers and customers. Partnering demands trust and openness and requires taking risks. Suppliers that want to be part of your team are going to invest time, money, and commitment to make improvements in their company that are suggested by supplier performance evaluations.

Broad statements such as, "Your prices are too high," "Your product quality is not good," "You never deliver on time," or "You never pay on time" are unacceptable in today's competitive marketplace. Details of problem areas in the suppliers' and their customers' companies must be shared so that each partner can pinpoint and completely eliminate problem causes.

The simplicity of buying directly from the supplier is no longer an option. Very few companies are able to take a product from the manufacturing level directly to the customer because it is a monumental investment. The practice of making products and blindly entrusting them to others for the continuation of the journey to reach the end user must stop. This is a costly and very poor business practice that can eventually result in the loss of profits and the demise of the supplier, as well as those in the supplier's distribution chain. Every link in that chain must be integrally locked into the next link and must be communicating back and forth to make the whole chain as strong as possible.

To be on the competitive edge, you must begin providing a means for multilevel manufacturer/supplier/distributor/end-user communication. Communication must flow from the end users through your company, through each level in your supplier chain, and back to the user, with focus on issues that are important to you. There are three types of information flow that affect you and your company:

- Product information—Information that flows from the supplier to the ultimate end user is generally product related. Unfortunately, product information does not flow from the ultimate user back to the supplier without a large expense to the supplier (when market research and extensive product testing are conducted), and even then the results may be marginal.
- End-user information—When product information begins with the ultimate end user who is trying to relay a problem back to the manufacturer, it can become distorted as it passes through each layer of the manufacturer's distribution chain. When this information is distorted or changed, it generally does not relay meaningful end-user suggestions for supplier performance improvement.
- Supplier evaluation information—Problems can be resolved when customer needs are relayed directly to the supplier's top management. Supplier evaluation identifies and documents problem areas specifically related to poor supplier performance and initiates cures to these problems by opening top-level supplier/customer communication.

By examining the Information Flow Chart in Figure 1-2, you can understand how a new industry has evolved at every level of the distribution chain and why they all have different needs. Remember, at each level of your company are supplier/customers with different needs to be assessed. Although these issues change from level to level throughout a distribution chain, they have one common trait—*All issues must be satisfied.*

Figure 1-2: Information Flow Chart

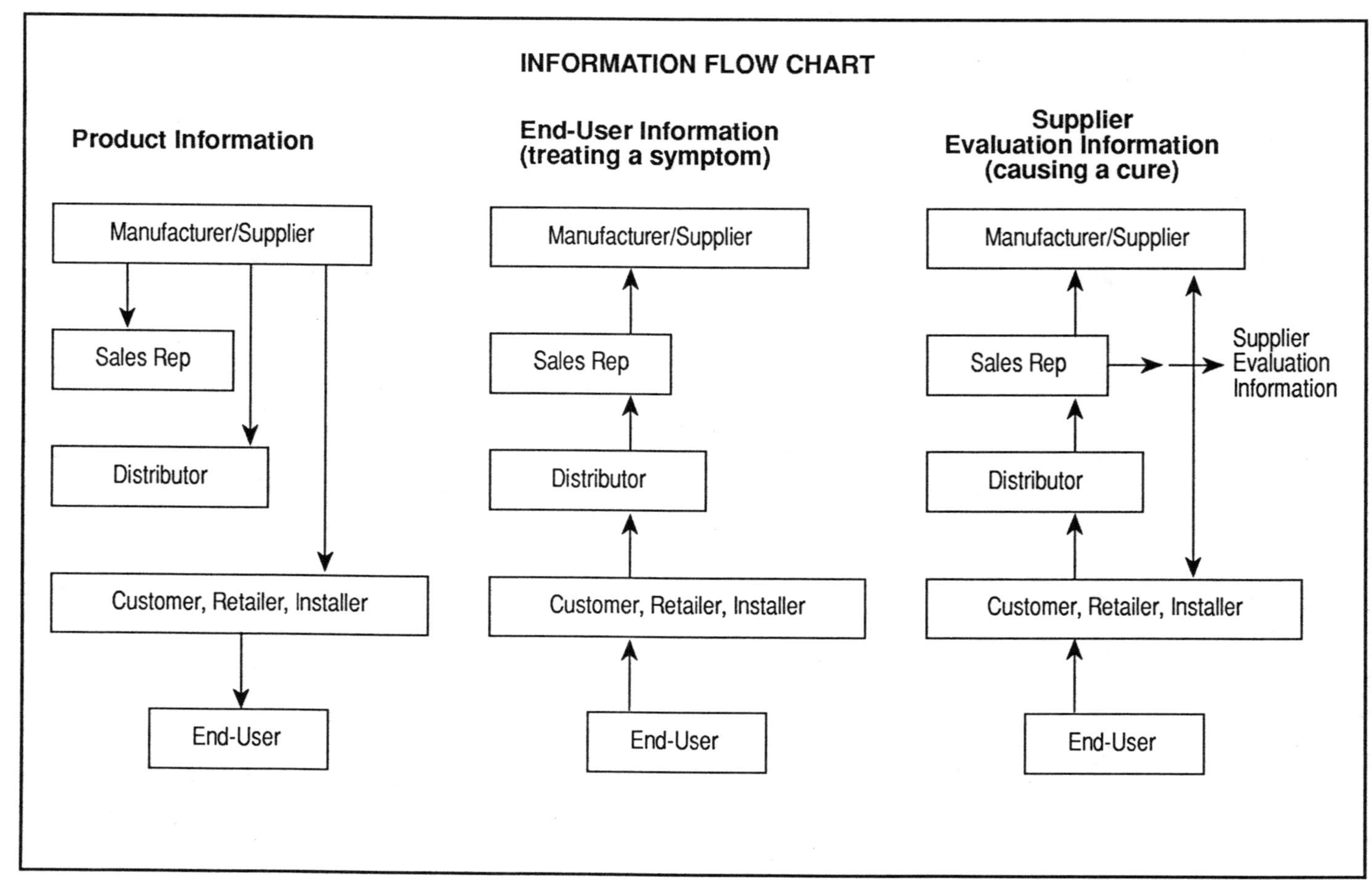

Notice your position in this sequence. You are in the middle. You pass goods and services from your suppliers to your customers. You also pass information from your customers back to your suppliers. In other words, you are the middle link in a chain of product and information flow. One of your most important jobs is to make this chain as strong and as informative as possible.

SHARING COMMON GOALS AND OBJECTIVES

Information that once was closely guarded must now be shared. For example, information about pricing, usage, design, markets, material, customer bases, competition, and strategies must be shared in a form that can be useful to all parties. Relationships of trust and unity of purpose are developed between partners through evaluations of supplier performance. These relationships produce the ties and the exchange of information that are required for successful partnering. When the managements of both supplier and customer agree to communicate, the results are a lasting and true partnering through which real problem solving occurs.

The revival of communication will enable you and your suppliers to share common goals and objectives leading to performance excellence, which is defined by:

- Lower product costs.
- Increased sales.
- Improved customer services.
- Higher profits.

This can be done quite effectively through the supplier performance evaluation and selection process when you understand the *total cost concept* of doing business.

UNDERSTANDING THE TOTAL COST CONCEPT

In today's competitive global market, the maximization of net profits is the result of total cost of supplier goods. While the price of goods is an important factor in supplier evaluation and selection, there are other product cost parameters that must be analyzed. It is no longer "dollar smart" for companies to make purchases or use their buying power just to achieve the lowest price for a product.

W. Edwards Deming's Principle 4, as stated in *Out of the Crisis* (1986), emphasizes this point. "End the practice of awarding business on the basis of price tag. Instead, minimize total cost." Dr. Deming's teachings point out that:

- The "low bid" is a fallacy.
- Purchasing managers must understand the "cost of ownership."
- Managers must share knowledge of quality improvement with suppliers.

The Importance of Educating All Levels of Management to the Total Cost Concept

It is imperative that you understand the total cost concept of doing business and the important role of supplier evaluation and selection in helping you and your company identify causes of poor performance and implement corrective actions to eliminate them. This process begins with educating all levels of your company's management. Only managers have the power to initiate the changes needed to eradicate causes of poor performance. When management believes that the present level of performance—whether it be the manufacturer's, the supplier's, or the distributor's—is not good enough and something can be done about it, changes will begin to take place. Let's review some managerial responsibilities:

- It is management's job to initiate and support quality improvement. Management must begin demanding the discipline needed to insure quality excellence in all phases of your operation.
- Management is responsible for informing every person in the organization about quality improvement through supplier performance evaluations. Employees need continuous support and reinforcement to establish the level of dedication needed for quality excellence.
- Once methods of improvement have been identified, corrective action must take place. The commitment to change is the proof that management is serious about quality performance from suppliers and employees.
- Management must be kept informed of the total cost of doing business. The purchasing manager should identify and pinpoint potential payback areas

by creating worksheets showing areas of potential savings such as freight charges, payment terms, better inventory availability, etc. By presenting your findings to the company president and department managers, you will ensure their support of your program.

Identifying Potential Payback Areas in Distributorships and Manufacturing Facilities

Begin identifying problem areas in your distributorship or manufacturing facility that are directly related to poor supplier performance. Create a worksheet for each area and analyze the results of your findings. For example, you might begin by reviewing costs directly related to your company's freight charges. You can get current inbound and outbound freight expenses from your controller or from the operating expenses shown on your company's financial statement. You will want to list suppliers and any problems directly related to their performance and estimate the savings to your company by eliminating these problem areas. A typical worksheet on freight charges might look like this:

Freight Expenses: Inbound Freight

Current Expenses = $500,000

Supplier	Problem areas identified by evaluation	Potential savings through reduced supplier charges as indicated by evaluation
Supplier X	The supplier's minimum freight breaks are too high.	$ 3,000
Supplier Y	The supplier does not allow freight.	15,000
Supplier B	Minimum breaks too high.	18,000
•	(Continue to identify problem areas.)	•
•		•
•		•
Total typical savings for inbound freight =		$75,000

Freight Expenses: Outbound Freight

Current Expenses = $250,000

Supplier X	The supplier has poor product availability.	$ 4,000
Supplier Y	Freight for warranty products is not recorded properly.	5,000
Supplier B	The supplier has excessive emergency shipments because of poor product availability.	3,500
•	(Continue to identify problem areas.)	•
•		•
Total typical savings for outbound freight		$ 50,000
Total typical savings for both inbound and outbound freight =		$125,000

Figure 1-3 illustrates potential savings in this area.

Figure 1-3: Potential Savings in Freight Charges

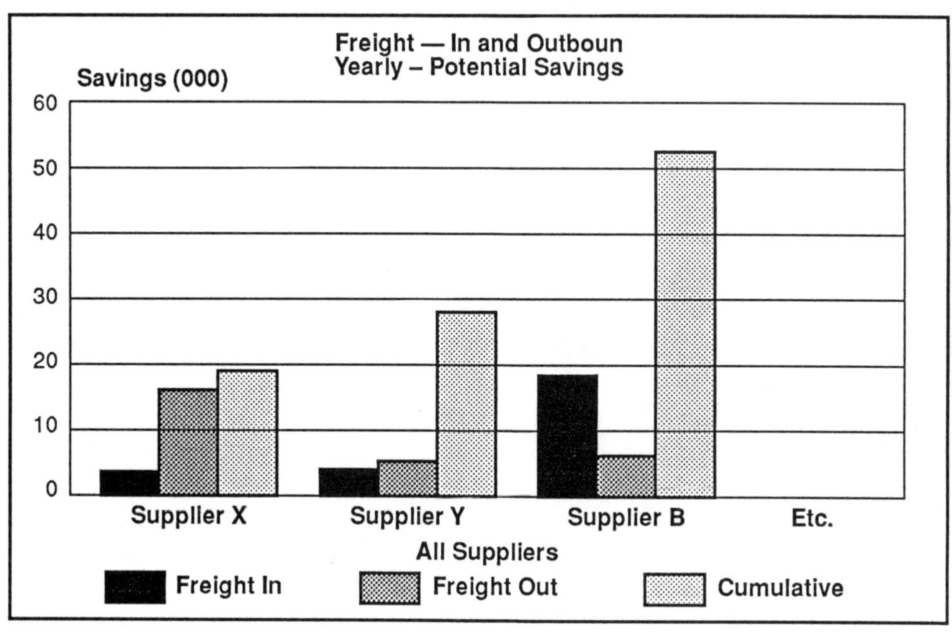

One of the major strengths of an evaluation program is that your company can realize savings in different areas, year after year. This happens when your suppliers begin aligning their performance to your company's expectations.

Identifying Supplier Causes and Expenses Incurred from Lost Discounts (Payment Terms)

Your controller or accounts payable supervisor can help you identify supplier causes and expenses incurred by your company from lost discounts on completed orders. A typical worksheet for lost discounts might look like this:

Lost Discounts (Payment Terms)

Estimated lost income because your company could not take advantage of payment discounts on completed orders = $50,000

Supplier	Problem areas identified by evaluation	Potential savings through supplier performance improvement
Supplier X	The supplier continually ships incorrect items.	$1,000
Supplier Y	The supplier does not include packing slips with shipments.	1,500
Supplier B	Orders are overshipped or undershipped.	1,000
Supplier A	Product costs do not agree with the supplier's quoted prices.	900
•	(Continue to identify problem areas.)	•
•		•
•		•
Total Typical Savings in Lost Discounts =		$7,000

Identifying Cost Savings in Warehousing and Material Handling

Your controller or materials manager can help you compile information from your company's financial statements pertaining to warehousing and material handling.

You will want to relate savings in this area to labor hours of savings. Determine the labor hours expended in material handling in each problem area. For example, if you have 15 people involved in material handling activities, calculate the total number of hours they work based on a work schedule of 252 days a year. That would be 30,240 labor hours, computed as follows:

15 people × 8 hours/day = 120 labor hours/day
252 workdays × 120 labor hours = 30,240 total labor hours

A typical worksheet for this area might look like this:

Warehousing and Material Handling Expenses

Warehousing and material handling personnel time = 30,240 labor hours

Current expenses including personnel relating to warehousing and material handling = $350,000 or $11.57 in expenses per labor hour ($350,000/30,240 = $11.57).

Supplier	Problem areas identified by evaluation	Potential yearly savings in labor hours through supplier performance improvement
Supplier X	The supplier does not have proper product identification on containers.	80 labor hours
Supplier Y	Package quantities are incorrect	35 labor hours
Supplier B	Material received has been damaged in shipment.	50 labor hours

Supplier D	There is erratic availability of supplier products.	60 labor hours
•	(Continue to identify problem areas.)	•
•		
•		•

Total typical savings in warehousing and material handling = 3,024 labor hours

By using the $11.57 expenses per labor hour and the estimated savings of 3,024 labor hours, we arrive at a savings of approximately $35,000. If your average warehouse employee earns $17,000 annually, then eliminating the identified warehousing and material handling problems would let you reduce your staff by two people.

Identifying Potential Sales Increases

Another area that can reduce revenue is supplier sales policies. When a supplier improves performance in this area, an increase in product sales is inevitable. You can obtain information for making this analysis from your sales manager and from your company's financial statements. A worksheet on supplier sales policies might look like this:

Sales Analysis

Prior Year's Sales Volume = $45,000,000

Supplier	Problem areas identified by evaluation	Potential increases in sales through supplier performance improvement
Supplier X	The supplier does not have representation in our market area.	$ 300,000
Supplier Y	The supplier has poor pricing policies.	80,000
Supplier A	The supplier does not provide incentive programs or product training.	100,000

Supplier D	The supplier's value/price ratios are poor.	75,000
•	(Continue to identify potential sales	•
•	increases.)	•
Typical sales increase =		$2,500,000

You can understand how these supplier-related problems can affect manufacturer/supplier/distributor sales. During our pilot program, it was not uncommon for suppliers and manufacturers to double their sales volume in just one year when they took the corrective measures indicated by their individual performance evaluations.

Identifying Supplier-Related Inventory Reductions

Suppliers can have an adverse affect on your company's inventory investment. You will want to include this area in your overall analysis. Your controller or materials manager can help you. A typical worksheet on inventory investment might look like this:

Inventory Investment

Current Average Inventory = $11,000,000

Supplier	Problem areas identified by evaluation	Potential inventory reduction through supplier performance improvements
Supplier X	The supplier does not provide information regarding market sales mix.	$ 70,000
Supplier Y	The supplier does not provide an inventory rebalancing program.	100,000
Supplier B	The supplier's product availability is poor.	75,000

Supplier C	The supplier does not provide assistance in handling obsolete and slow-moving items.	50,000
•	(Continue identifying problem areas.)	•
•		•
Typical inventory reduction =		$1,100,000

If your average gross margin in this example is 25%, then this reduction of average inventory would increase your inventory turns from 3.2 to 3.4 by reducing your average investment in inventory by 10% without an increase in sales. Refer to Chapter 5 for additional information on inventory turns and earns.

Summarizing Potential Savings and Increases in Profits

You will want to summarize your worksheets to show the total potential savings and increases in profits your company can derive by implementing a supplier evaluation and selection program. A typical summarized worksheet might look like this:

	Potential increases in revenue through supplier performance improvements
Freight (Inbound and Outbound)	$125,000
Earned Discounts	7,000
Warehousing & Material Handling	35,000
Increased Sales	625,000 ($2,500,000 × 25% G.M.)
Inventory Savings	$198,000 (1,100,000 × 18% cost of carrying inventory)*
Total Estimated Increase in Revenues =	$992,000

Estimated Expenses on Sales Earnings Increase =	156,000
Total Estimated Earnings Before Taxes =	836,000

*The cost of carrying inventory includes interest costs, insurance, inventory space, utilities related to inventory, taxes, computer expenses, and expenses related to the average cost of carrying inventory.

Take this analysis through to the bottom line. For example, last year's sales were $45,000,000, and net profit was $2,250,000, which is 5 percent. From the examples of supplier improvements net profit was increased by:

Increased earnings before taxes = $836,000
Percent of increase in earnings = 37%

If your company realizes a 5% earnings before taxes, it has the potential to increase that percentage by 37% through improved supplier performance.

REVIEWING TOTAL PRODUCT FLOW IN MANUFACTURING FACILITIES

A payback analysis for a manufacturing facility is basically the same as for a distributorship. However, you will want to look at the total product flow to review two additional areas:

- You will want to analyze every step in manufacturing's product flow to determine which outside influences are the most prevalent in the product flow.
- You will want to determine how an emphasis on supplier evaluation can bring about continual, controlled, constructive change in product flow.

Review the illustration in Figure 1-4 that shows the flow of product through a manufacturing facility. Keep in mind that your ultimate goal is cost reduction through evaluation of the total product flow. There are five areas you need to review:

- Raw material
- Work-in-process
- Assembly areas
- Finished goods
- Component parts storage

Figure 1-4: Material Flow Through Manufacturing Facilities

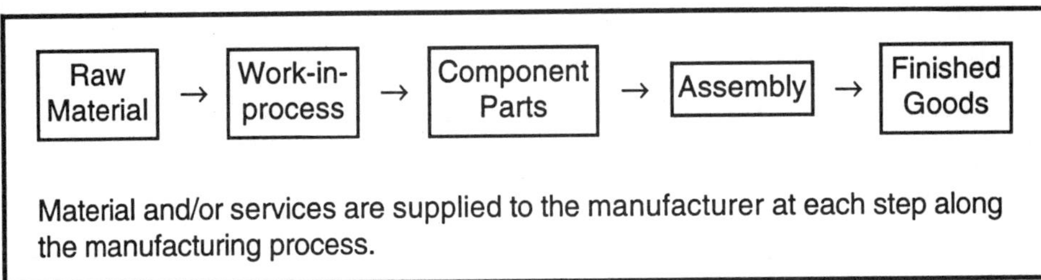

Material and/or services are supplied to the manufacturer at each step along the manufacturing process.

RaRaw Material Usage

To effectively analyze raw material usage, you must determine the answers to the following questions about material costs.

- How many suppliers currently sell you raw material?
- How many of your total suppliers are actually capable of supplying identical raw material?
- Do you have more than one supplier give you quotes on this type of material?
- Has your engineering department ever talked to your suppliers about the advantages and disadvantages of using alternate material?
- Do your suppliers ever suggest better methods of delivery, better terms of payment, different packaging, shorter lead times, or smaller order quantities?
- Have you ever checked on duty-free zones that can provide nearby storage of raw material from foreign sources, thereby reducing your carrying costs?
- Do you ever invite your suppliers into your facility to see your raw material storage area?
- Have any of your suppliers ever suggested better methods for improving material receiving, storage, or movement?
- Have they ever offered to totally unload and stack material for you as part of a total price package?

Ask your suppliers to quote you a total package on the material they are furnishing to you and begin making comparison analyses. For example, a typical raw material comparison analysis might look like the one illustrated in Figure 1-5. By comparing all the issues addressed in the comparison analysis you may discover savings that are not apparent when you are given the price only by suppliers.

Figure 1-5: Analysis of Raw Material Suppliers: Total Cost Packages Offered to a Manufacturer by Four Suppliers

Supplier	A	B	C	D
Material	**steel**	**steel**	**steel**	**steel**
Price	$1.015/lbs.	$1.05 to $1.0 %/lb.	$1.011/lb.	$1.02/lb.
Payment Terms	Net 30 days	2% tenth Prox.	1% tenth Prox.	Net 30 days
Packaging	100 ft. rolls	25, 50, 75, and 100 ft. rolls	75 ft. rolls	sheet material
Handling	crane needed	fork truck	crane needed	fork truck
Storage	local warehouse	no local warehouse	local warehouse	distributor warehouse
Availability	lead time 30 days	lead time 60 days	lead time 45 days	lead time 15 days

CASE EXAMPLE

I did a raw material comparison analysis for a plumbing manufacturing facility in central Arkansas whose first operation from raw stores was an automated cutting operation of tubular material. The product was most available, best packaged, and most easily handled in twenty-foot lengths. The automatic saw rack used for cutting was made to handle this length of tubing. For several years the plumbing manufacturer had purchased twenty-foot lengths of tubing from a domestic manufacturer. By purchasing *approximately* twenty-foot lengths of tubing, the per-pound cost of the material was significantly reduced. However, the domestic manufacturer varied the length of the tubing by as much as 12 to 14 inches. This resulted in more scrap and less output. Furthermore, the plumbing manufacturer's automatic saw did not handle the odd lengths of tubing properly.

The comparison analysis with other tubing suppliers showed that foreign manufacturers made the same price concessions for approximate lengths as the domestic manufacturer did. They also were required to hold the length differential to less than two inches. By changing suppliers, the plumbing manufacturer realized a substantial savings on raw material purchases, scrap was cut, and saw operations were maintained. In addition, it was able to use a duty-free zone in the area to its advantage in storing material from the new supplier.

Don't forget to get receiving, quality control, and accounting involved in this process.

They can evaluate and answer the following questions for you:

- How is raw material received?
- Are packing slips always included in shipments?
- Do quantities shipped always agree with quantities ordered?
- Does the supplier always ship the correct material?
- Is the material always consistent in size, color, and other important matters?
- What is quality control's opinion about your raw material suppliers?

Your accounting department can give you input as to your manufacturer's payment terms, invoicing, and other payment/credit matters that can affect the overall cost of raw material.

Work-in-process

Many different suppliers provide goods and services to the work-in-process product flow of a manufacturing facility. Your accounting department can furnish you with a list of suppliers for your operation. For example, a typical list might include some of the following suppliers:

- Tool and die manufacturers
- Tool suppliers
- Material handling devices
- Carts or material racks

- Storage materials
- Different materials used in the manufacturing process, for example,
    - Solder
    - Freezing materials
    - Chemicals used for cleaning or plating
    - Hazardous waste handling or dispositions

These materials add a large portion of direct or indirect costs to the total cost of your products. Direct costs are labor or material costs that go into a manufacturer's products. Indirect costs are applied to product costs through the application of overhead rates or listed in other expenses. Reductions in work-in-process will reduce product costs and increase profits.

Assembly Areas

Study your assembly area in the same manner as the work-in-process analysis. You will need to separate assembly costs from the cost of material added during assembly that actually goes into the unit cost of goods produced. For example, you need to separate the following costs by supplier and measure the dollars spent with each one to help you compare and evaluate your top supplier's performances:

- Work station material (indirect)—material used in the process of product assembly
- Tools (indirect)—hand or automated tools used to assemble products
- Packaging materials (direct)—package materials that are added directly to product costs
- Shrink-wrap material (direct)—material used in the packaging of a product (machinery costs are usually a part of indirect costs)
- Stenciling supplies (indirect)—material used to date, code, and identify products
- Labels (direct)—material used in the identification of a finished product that adds directly to unit costs

Figure 1-6 is a chart of typical assembly area costs.

Figure 1-6: Assembly Area Costs

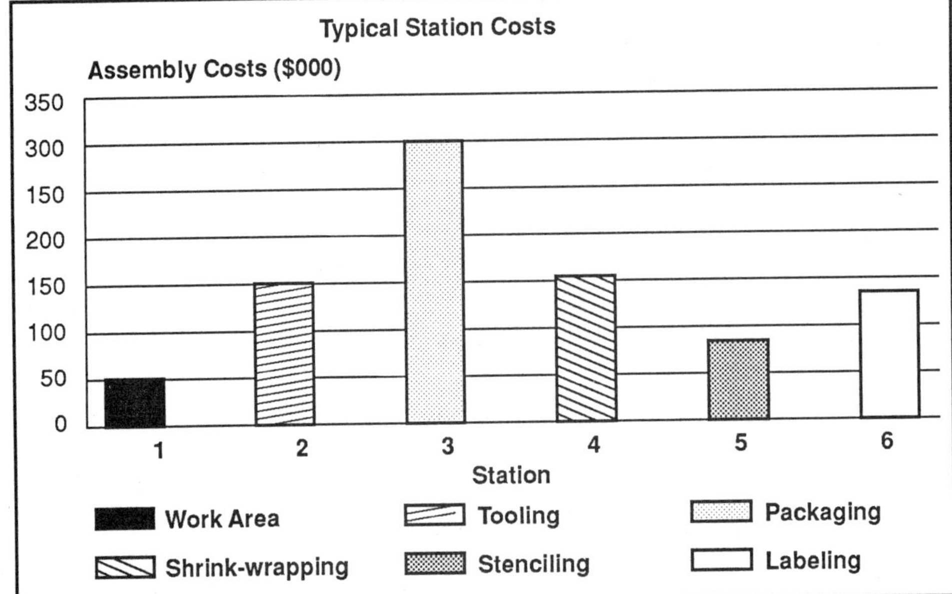

Finished Goods and Component Parts Storage

The previously discussed approach can be used in finished goods, also. Look at handling, storage techniques, retrieval methods, and storage areas. Who supplies goods or services? Their performance can and should be evaluated.

Component parts storage will usually account for the majority of your suppliers. It represents all the parts and pieces that go into your product that are not manufactured at your facility. This area can be represented by many different suppliers, including sister facilities (other plants in your company family that supply material to you). Look for consistent availability of material, correct package quantities, easy-to-read identification labels, good product protection in packaging, and bar code identification.

Now that you have identified issues that are part of the total product flow, from raw material to indirect parts and services to component parts, you are ready to summarize the areas of potential savings and introduce your supplier evaluation and selection program to upper management.

PRESENTING YOUR FINDINGS TO COMPANY MANAGEMENT

Compile all the information you have gathered into a format suitable for making a presentation to your company president and department managers. You want them to understand what poor supplier performance is costing your company in dollars and time and to see the potential savings that can be derived by monitoring supplier performance. You will want to include the following information in your presentation:

Worksheets. Include in your presentation your worksheets and the summary sheet showing the total costs of doing business and the potential savings. Be sure you reduce all your information to dollars of savings. Figure 1-7 is an example of a worksheet summary that can be used in your presentation. Figure 1-8 is a graph showing potential savings as a result of improved supplier performance. It and the graph in Figure 1-9 are examples of graphs that can be used as visual aids to your worksheets.

Explanations. Explain how poor supplier performance can affect every department in your company. For example, proper product identification is important in three areas of your company:

- It may significantly reduce storage and retrieval time, thus reducing material handling and warehousing expenses.
- It can reduce the material shrinkage factor of physical inventory in the inventory control department.
- It can also have an impact in your customer service department when a customer gets the wrong product, etc.

Explanations will enhance the data you have summarized for your management as justification for a supplier evaluation and selection program.

Supplier comparison chart. Select several suppliers who are competitors and make a supplier comparison sheet similar to the one shown in Figure 1-9. This chart shows the product with the highest piece cost ending up with the least total cost. It also shows non-financial consideration, such as co-op advertising and availability of emergency services.

Manufacturers will want to include a comparison analysis of raw material suppliers similar to the one illustrated in Figure 1-5.

Figure 1-7: Summary Worksheet

Area of review supplier contribution		Current cost of inadequate supplier service	Estimated savings by improved supplier performance	Data supplier
Material Handling and Warehousing	• proper product identification			• Materials Control
	• correct count of items			
	• damaged material			
	• cannot plan warehouse space because of poor product availability			
	• excessive material handling expenses			
	• other			
Warranty Returns	• insufficient product training			• Quality Control Manager • Warranty Administrator
	• warranty procedures are too complicated			
	• sub-standard product quality			
	• warranty does not reflect customer needs			
	• other			
Inbound and Outbound Freight Expenses	• excessive emergency shipments			• Shipping Manager • Traffic Manager • Controller
	• poor product availability			
	• excessive warranty returns			
	• excessive freight allowances			
	• other			

Area of review supplier contribution		Curreny cost of inadequate supplier service	Estimated savings by improved supplier performance	Data supplier
Lost Payment Discounts	• shipping incorrect items			• Accounts Payable • Controller
	• no packing slips with shipments			
	• incorrect product quantities shipped			
	• incorrect purchase order references			
	• incorrect product costs on invoices			
	• other			
Sales and Customer Service	• inadequate product information			• Sales Manager
	• no provision for product training			
	• customer complaints are not handled by reps			
	• poor pricing policies			
	• customer perceives value to price ratio is excessive			
	• other			
Inventory Investment	• inadequate product identification			• Materials Control Manager • Controller
	• product availability is inconsistent			
	• product mix does not match demand			
	• inventory rebalancing is not available			
	• obsolete inventory is too high			
	• average inventory investment is too high			
	• other			

Figure 1-8: Potential Savings as a Result of Improved Supplier Performance

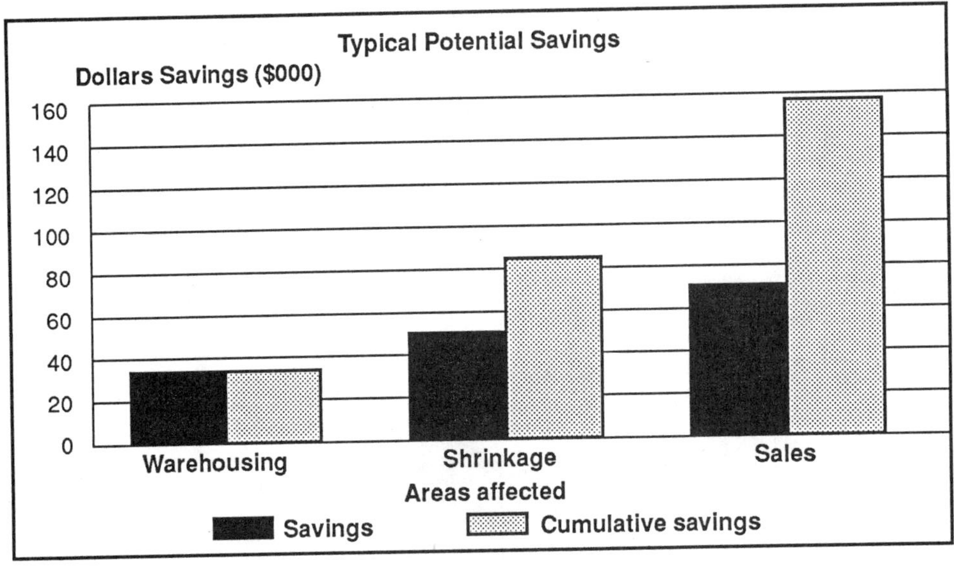

Figure 1-9: Price Comparison Chart of Competitive Products

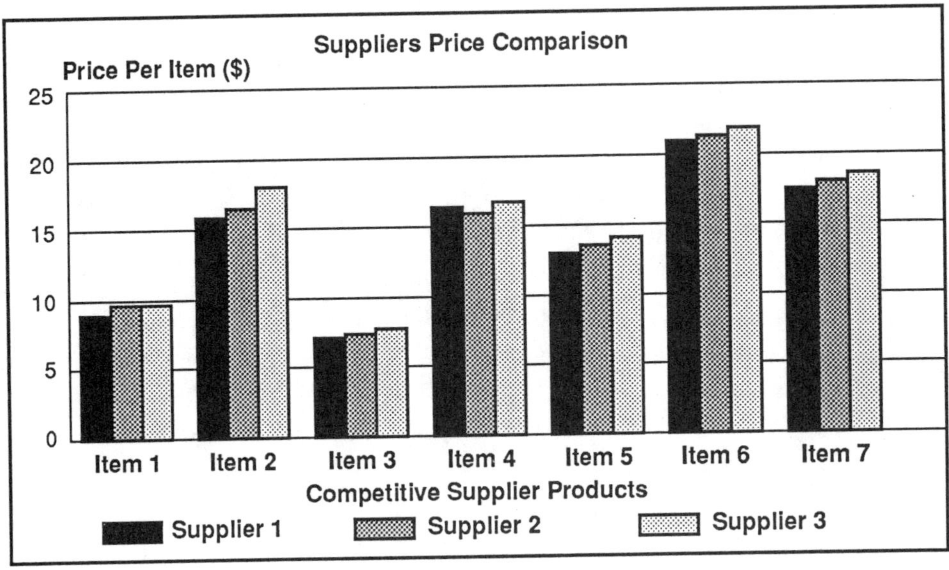

Parameters of prime importance. Discuss parameters that are of prime importance to each department manager. Include comparison charts for issues that affect each department.

Price analysis. Compare the product pricing of competitive suppliers. Refer to the Price Comparison chart in Figure 1-9. By applying the analysis in Figure 1-10, you may find that the lowest priced item is not the best value. For example, after calculating the deductions or additions to the cost of each item in Figure 1-10, the higher priced unit cost item turns out to be the best value. The unit total cost of the highest priced item drops to 98 cents while the total cost of the lower priced item increases to more than $1.00.

Savings/cost ratios. Discuss cost savings showing the ratio of savings to cost involved in supporting an evaluation program.

You will also need to stress three major points in your presentation:

- The evaluation process is an iterative process that will produce savings for your company every year.
- The evaluation process is geared to put emphasis on your top supplier's performances. By doing so, your company can show significant dollar savings each year. Figure 1-11 gives a graphic view of the potential increases in revenue. Add this chart to your presentation to management. It can be impressive to see the potential for savings and the resulting increased revenues.
- The impact of supplier evaluation is the attention it directs to problem areas and the visibility it gives to your supplier's management groups.

When you complete your presentation on the total costs of doing business with your suppliers and the potential savings your company can experience every year by implementing a supplier evaluation and selection program, upper management will be more than ready to make a commitment to performance excellence and dedicate themselves to the success of your program.

Your company president cannot achieve and maintain a reputation of heading a "quality" organization dedicated to performance excellence when you continually deal with suppliers whose level of performance is considered "below par." A commitment to performance excellence within your organization cannot be achieved as long as substandard performance by suppliers is allowed to continue.

Management involvement projects the emphasis needed to insure supplier participation and communication for continual, controlled, constructive change. The commitment your organization makes to total performance excellence is a signal to suppliers—*get better or get out!*

Figure 1-10: Supplier Comparison Chart

The following chart compares the performance of three suppliers and the total cost of purchasing 1,000 pieces of material from each supplier.

	Supplier X	Supplier Y	Supplier Z
1,000 pieces of material (cost per item)	$1.00 ea. = $1,000.00	$.98 ea. = $980.00	$.95 ea. = $950.00
Freight Charges (3% rate)	no freight charges	29.40	29.40
Payment Terms	2% tenth Prox. = {20.00}	1% tenth Prox. = {9.80}	net 30 days = 0
Order Placement (phone, fax, etc.)	phone toll-free = 0	phone toll-free = 0	phone charge = 2.50
Expediting Charges	always on-time = 0	2.50	5.00
Excess Inventory Carrying Costs (the result of poor product availability)	none	17.64	25.65
Total Cost	$980.00	$1,019.74	$1,012.55
Unit Total Cost	.98	1.02	1.01

OTHER CONSIDERATIONS: Terms and Conditions of Purchase

	Supplier X	Supplier Y	Supplier Z
Co-op Advertising Allowance	2%	1%	none
Availability of Quantity Pricing	available	none	available
Freight Allowance	c $1,000.00	c $5,000.00	none
Payment Terms	2% tenth Prox. net 30	1% tenth Prox. net 30	net 30 days
Toll-Free Phone or Fax for Order Placement	phone available fax available	phone available fax—none	none
Perceived Quality	customer preference	good substitute	no quality image
Emergency Services	yes—100% delivery extra charge	yes—95% delivery extra charge	yes—50% delivery no charge
Comparative Unit Price at Quantity Levels	$1.00	$.98	$.95
Inventory Rebalancing	yes—no reorder required	yes—with reorder	not available

Figure 1-11: Increased Revenues from Improved Supplier Performance

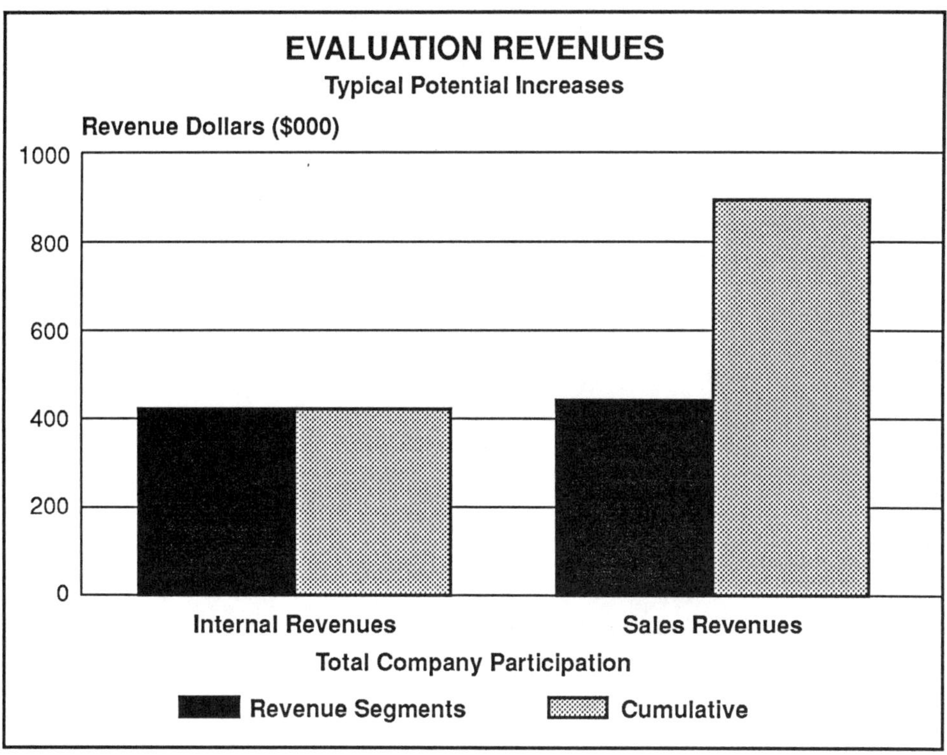

CHAPTER 2

AUDITING THE SUPPLIER—VISITING MANUFACTURING FACILITIES AND EVALUATING OPERATIONS

On occasion, particularly when evaluating a manufacturing supplier, it is not possible to assess the supplier's potential to be a partner for performance excellence without an audit. For example, an audit is necessary when you are selecting a major supplier or trying to determine why your current supplier is unable to meet your standard of performance.

Supplier auditing is done by making on-site visits to the supplier's manufacturing facility and evaluating supplier operations. Personal observation of the supplier's operations and communication with the manufacturing and material control management will give insights into issues governing product availability, the supplier's dedication to quality, and the commitment to customer satisfaction. Thus, the supplier audit is an important adjunct to the Supplier and Evaluation Selection Program.

Defining your objectives for plant visits and setting measurement standards and grading procedures for potential suppliers are vital for successful supplier auditing and the selection of quality suppliers. This systematic method will help you find suppliers to be partners in performance excellence.

ESTABLISHING AUDIT PROCEDURES

The first step in implementing auditing procedures is a planning session to lay the groundwork necessary for successful audits. During this meeting you and the president of your company have the following responsibilities:

- Define objectives—Define your expectations of supplier manufacturing facilities.
- Determine key issues—Determine what issues you want to address during the audit.
- Establish standards for grading and evaluation procedures—Grading standards and evaluation procedures have to be set for measuring the quality of a supplier's manufacturing facility.

Defining Your Objectives for Successful Plant Audits

You cannot continue to be a quality distributor when new or current suppliers fail to provide you with quality products and service. Plant audits can help in the selection of quality suppliers and/or determine why a present supplier is unable to perform to your standards of excellence.

By auditing supplier manufacturing facilities, you can determine if potential suppliers have the ability to perform to your standards and meet your needs as a customer on a continuing basis. An audit of a current supplier's manufacturing facility can help you determine if supplier problems can be remedied or if you need to find another supplier.

Determining Key Issues for Successful Plant Audits

You can determine a supplier's ability to perform to your standards of performance by auditing four areas in the supplier's manufacturing facility:

- Plant capacity— Is the plant capacity of a supplier's manufacturing facility large enough to provide the volume of product your company needs on a continuing basis?

- Work force— The attitude and appearance of the supplier's work force give you an indication of the supplier's dedication to the manufacture of quality products. Problems in work force relationships, skills, and habits affecting supplier performance will be apparent.
- Machinery and automation levels—The age and condition of machinery and automation levels are good indicators of product flow. The ability of the supplier to meet an increase in orders and to operate with a minimum of equipment repairs or downtime is an important issue in supplier selection.
- Housekeeping—Observe the general housekeeping of the manufacturing facility. This is one of the most revealing characteristics about the discipline of the manufacturer. It will give you an indication of the supplier's commitment to produce quality products on a consistent basis.

DETERMINING PLANT CAPACITY

The supplier being audited must have the ability to supply material to you on a continuing basis. By auditing the supplier's plant capacity you can determine if your current and future product demand can be supplied.

Plant management will be able to provide your auditors with information about the plant's daily output. If your daily needs do not exceed 10 percent of the supplier's available output, then the supplier's plant capacity should be sufficient to supply you with product. For example, you know how much of a supplier's particular product your company uses in a given time period. Ask the supplier's management how many of these items can be produced in the same time period. Suppose you use an average of 700 pieces of the manufacturer's product per month. If the manufacturer produces an average of 10,000 pieces of this product per month, your needs represent 7 percent of the manufacturer's total output for this product. When your needs exceed 10 percent of the plant output, you need to determine if additional output can be maintained or find another supplier. An increase of 10 percent output at a facility, especially if it is operating at planned efficiency levels, will dictate planning changes.

Five Methods of Obtaining Additional Output Capacity

If a current or potential supplier does not have the capacity needed to supply material on a continuing basis and you still are interested in its product, you need to determine its additional capacity capabilities. Capacity additions may be easy to obtain and quickly initiated, or they can be very expensive and require an extended length of time to produce extra product. For example:

Overtime. This is an inexpensive way to gain more capacity. This increase is also quick but, unfortunately, is limited as a continuous or permanent cure to capacity problems. However, capacity expansion is marginal when employees are required to perform continuous overtime.

Additional shifts. This method is more costly than overtime and can be limited by the availability of the needed work force and supervision. However, it is quick to implement and can afford a long-term solution to capacity problems.

Improved efficiency or increased utilization. Improved efficiency and increased utilization are the most economical methods of increasing capacity. However, they may be the most difficult to obtain. A study of work habits and standards of operation is required to identify areas that can be improved. The process is time consuming, and final results still depend on the attitude of the work force to change in operations.

Additional machinery. Adding machinery can increase output. This method is costly, and the lead-time for new equipment can be long. Employee training on new machinery can also extend the time needed to improve output.

Plant expansion. The most expensive method of adding capacity is through plant expansion or new facilities. This is also the most time-consuming method of obtaining increased capacity.

If these methods of obtaining additional output capacity are unacceptable to you and the supplier cannot otherwise meet your requirements, you need not continue audit and evaluation procedures. It is advisable to find an alternate supplier capable of performing to your set standards.

AUDITING THE SUPPLIER'S WORK FORCE

When a supplier has a good working relationship with its employees, fewer problems will surface in supplier/manufacturer/distributor relationships. In the manufacturing arena, the focus of the work force has been highlighted greatly by the introduction of the Just-In-Time (JIT) concept. JIT considers anything that is a waste to be contrary to the optimal production of goods and services. Of course, to hinder utilization of the human resource either by misplacement or poor utilization is strictly against the JIT concept.

By evaluating the supplier's work force you can identify and address six potential labor problems that can affect product flow:

Unstable employee relationships. Unhappy employees result in tense working conditions and work stoppages. In some instances, strained relationships with a union work force can telegraph the potential for production delays. Always inquire about labor relations with a union shop.

Inadequate employee training. An employee who lacks proper job training will produce shoddy work and hamper product flow. One sign of this is overly large queues of work at different work stations, which also may stem from inadequate machinery maintenance or faulty plant layout. Whatever the problem is, it can be determined by observation during a plant audit.

Unacceptable skill levels. Unskilled employees produce substandard products. If a product requires a high level of machine tolerance with strict attention to design and engineering specifications, a highly skilled, properly trained work force is mandatory. If the supplier of this product is located in an area that cannot provide the proper employee base, then a concern must be voiced by the auditor. The skill level of a surrounding area can change drastically over a given period of time. Your plant auditors must be able to recognize these potential problems in their audit activities.

Plant location. The location of a supplier's manufacturing facility may limit the availability of skilled workers needed to increase the work force. For example:

- Plants might be subject to work stoppages due to civil unrest.
- Population patterns may have changed in the area where the plant is located, making it difficult to attract workers with suitable skill levels.
- There may be environmental problems that need to be addressed because a manufacturer is producing hazardous products. For example, work stoppages due to nuclear energy protesters, problems over the selection of sites for hazardous waste disposal, and the actions taken to control the depletion of the ozone layer all have profoundly affected output all over the world. This will continue and become more intense in the future.

Attitude and appearance of the work force. The attitude and appearance of the work force are strong indicators of the quality of product they will produce. You can determine the employees' neatness in appearance and their attention to job requirements by observation. Workers will telegraph confidence in their training and abilities as they perform their duties.

Age level and age mix of the work force. Another factor to consider is the age level and age mix of the work force. This does not suggest that manufacturers discriminate because of an employee's age. It simply means that where an older working group may be more skilled to do specific jobs, pending retirements could disrupt product flow because the more experienced employees are difficult to replace.

On the other hand, a younger work force may signal a lack of needed skills to produce and maintain quality output.

CASE EXAMPLE

There was an unusual slump in output by one of our suppliers. The supplier, a major provider of refrigeration components, was having problems supplying product in a timely manner. After we started our supplier evaluation program, we asked for a supplier visit.

When we arrived at the supplier's location in north Texas, it was apparent that everything was being done manually. There was no automation, and the appearance of the production area showed a complete lack of discipline. The majority of the work force consisted of unskilled persons who were working illegally in the area. The slump in output had occurred when the work force was depleted by a visit from the border patrol! Production stopped for a week or more until the labor force was replaced. The supplier was also violating the law by hiring illegal immigrants.

Production scheduling was nonexistent; everything was done on an emergency basis. The problems were so numerous and so deeply ingrained that we were forced to look for another supplier. This is a perfect example of where the lowest cost resulted in higher total costs for the distributor.

The new supplier provided better quality, more timely receipt of product, and, as a result, sales increased, quality improved, and warranties were reduced. Of course, our unit cost went up. Was it worth it? You bet! Our total cost went down. While this is an extreme case (in most cases suppliers are able to make necessary improvements), it shows how spending the time to grade performance and visit your supplier can save your company money and improve your return on investment.

AUDITING PRODUCT FLOW

The age and condition of machinery and the level of automation in a manufacturing facility can affect product flow. These are vital issues in supplier selection.

Observe the age and condition of the supplier's equipment. Machinery that is new is easy to spot. Most of the machines will be working and will show little wear.

Machinery that is not new should be clean in appearance and require minimum downtime for repair. Suppliers with this type of equipment are dedicated to preventive maintenance, which is a definite asset.

On the other hand, when the supplier's equipment is dirty, worn out, and the work stations are sloppy, concern must be voiced. This type of machinery will hinder the supplier's production flow, and there will be excessive queues of work at the work station.

Observe the product flow at individual work stations and the methods of manufacture. An excessive use of manual operations indicates an excessive labor content in the final cost.

CASE EXAMPLE

XYZ, Inc., a supplier participating in the supplier evaluation and selection pilot program, provided a visit and tour of its manufacturing facility in 1983. During this fact-finding trip, the methods observed to manufacture components showed that the labor content of unit cost was significant. An inquiry of management determined that standard costs were used and that the labor portion of total cost was too high. Further inquiries revealed that XYZ, Inc.'s management was in the planning stages of modernizing the plant, which included automating many manufacturing operations that were currently being done by hand.

Overall, the unit price of the manufacturer's product was too high in relation to the product's name recognition in the marketplace. The fact that the supplier was aware of the problem and was in the process of remedying the situation was important. The members of the audit team recommended continuing the distribution of the manufacturer's product.

Within two years the modernization of XYZ, Inc.'s facilities was completed. The manufacturer's unit cost decreased, and it was able to provide a competitive product in the marketplace.

OBSERVING THE SUPPLIER'S GENERAL HOUSEKEEPING

Plant housekeeping is an outward sign of the supplier's commitment to total excellence. The discipline needed to keep a facility in good appearance on a daily basis is the same discipline manufacturers need to maintain sound business practices.

A group of graduate students at Stanford University conducted a study to determine if there were any traits common to successful companies and companies that were failing. Fifty companies of varying sizes and types in both categories were selected for the study. All aspects of every participating company were analyzed: management personnel, management styles, facilities, production process, and material control. When all parameters were analyzed, only one common trait came to the surface—housekeeping. The companies considered successful had facilities that were well-kept and maintained. Failing companies were sloppy in all their housekeeping activities.

You should audit four areas pertaining to a manufacturer's housekeeping habits:

Plant appearance. The outside appearance of the manufacturing facility will give you an indication of the the importance the supplier places on plant maintenance. Grounds and surrounding areas should be clean and properly maintained. Buildings should be in good repair and neat in appearance.

Facilities. Cleanliness in all work areas and proper disposal of scrap material are important safety factors. Work areas should be clearly marked and work-queued material neat and properly stored at all plant locations, including shipping, receiving, and the warehouse.

Automated flow. Product and people flow should not be hampered by poor lighting or poor work area layout. Safety precautions should be evident.

Restrooms. Unkempt restrooms with receptacles that need attention are health hazards and show a lack of detail discipline on the part of the supplier.

TWO KEYS TO EFFECTIVE SUPPLIER AUDITS

There are two keys for effective supplier audits: simplicity and communication. Suppliers cannot perform to your standards when they don't know what they are. Focus on the issues that are important to your company, not on the latest mathematical techniques that might be difficult for your suppliers to understand. Statistical methods indicate the need for an audit. Keep your audits supplier friendly! Suppliers can understand something as basic as the need for a packing slip to be included with every shipment they make to your company and that you expect shipments to be on time, so keep your standards simple. Don't waste your time and their time by trying to explain how the audit team will technically grade every phase of their manufacturing facility. They will doubt whether you really can effectively audit the place! Let the management of the manufacturing facility you are auditing grade its own performance (using your standards) along with your audit team, if it wishes. Those that don't will probably do it after the audit team leaves.

ESTABLISHING A GRADING SCALE AND APPLYING IT TO AUDIT PROCEDURES

You can use a grading scale in supplier auditing. This is done by setting simple numerical values to key issues that directly affect the ability of manufacturers to provide you with quality products on a continuing basis. For example, you can set a grading scale range of 0 to 10.

- Zero to 4 are the lowest grades suppliers can receive in the manufacturing process and indicate very poor performance. Suppliers receiving grades in this range are definitely not suitable for selection.
- Designate 5 as your midpoint value, indicating average manufacturing abilities. Suppliers receiving grades of 5 may not have the needed plant capacity to provide you with quality products on a continuing basis, but they can have positive points in other areas such as the lowest price, best quality, or priority products, and can still be considered as potential suppliers.
- Grades 6 through 9 indicate that a supplier has the ability to supply quality products to you or is capable and willing to make necessary changes in the manufacturing process to meet your needs.
- 10 will be the highest grade attainable and is given for performance excellence. This grading scale will become a permanent part of the Supplier Audit Work Sheet that is illustrated in Figure 2-1.

Figure 2-1: Supplier Audit Worksheet.

SUPPLIER AUDIT WORKSHEET

Date of Audit: ______________________
Supplier: ______________________
Plant Site: ______________________
Supplier Rep: ______________________
Product: ______________ Estimated Usage: ______________
Auditor: ______________________

Supplier manufacturing facility standards are set in four areas of importance: plant capacity, work force, machinery and automation levels, and general housekeeping. They are listed in order of importance, and the following grading scale is used:

Grading Scale
0–4 = Very Poor
5 = Average
6–9 = Above Average
10 = Excellent

Suppliers can be awarded extra points (additions) when their manufacturing facility earns excellent grades in specific areas, or they can have points deducted (deductions) from their grades when their manufacturing facility is below distribution's expectations.

Explanations of each area being audited and the point values given are as follows:

GRADING STANDARDS FOR A CAPACITY ANALYSIS (Grade one statement only.)	Point Value	Actual Grade
____ Distribution's current product demand does not exceed 10 percent of the manufacturer's plant capacity.	10	________
____ Plant capacity can be obtained by overtime, added shifts, improved efficiency, or increased utilization.	8	________
____ Additional machinery can be added to improve the manufacturer's product capacity.	6–7	________

Figure 2-1 (Continued)

____ Major changes must occur before the manufacturer can produce additional product (plant expansion, new facility, etc.). 4 ________

DEDUCTIONS (–):

____ The time period needed for the manufacturer to institute needed changes is unreasonable. –2 ________

____ The supplier is not willing to make suggested changes to meet distribution's needs. –2 ________

____ Other suppliers can supply a product of equal or superior value. –3 ________

* A grade below 5 indicates unacceptable supplier performance in this area.

COMMENTS: ____

____

____

GRADING STANDARDS FOR WORK FORCE
(Grade each statement.)

____ Shop personnel are neat in appearance and attentive to job activities. 2 ________

____ Work activities indicate good training and acceptable skill levels. 2 ________

____ Age level and mix are reasonable throughout the work force. 2 ________

____ Employee relations are stable, and work stoppages are non-existent or very rare. 2 ________

____ Plant location provides adequate availability for additional skilled work force. 2 ________

DEDUCTIONS (–):

____ The supplier has a history of frequent work stoppages. –2 ________

* A grade below 5 indicates unacceptable supplier performance in this area.

COMMENTS: ____

____

____

____

Figure 2-1 (Continued)

GRADING STANDARDS FOR MACHINERY AND AUTOMATION LEVELS
(Grade one statement only.)

____	The equipment is new and/or is in excellent condition. Work operations are automated and product flow is well engineered. Product queues are small and evenly distributed.	10	________
____	Machinery is old but well-maintained. Preventative maintenance is evident, and automation levels are acceptable.	8	________
____	Machinery is adequate but needs attention. Preventative maintenance is not practiced. Improvement in product flow and reduction of work queues are needed. The supplier is willing to take corrective measures.	6	________
____	Machinery is in poor repair and additional machinery is needed. Most plant operations are done manually, and product flow is poor. Major changes must occur to correct problem areas.	0–5	________

* A grade below 5 indicates unacceptable supplier performance in this area.

COMMENTS: ____

____

____

GRADING STANDARDS FOR GENERAL HOUSEKEEPING
(Grade each statement.)

____	Outside area of the manufacturing facility is well maintained. Grounds are well kept, and the outside of buildings is clean and neat in appearance.	2	________
____	Inside office and work areas are clean, properly lighted, and uncluttered.	2	________
____	Manufacturing areas are clean and work stations are not crowded. The floors are clean; scrap and trash are disposed of properly.	2	________
____	Work stations are properly lit, and work queues are properly arranged. Management encourages and provides safety precautions.	2	________ ________

Figure 2-1 (Continued)

____ Restrooms throughout the entire facility are well maintained. Receptacles are clean, and hand towels and soap are available. 2 ________

* A grade below 5 indicates unacceptable supplier performance in this area.

COMMENTS: ____

____

____

TOTAL POINTS:

CAPACITY ____

WORK FORCE ____

MACHINERY & AUTOMATION ____

HOUSEKEEPING ____

GRAND TOTAL ____

AUDITOR: ________________________________
(signature)

Auditing and evaluating plant capacity, work force relations, machinery, and automation levels and housekeeping are critical. A grade of 5 or less in any category indicates serious problems in the manufacturing facility that will affect the supplier's ability to supply your company with a quality product on a continuing basis.

Often, a supplier is willing to make necessary changes to meet your performance standards. When this happens there are two additional points to consider:

- Management—Management may need to be changed before the manufacturing facilities can be improved. For example, faulty practices might be so ingrained in current management that a change in management must take place before corrective measures can be taken to improve the facilities.
- Time—The time needed to make the necessary changes in the manufacturing facility may be longer than you care to wait for quality performance.

In both cases, your company may not want to invest the additional time needed for a supplier to implement these changes.

ORGANIZING AN AUDIT TEAM

Determining the Size of Your Audit Team

The size of your audit team depends on the number of areas in the supplier's manufacturing facility you plan to audit. For example, we have identified four areas of major concern. Therefore, you must assign an auditor to each of these areas and have a team leader to monitor auditing procedures. In this case, your audit team would have five members.

Selecting Members of Your Audit Team

The purchasing manager will be the audit team leader. You might want to enlist the aid of your company's president in selecting your audit team members. Remember, the auditors represent you, your company, and its interests. It is your job to educate them about the importance and purpose of supplier audits and how to recognize and ask detailed questions about the manufacturing process.

There are two requirements for audit team members:

- They should have the analytical skills needed to perform audits.
- They should have a working knowledge of the areas they will be auditing.

Carefully choose your audit team members from the following departments: engineering, material control, manufacturing, quality control, and purchasing. Employees from these departments will already have a working knowledge of the areas chosen for auditing because they have close working relationships with the same areas in your company. This will enhance their abilities to audit and evaluate supplier manufacturing facilities successfully. For example, they already have a working knowledge of suppliers, supplier products, material flow, cost components, product design, plant layouts, and manufacturing processes.

A detailed list of responsibilities for audit team members is shown in Figure 2-2. These team members will become a permanent part of your audit team.

Figure 2-2: Audit Team Responsibilities

Name of Employee: ______________________________
Department: ______________________________
Supervisor: ______________________________
Job Title: Supplier Auditor

This person will be a permanent member of an audit team. Candidates for this position can be chosen from the following list of departments:

- Engineering
- Materials control
- Manufacturing
- Quality control
- Purchasing

POSITION QUALIFICATIONS:

- Five years' experience in a manufacturing, industrial engineering, or materials control environment is the minimal requirement.
- A college degree is preferred.
- Direct contact with suppliers, their representatives, the manufacturing facilities they represent, and familiarity with all supplier products is vital to this position.
- A good understanding of the supplier auditing program, grading process and of good communication skills is essential.
- A working knowledge of the manufacturing process flow, machine capabilities, and labor power requirements is essential.
- Being capable of estimating skill levels needed to perform the manufacturing process is needed.

Other characteristics of supplier auditors are:

- An even temperament.
- The ability to work with people with varying backgrounds and educations.

POSITION FUNCTIONS AND RESPONSIBILITIES:

This position's specific functions include:

- Monitoring the grading of a specific area of the supplier's manufacturing facility.
- Performing supplier audits in each area being audited.
- Preparing a graded evaluation of the audit.
- Making an analysis of the supplier's manufacturing facility.

Defining Team Responsibilities

The auditors, under your direction, will audit and evaluate each area of the manufacturing facility that directly affects product availability. You will want to plan a training session for your team members to:

- Explain the purposes of supplier auditing.
- Make sure team members understand audit procedures.
- Delegate responsibilities to your audit team members.

Your auditors have three responsibilities:

- Each auditor will have primary responsibilities in a specific area, for example, housekeeping. The auditor in charge of housekeeping will conduct auditing procedures in that area. He or she will make sure each auditor understands grading in this area.
- Each auditor will audit and grade every area being audited. Each one has a primary area to audit and grade, and is encouraged to review every area and make comments when needed.
- Auditors will report their findings to you and your company president.

BEGINNING YOUR AUDIT

Meet with your audit team before each audit and review the issues at hand. You will want to share any information you have about the manufacturing facility to be audited. For example, if you are planning to audit a potential supplier's manufacturing facility, you might already know the plant size and current capacity.

When you plan to audit a current supplier, discuss problem areas with your team members and discuss the actual documentation of the problem areas. Perhaps a current supplier has mishandled 5 out of the last 10 orders delivered to your company. This supplier can understand the problem perfectly when you and your team members can produce documentation.

It is also your responsibility to contact current or prospective suppliers and make arrangements for you and your audit team to visit the manufacturing facility.

The success of your audit depends on supplier/manufacturer/distributor communication. The supplier will want to know:

- Why you want to do an audit of the manufacturing facility.
- Details about your audit and grading standards.
- The results of your audit.

Arrange a meeting with the supplier's upper management during the audit to talk about the audit procedures and any problem areas. Give them a copy of your Supplier Audit Worksheet (Figure 2-1). The worksheet will help explain your expectations for quality suppliers. It is not uncommon for the supplier's upper management to audit its own manufacturing facilities using your grading procedures.

ANALYZING AND SHARING AUDIT RESULTS

After the audit has taken place, meet with your audit team and review their individual audit sheets and their recommendations. Summarize all the audit information presented to you and present the information along with your own observations and recommendations to your company president for review and final action (see Figure 2-3). This worksheet summary will detail the information obtained during the audit. It will supply a snap-shot picture of the audit team's cross-section view of each area. Make sure the information you present is in a factual and concise package. Your company president is responsible for making the final decision to add a new supplier or to replace an inadequate supplier.

Remember that your recommendation to replace or select a new supplier is a very serious matter. Not only will it affect your company, but you will be contributing to a change in your customer's thinking. You can create a bad image for your company in your market area by continually replacing current suppliers.

When an audit indicates that your current supplier cannot or will not make the necessary changes required for performance excellence, it is time to make a change. This is always a difficult decision to make because long-time supplier/manufacturer/distributor relationships can be at stake. Even so, it must be done if your company is going to survive in today's competitive global market.

Searching for suppliers that share the same commitment to performance excellence has financial rewards for you and for your suppliers. When you locate such suppliers, you must be sure that the goals you are striving for are also shared by your customers. The next chapter focuses on the concept of quality and how your customers' perception of quality in products and services can be used to improve your performance and that of your suppliers.

WORKSHEET SUMMARY
(Final Auditor's Report)

Date: ____________________
Supplier Audited: ______________________
Audit Team Members: ____________________________________

GRADING SUMMARY

Issues	Auditor 1	Auditor 2	Auditor 3	Auditor 4	Audit Leader	Total Points	Average Grade
Plant Capacity							
Work Force							
Machinery and Automation							
Housekeeping							

Comments: ____

Recommendations: ____

Audit Team Leader: ______________________________________
(signature)

CHAPTER 3

UNDERSTANDING YOUR CUSTOMER'S CONCEPT OF QUALITY

Quality is a degree of excellence or superiority manufacturers and distributors strive to achieve in all levels of their companies, their work force, and the products they manufacture and/or sell. It is important to be known as a "quality" manufacturer or a "quality" distributor in today's competitive global market because quality is the number one issue of every company and purchasing group and their customers and ultimate end users.

Manufacturers and distributors view quality as an engineered tangible asset. On the other hand, to customers or product end users quality is perceived value. Simply stated, *perceived quality* equals *total value* in the customers' minds. Supplier evaluation and selection is the measuring stick and vehicle by which these opposing views of quality can be tied together.

In 1982, the American Productions and Inventory Control Society (APICS) held its 25th annual international conference. During this conference, only one article on quality was presented. By 1989, APICS had a full section of 17 papers on quality, with the subject being addressed in many other presentations as well. The concept of total quality management (TQM) is coming to the forefront.

COMPARING QUALITY FROM CONTROL TO MANAGEMENT

Labor or material problems relating directly to the manufacturing process of a product are identified and corrected by manufacturers and suppliers through quality improvement programs. The degree with which they implement quality procedures determines the total value of the product. That is, they implement quality control that relates only to the functional quality of a product. By implementing quality in all their operations, the value of their product increases.

Reviewing Traditional Quality Control

The traditional form of quality control is one of detection. In other words, manufacturers take material through a manufacturing process that ends with product inspection. If the product passes final inspection, it is ready to sell. If it fails final inspection, the product is either reworked or sent to the scrap heap.

There are several major shortcomings in traditional quality control:

- The manufacturer's quality control department has the burden of being totally responsible for the quality of parts and services.
- Traditional quality control does not identify or eliminate the causes of why defective products have to be reworked or scrapped until after they fail inspection.
- Defective products play an important role in product availability. When customers are faced with delays in product deliveries, they become angry with the manufacturer and purchase alternate products elsewhere.
- There is a customer recognition problem in a quality control environment that needs to be corrected. For example, workers believe their customer is the final consumer. Therefore, they are more concerned with production quotas. They let quality control worry about the condition of the finished part before it goes to the final consumer. In this setting it is difficult for workers to grasp the concept of producing value (quality) in every phase of production.

This does not mean that workers are not concerned about quality. It simply means that production goals set by the manufacturer have more emphasis in the quality control environment. With the advent of Total Quality Control, the emphasis changes, proving that both quality and production goals can be obtained simultaneously. In fact, a production goal is much easier to obtain when quality goods are produced the first time around.

When defective components are not detected during the final inspection process and are allowed to be shipped to customers, there can be more disastrous and costly results:

Work stoppages. When contractors receive defective material, they can be faced with shutting down entire projects and eliminating many workers.

Loss of revenues. Every level of distribution can experience loss of revenues when defective material has to be returned to the manufacturer for replacement.

Excessive costs. The loss of material value is small compared to the subsequent costs caused by faulty material, such as plant shutdowns and the loss of customers.

Delivery delays. Every process has a time constraint. Those using the Just-In-Time (JIT) philosophy cannot accept delays caused by defective parts. The flow-in- process activities are dependent on the timely delivery of product.

Physical injuries. Manufacturing and receiving defective material can result in physical injuries and even deaths throughout the entire distribution chain. When this occurs, manufacturers and distributors may find themselves faced with costly lawsuits by employees as well as customers.

Accounting nightmares. Accounting plays a major role in the receipt and return of defective shipments. Accounting staffs are faced with billings and credits and can end up with endless audit trails trying to keep up with the costs involved in returning defective shipments to the manufacturer.

None of these consequences is acceptable, nor can they be tolerated by customers.

Understanding Customer Compensation

Many manufacturers are willing to give some kind of customer compensation when defective products are inadvertently shipped to their customers. For example, a manufacturer might agree to take defective goods back and pay the return freight costs, or it might offer a discount on the next order placed by the customer.

Neither of these policies totally compensates the customer because there are many added internal costs that the manufacturer does not take into consideration:

Receiving. The recipient of defective material has receiving costs but does not produce revenue from the defective material to offset these costs.

Material handling. When defective material is received, it often has to be moved from one area to another to get it out of the way until it can be returned to the manufacturer.

Storage. The cost of storing defective material is greater than storing good material because care has to be taken to insure that defective material is not mixed in with good material.

Repackaging. Original packaging is usually ruined by the time defective material is discovered, and the costs involved in repacking defective goods are expensive.

Reshipping. Reshipping defective material is more expensive since it has to be handled differently and often has to be directed to different locations specified by the manufacturer.

Analyzing Total Quality Control (TQC)

TQC relates to quality in every phase of a company's operation—from the receipt of raw goods through product production to the accounting operation. This concept uses employees from every level of the company to identify and solve problems. Not only are engineers and technicians used, but small teams of employees from all areas of the company are assigned the same tasks. Workers directly involved in putting a product together also work as a team to solve related product and process problems.

The TQC concept focuses on such issues as product reliability, form, and function. It encourages new ideas and innovative approaches to solving product-related problems. However, the new ideas and innovative approaches must be tried and proven in a disciplined atmosphere. Every company using TQC is responsible for setting the guidelines through which change can take place to keep pace with an ever- changing global marketplace. Every person in the distribution chain must be encouraged to make suggestions without feeling threatened by change and must be trained in customer recognition. The person who receives output from each specific function is that function's customer. The diagram in Figure 3-1 illustrates internal relationships that can be established by total quality control. The saying "Garbage in, garbage out" is changed to "No garbage will be tolerated!"

Figure 3-1: Internal Relationships Established by Total Quality Control

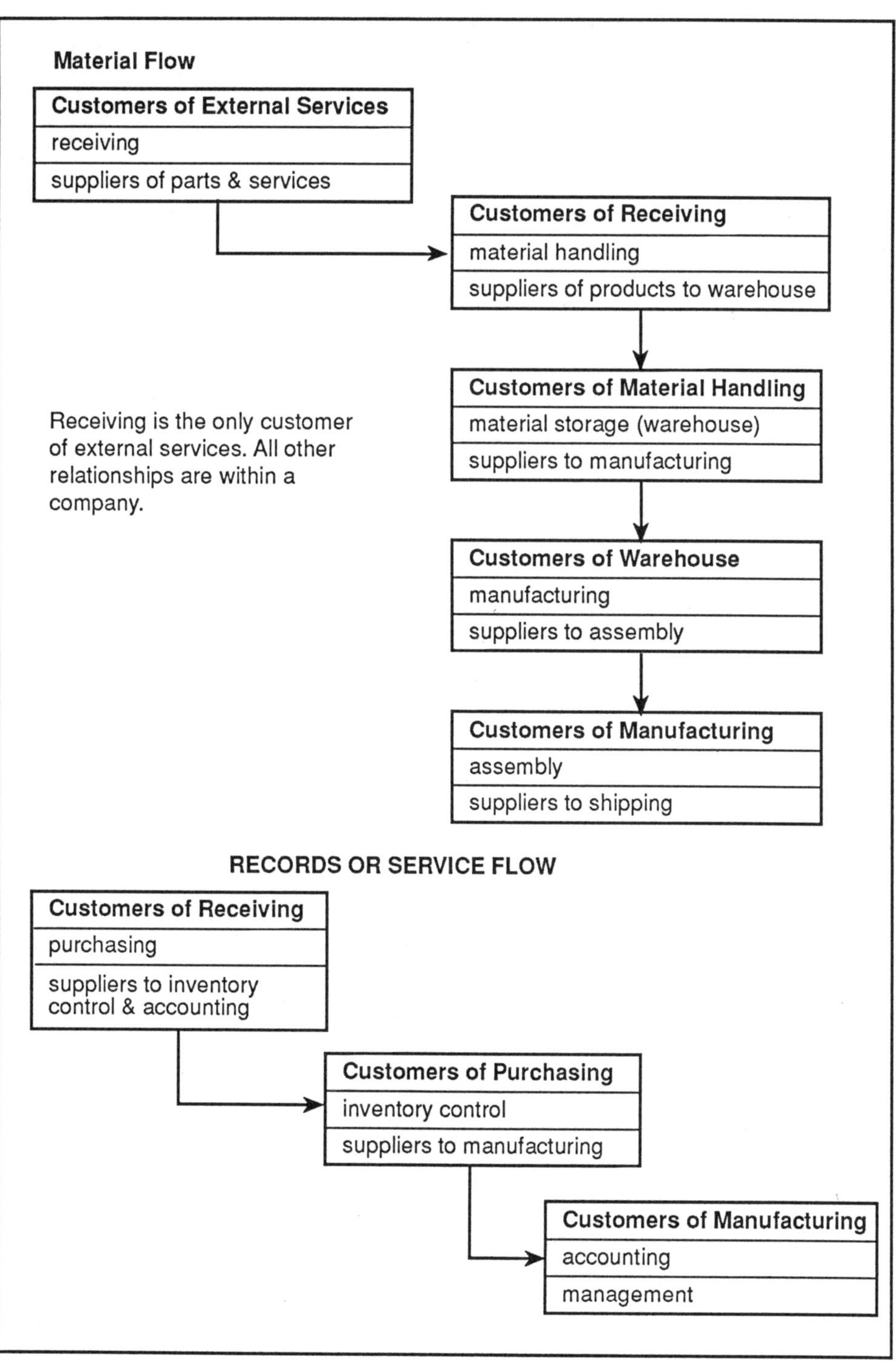

Material Flow
Customers of External Services
receiving
suppliers of parts & services
Customers of Receiving
material handling
suppliers of products to warehouse
Customers of Material Handling
material storage (warehouse)
suppliers to manufacturing
Receiving is the only customer of external services. All other relationships are within a company.
Customers of Warehouse
manufacturing
suppliers to assembly
Customers of Manufacturing
assembly
suppliers to shipping
RECORDS OR SERVICE FLOW
Customers of Receiving
purchasing
suppliers to inventory control & accounting
Customers of Purchasing
inventory control
suppliers to manufacturing
Customers of Manufacturing
accounting
management

Review the comparison chart in Figure 3-2. It compares the customer's perceived quality to traditional product quality, showing major aspects of both. Both of these quality identification programs are controls. They correct problems *after* they have been detected. Total Quality Management (TQM) identifies and corrects potential problems *before* they cause product difficulties.

Understanding Total Quality Management

TQM is a management tool that plans performance excellence in every phase of the manufacturer's and distributor's businesses. It expands Total Quality Control and encompasses the manufacturer's distribution chain, including end users, by including supplier evaluation as an integral part of managing quality. The management of every phase of these businesses (internal, external, suppliers, customers, products, service, and quality) are all vital parts of TQM. When you understand that customer value is one of perception and incorporate it into your company's TQM program, you have an even more effective method of problem identification and correction throughout your business chain reinforcing each link.

TQM includes supplier evaluation as a vital part of managing quality. The Supplier Evaluation and Selection Program becomes the vehicle that ties your customers' expectations (perceptions) to supplier performances. Look at the benefits of TQM and the Total Value Concept, which includes the Supplier Evaluation and Selection Program as an integral part of a total value package. TQM actually takes a product or service from conception to consumption. It will:

Figure 3-2: Traditional Quality Vs. Perceived Quality

	TRADITIONAL PRODUCT QUALITY	CUSTOMER'S PERCEIVED QUALITY
Product Initiated	X	
Customer Initiated		X
Sales Related		X
Marketing Efforts		X
Product Reliability	X	X
Product Availability	X	X
Material/Workmanship Based	X	

- Identify key problem areas that need immediate attention.
- Set realistic goals for solutions to these problems.
- Select teams to analyze problem areas that have been identified.
- Provide the tools needed for problem correction.
- Provide progress benchmarks.
- Reward achievement.

In essence, TQM relates to the total value package you want to offer your customers, while supplier evaluation ties customers' total value to total quality. This total value concept is composed of four basic issues:

- Services provided—Are your customer's expectations of added value being met?
- Products offered—Do your products fill your customer's basic functional needs?
- Product quality—Are your products or services free of defects?
- Product pricing—Is it fair and reasonable?

The formula for total value, as your customer sees it, looks like this:

Product + Pricing + Services Provided + Quality = Total Value

Remember, value is customer defined and customer measured.

Very few of your customers supply a measuring stick or even discuss performance measurement. When you apply supplier evaluation and selection as a part of TQM, you are actually providing your suppliers with a measuring device to gauge their performance by using your standards. They are getting a customer's view of their business performances.

Identifying Services and Their Role in TQM

Services can be extremely hard to identify as part of TQM. They are sometimes intangible, often perishable, very complex in nature, or dependent on time. Services also have quality expectations associated with them. Quality services are measured with such terms as:

Reliability. The manufacturer or distributor can be counted on to always have the product available that customers need.

Responsiveness. Manufacturers or distributors help satisfy customers through services, products, or both. They are proactive rather than reactive.

Competency. Well-trained personnel who know the products and understand customer problems are made available by manufacturers and distributors. They are able to make product applications to meet customers' needs.

Courtesies. Personnel have a good attitude and are always pleasant when assisting customers. They take a personal interest in customers and their problems. They must communicate, understand, be accessible, and, in some cases, offer security.

Services relate to many areas. Some examples are:

- Product pricing
- Product packaging and labeling
- Product knowledge and training
- Product warranties
- Customer credit and payment terms
- Product availability
- Emergency services

These are areas that can be monitored and measured as part of your supplier's quality performance in supplier evaluation and selection. These are also parameters that can be measured throughout your internal process flow. Imagine what can happen to your operation when each person realizes who his or her customers really are!

UNDERSTANDING THE IMPACT YOUR CUSTOMER'S PERCEPTION OF QUALITY HAS ON MANUFACTURED PRODUCTS AND SERVICES

Perceived quality has always been the driving customer force. It is the customer's perception of a product or service that determines demand.

People keep using a brand of product for various reasons:

- A certain brand of product may suit their needs better than a like product from another manufacturer.

- They may have used a particular brand of product for several years without having product-failure problems.
- Perhaps a certain brand of product looks better to the customer than other similar brands.
- Customers might base product preference on price, or what they consider is fair value, not necessarily because it is a "quality" product in the eyes of a manufacturer. Remember, they use their measure, not the manufacturer's.
- Distributorships often develop brand loyalties over time and tend to stick with these brands until jolted out of their rut.

Manufacturers are now beginning to realize that the traditional methods of identifying product quality are no longer acceptable. They are becoming aware of the vast difference between their concept of product quality as tangible assets and the customer's view of perceived value.

Understanding the Importance of the Customer's Role in Product Design

Many suppliers use advisory groups composed of members of their distribution network for input about product design and packaging. One of the main purposes of these advisory groups is to identify customer needs and present them to the supplier's engineering department to be outlined, analyzed, and engineered into existence.

Manufacturers will include input from the following departments in the manufacturing facility to help the advisory committee determine what product (or products) should be produced and how to produce it (them):

DEPARTMENT	INPUT
Engineering	product design, including: shape, appearance, functionality, durability, safety features, material content, machine, or process flow
Materials Control	shipping methods, receiving, material handling, material storage
Purchasing	material availability, material price, supplier selection
Production	material process flow, manufacturing process, work force needs, machinery requirements

Marketing	marketing needs for product distribution networks, sales pricing, customer services
Accounting	method of cost accounting, accounts payable, accounts receivable, cash flow modules

The missing link here is the customer or end user.

Manufacturers seldom include customers or end users in these advisory groups to provide input for the design of new products or the redesign of current products.

Every supplier planning to produce a new product can benefit greatly by utilizing information gathered from the *entire* distribution chain about product design, form, fit, and function. The ultimate end user will have valuable input. After all, customer needs are what spur the introduction of new products and the redesign of current products that are not selling well—"Necessity is the mother of invention." Unfortunately end-user input is usually as a result of sales or lack of sales, which is after the fact, and can be very costly to the product manufacturer.

Understanding the Relationship Between Price and Quality

There is a definite relationship between price and quality that stays with the customers and end users of the products you manufacture, sell, and service. It can be identified as "perceived quality" or what these people "think" about product quality. In other words, your prices must reflect value to your customers.

Pricing is an important factor at every stage of a product's distribution chain. Product pricing will vary as the product continues its journey along the distribution chain. It often relates to different issues in value judgment at each distribution point. The chart in Figure 3-3 illustrates the price expectations for different levels of distribution.

The evidence of the price-value relationship is whether or not customers are willing to pay more for products that are considered by suppliers to be "top-of-the-line" or "quality" products. If customers perceive that quality is better in a certain brand of product, they are willing to pay more for that specific product. However, they are not willing to pay the same amount of money for substitute products. For example, quality can be ranked in the following manner:

Top quality. These products are recognized as quality leaders. Customers pay more for these items and will not accept substitutions. The companies that own these products are very conscious of their image and

Figure 3-3: Price Expectations for Different Levels of Distribution

	PRODUCT OR SERVICE			
DISTRIBUTION LEVELS	**Product Availability**	**Credit**	**Expertise**	**Product Reliability**
Manufacturer	X			X
Distributor	X	X	X	X
Retailer	X	X	X	X
End User	X	X	X	X

X indicates what each level of distribution expects to receive for the price paid for a product or service.

maintain high levels of quality assurance. They demand and get higher prices for these products in the marketplace. These companies offer a whole package—better advertising, more product information, better availability, emergency services, and more reasonable warranty service—all at a price the customer is willing to pay.

These top quality products are known as the "Cadillacs of the industry." Cadillac has enjoyed the image of being the best quality American-made automobile for many years. It has a perception of top quality to consumers.

Average quality. These products are serviceable. They are not known as the highest quality products, but they are considered good, acceptable substitutes for top quality products. The majority of industries usually have two or three brand names in this category. Pricing is less than for products known for quality, but average quality products do not have the cheapest prices in the industry. For example, Oldsmobiles, Buicks, and Thunderbirds are good quality products. They might not have as many options or be as expensive as Cadillacs, but consumer perception of these cars is good.

Low quality. The items at this level are known for price. They will be the lowest price in the total product group. Even though they provide functionality, product life is shorter, and the product cannot be used for heavy duty service. Packaging and identification are poor, availability is a problem, and product warranties are nonexistent. For example, a supplier will not give the same level of service on a low-end product as on average or high-end products.

Understanding Packaging and Labeling as Perceived Quality Issues

Packaging and labeling are very important to customers at each level of the distribution chain. For example, intermediate distribution is interested in several things:

- Products that are designed for ease of handling and maintenance.
- Products that are packaged for customer and product protection.
- Shipping and receiving ease.
- Ease in product storage and retrieval.
- Proper identification of part numbers and proper labeling.

The ultimate consumer has many other considerations, such as:

- Date codes and product freshness.
- The latest design.
- Product and customer protection.
- Adequate instructions for product assembly, specific doses of medicine, proper use of products, or instructions on proper disposal of hazardous materials.

These are areas that manufacturers must consider when they purchase material and/or services that affect the packaging and labeling of products they are manufacturing.

Understanding How Customers Relate Quality to Product Knowledge Through Product Training

One of the surest methods of improving the quality image of a product, a manufacturer, or a distributor is through the availability of proper product training. This is a valuable part of customer service and should not be overlooked as part of your customer's quality perception. For example, product training is of prime importance to the intermediate stages of product distribution: the distributor, the wholesaler, and/or contractors. This covers everything from product function and installation to selling techniques. If supplier networks do not have good product training programs available, their product will be doomed before it ever reaches the customer. Make sure that the sales distribution network you choose is not only well informed about your product but that the participants are committed to sharing that information with their customers. Only those who realize the importance of product training and information sharing will make good partners.

The entire distribution industry is faced with many problems due to inadequate product training. For example, a large portion of warranty product returns is due to improper use of the product in the following ways:

- The item was not assembled properly by the customer.
- A product might have been installed incorrectly.
- The item was subjected to improper use by the purchaser.

The lack of product knowledge by the customer contributes to product failure in these instances. A good example of this happened in the early 1970's. A major producer of plumbing products decided to introduce plastic nuts to use as connectors in trap and drain areas. This idea had good potential for reducing connector and installation costs. However, marketing research and customer input was not sought. Within six months, the use of plastic nuts had to be abandoned. The manufacturer had failed to furnish product training to explain the makeup and proper installation procedures for the plastic nuts, and they were being destroyed by plumbers using heavy pipe wrenches for installation. After this the manufacturer decided to provide proper training for customers. Today, many homes have entire plumbing networks made out of plastic pipe as well as fittings because manufacturers and suppliers are providing proper training for plumbers.

When you purchase a product, you expect the manufacturer to include instructions pertaining to product assembly, product care, etc. When this information is omitted or you cannot understand the instructions that are included, you generally will use your own judgment about what to do with the product. In the end, the customer's estimation of a quality product includes product knowledge and product training.

Understanding Warranty as Perceived Quality

Customers want a measure of product assurance and take supplier warranties into consideration when making major purchases. Warranties are a measure of product assurance to customers. They state the degree of confidence manufacturers have in their products or services.

A manufacturer's warranty will generally cover defects in both material and workmanship and span the entire distribution chain, making restitution at all levels. Distributors, contractors, and ultimate end users view the warranty from different perspectives:

- Distributors—Warranties mean ease of product replacement or a method of accounting for defective merchandise to distributors.
- Contractors—Smooth, easy, quick replacement of warranty material is important to contractors.
- End users—They are interested in warranties as a reasonable method of making adjustments to an unacceptable situation when defective material or services are encountered.

Warranties are also a measure of product assurance to customers. Customer expectations of product warranties are:

Reasonability. Customers want product warranties to be reasonable. For example, a supplier might require that customers purchase a warranty or extended warranty policy with the purchase of a product. However, this might not be advantageous for the customer. It might be cheaper for the customer to "junk" the product rather than pay for maintenance or emergency services on it.

Quick warranty resolutions. A customer expects quick problem resolution and proper accounting for any inconvenience a product failure might cause. For example, a customer might use a power drill several hours a day, every workday. A warranty that states that a defective drill has to be returned to the supplier for credit or repair would not be reasonable to this worker. The supplier that makes a replacement tool available while a faulty one is being repaired or allows for an over-the-counter exchange would be resolving the issue in a way quite acceptable to the customer.

Reviewing Manufacturer Product Warranty Policies

All manufacturers can benefit by reviewing their product warranty policies on a regular basis. They cannot afford the old approach of "set it and forget it," and neither can you.

Evaluate your manufacturers' or suppliers' product warranty policies. Do they meet the standards of your company's final warranty statement regarding each product you sell? You cannot allow any of your suppliers to offer product warranties that do not meet the conditions in your company's final warranty statements. This type of evaluation will begin to bring about continual, controlled, constructive change in two important areas:

- The manufacturer will begin changing inadequate product warranty policies to meet customer requirements.
- Your company will begin requiring changes in poor warranty procedures caused by the manufacturer's inadequate product warranty policies.

This is an area where your sales and marketing departments must supply continuous information about customer needs and the changing market demands concerning product warranties.

Incorporating Innovative Warranty Approaches to Achieve Quality Images

Many manufacturers and distributors are beginning to take innovative approaches as they strive to become known for having a total quality image. They want to be *the* company everybody likes to buy from.

Here are a few innovative ideas being used by some distributors:

- Some distributors have begun offering loaner products to customers to use while their faulty products are being repaired.
- A group of manufacturers in the Houston area has monitored the failure rate of its products for many years. The group allows deductions of the same percentage as the percentage failure rate on each of their distributor's purchases of that product. For example, if the failure rate for a particular product is 1 percent, then distributors can deduct 1 percent from their invoices every time this item is purchased from the supplier. By doing so, the distributor has credit up front and can really service the customer by simply replacing the defective product over the counter and disposing of the defective product.

Look at some of the other paybacks in this approach:

- Defective material can be disposed of more quickly and more efficiently without affecting the inventory of the manufacturer or the distributor. Laborious product failure documentation can be avoided, material can be field scrapped, and material storage and freight costs on returns can be avoided.

- Accounting records are easier to maintain since credits are issued at the front of the transaction and elaborate methods of tracking returned material are not necessary.
- Sales personnel of the manufacturer and distributor have more time to concentrate on sales and customer satisfaction issues. They no longer have mounds of paperwork to fill out to make sure everyone gets the proper credit.
- Customers are happier since they get the faulty product replaced on the spot. The hassles in getting correct invoices and having to wait to get proper credit or material back are eliminated.

Did the quality of the product change? No, but the quality of customer service made a major leap. Manufacturers cannot expect their customers to do without a product that is used daily. Instead, customers will purchase a different brand of what they consider equal or better value for their money.

It is the job of quality manufacturers or distributors to inform their suppliers about such problems. Every manufacturer and/or supplier should also demand and require this type of customer feedback from distributors because they are partners in marketing their products. This is an area where distributors have the opportunity to establish a solid quality image with customers. Customers deserve and expect these services and assistance.

Understanding Terms in Relation to the Customer's Quality Perception

The customer's cash flow is affected by your payment terms. A quality manufacturer is willing to make allowances for varying types of payment terms when dealing with distributors. The same is true of companies that supply material to manufacturers. It is important for customers to have flexibility in determining the form and timing of payments. It is unreasonable to expect a market segment to use the same payment terms all the time.

Terms are related to many issues:

- They may relate to cash discounts to customers when payments are made quickly.
- They may relate to the length of time over which payments can be extended.
- Terms can be included in profit margins if they are included in product costs.
- The end user will see terms most often reflected in the form of pricing concessions.

Why not offer a payment program that meets each of your customers' particular needs? Talk to your suppliers. Explain the importance of addressing the needs of your customers in an individual manner. For example, a new business might have a problem with cash flow, or a more established firm might always discount. Payment terms are an important part of cash flow, whether it is your cash flow or your customer's. Let your suppliers know what your expectations are in this area. You and they must realize that payment terms are subject to change when the economy has a prolonged swing in one direction.

During a recent economic downturn, a large manufacturer was experiencing a cash flow problem. Its purchasing department was instructed to send the following letter to all suppliers:

> Dear Supplier:
>
> We are currently experiencing a cash flow crisis similar to that of other manufacturers in our industry as a result of the recent economic downturn. We expect this situation to continue for the next 12 months. During this time frame, we would like to ask your assistance in a temporary revision of our payment terms.
>
> We would like to extend the payment of invoices to a 90- day period. All of our suppliers will have the same consideration, and all invoices will be paid at the end of each 90-day period. At the end of the 12-month period, or when economic conditions improve, we will return to regular payment terms.
>
> You are greatly appreciated as a supplier, and we would like your reply on this proposal within the week.
>
> Yours truly,
>
> A. Friend

Without exception, everyone of the manufacturer's suppliers accepted the proposal for extended payment terms. There were four factors that led to such favorable responses:

- The manufacturer had an excellent payment history with all suppliers.
- The manufacturer was considered to be a solid performer in the industry.
- The manufacturer did not use company size or buying power to dictate terms in a stressed market environment.

- The manufacturer had the reputation of *always* keeping business agreements to the letter.

Some of your customers will discount all the time, while others may choose to pay at the end of the pay period. Ask your suppliers to help you prepare a more flexible payment-terms package for your customers. Your customers will perceive added value when you provide this assistance for them.

Understanding the Relationship of Product Availability to Perceived Quality

Your customers expect to purchase a product when *they* want it, not when the supplier decides to furnish it. While product availability is of prime importance to all concerned, the driving force in product availability is the *end user.* Some examples of how manufacturers, distributors, and end users deal with product availability are:

Manufacturers—Manufacturers can adjust their manufacturing processes or finished goods inventories to fluctuations in product demand.

Distributors—Distributors can use safety stock to cover inadequate supply or exhaustive demands.

End Users— Material must be available when the end user needs or wants it.

However, end users may very well decide to find another supplier if you don't have product availability when their needs arise. Then they apply their own concept of value added or perceived quality, and the result is change in the market share of particular products. Make sure you understand who your customers are. Refer back to Figure 1-1 to properly identify customers in the production/distribution chain.

Manufacturers are especially vulnerable in this area. As orders from customers are accepted, they begin to purchase material to manufacture goods. If at any point in the manufacturing process one of their suppliers fails, the effect can be monumental:

- Lead times have to be extended.
- Inventory becomes unbalanced.
- Expediting costs increase.

- Customer complaints begin to backlog.
- Orders are cancelled.
- Layoffs may be forced on the work force.
- Excess inventory occurs—even to the point of obsolescence.
- Future business is hurt since an unfavorable reputation is formed.
- Market share decreases.

In the just-in-time manufacturing environment, supplier performance in every area is critical. Transportation suppliers must perform on schedule, indirect materials must be available exactly when needed, outside services must be performed on time, and customers must be satisfied.

Just-in-time flow of products has three basic elements that must flow uniformly and must always be on time:

- Component parts and services needed to manufacture products should always be delivered on time and in the correct quantity.
- Manufacturing should always be on a designated production schedule to have a steady flow of finished products available.
- End-user demand patterns should be consistent. When a change in demand occurs, it should be predictable.

The manufacturer cannot produce products when suppliers fail to provide the goods or services needed for production. A change in any portion of this flow causes inventory problems, shuts down plants, and sends the work force home.

An aerospace firm I was working for was nearing the end of a contract with the federal government. It had designed and bid on another contract job that would last for several years. The bid was accepted, and the firm set about preparing the changeover of material and machinery to supply the product for the new contract.

The machinery supplier fell behind on the stated delivery time for the new machinery by several weeks. Literally thousands of people were laid off for that period of time. The aerospace firm lost many good employees who could not wait to be rehired. The cost to hire and train new employees from scratch was much higher than anticipated. This extra expense should have been shared by the machine supplier since its inability to deliver product on time had caused the extended layoff.

You have to be willing to stay tuned in to your customer's current and future needs. The customer, whether it is the manufacturer, distributor, contractor, or retailer, realizes it cannot afford to carry excess inventory to hedge against the inability of the supplier to supply product on a continuing basis. When manufacturers do not have or cannot produce the products their customers want, they become unhappy because product sales suffer, and distributors become disgusted because excess inventory expenses are out of control. The distributor, as well as the manufacturer, begins to lose the quality image it has tried to maintain. To make matters worse, the customer goes elsewhere for future purchases.

Distributors must ask their customers what products they use on a continuing basis and keep an adequate supply of those products in stock, instead of trying to stock everything the manufacturer offers. Customers do not use all of a supplier's products continually, and distributors tie up precious inventory funds when they try to "carry everything just-in-case." The customer's quality image of a company and its product value go hand in hand with product availability.

Understanding Quality Perceptions in Emergency Services

Suppliers often consider emergency services a necessary evil. Emergency services can be costly and difficult to maintain as they are usually performed outside the regular process of providing products or services. However, they are one of the characteristics that customers attribute to quality suppliers.

Emergency services apply to many types of conditions. For example, emergency situations can warrant:

- Quick delivery of products.
- Provision of product information.
- Corrective measures.
- Maintenance assistance.

They can:

- Save lives.
- Prevent untimely delays.
- Replace faulty components.
- Dispense information.
- Correct mistakes.

DETERMINING YOUR QUALITY RATING

How do you rate as a quality company? Rate yourself on the quality of services you offer your customers. Ask your company managers for their views of how well your company services its customers. You can learn how your company's services are perceived by customers by doing a customer survey. You want your customer to understand that the information you are asking for has value for you and them. Your survey sheet might look like the one shown in Figure 3-4. You must know how your company's services are perceived by customers. Let your customers know that their opinions are valuable and welcome.

An easy and effective way of getting the survey to your customers is to mail it with your billing statements. You might consider offering your customers an incentive for returning the completed survey (such as a discount on their next purchase), but this is not mandatory.

You will find out exactly what your customers' perceptions of your company are by reviewing the returned survey sheets. If customer perceptions are not good, supplier evaluation and selection is a tool that can help your company gain a quality image by striving for performance excellence in all areas of your business, including your suppliers.

There are two additional ways to get input information on quality:

1. You can include some of your key suppliers at quality meetings so they can get firsthand information about your current needs. You will find them helpful in making suggestions that can save money and improve performance to the end user. If your materials suppliers are not interested in these activities, it's time to look for different suppliers.
2. You can also include some of your customers at quality meetings to provide firsthand information about their current needs.

USING SUPPLIER EVALUATION AS AN EFFECTIVE METHOD FOR RECONCILING AND MEASURING OPPOSING VIEWS OF QUALITY

Manufacturers will have to change their views of quality in the 1990's to survive in the competitive global market. Product quality has to move from being the manufacturer's "claim to fame" to being a competitive, value-

Figure 3-4: Customer Service Survey

Customer Service Survey

Our goal is to give you the best service in this area. As you are a valued customer, we would appreciate your input on the quality of the services we offer.

Please answer the following questions and return the survey sheets to us by return mail or in person. A 10% discount will be given to you on your next purchase.

- Return Mail—We will send a 10% discount card to all participants returning the survey by mail. (Be sure to include your name and mailing address on the survey sheets).
- In Person—A 10% discount on your next order will be given to those participants returning the survey in person.

	Below Average	Average	Above Average
Sales Assistance			
• Courtesy—Are we easy to do business with?			
• Timeliness—Are we quick and efficient?			
• Helpfulness—Do we have the "whatever-it-takes" attitude?			
• Product Knowledge—Do we solve your product problems?			
• Follow-up—Do we follow up with you in a reasonable length of time?			
• Returns—Does our service on returned products meet your expectations?			
Product Issues			
• Mix—Do we stock the products you need?			
• Quality—Are our product brands acceptable to you?			
• Availability—Do we always provide product when you want it?			
• Pricing—Do we provide fair product value?			

Invoicing Procedures

- Timeliness—Do you receive our invoices on time?
- Accuracy—Do our invoices always reflect what you actually purchased?
- Credit—Are product returns posted promptly?
- Terms—Do our payment terms meet your needs?

Additional Comments: ____

____

____

____

____

Name:

Mailing Address:

added component that addresses the needs of every link in the distribution chain, ending with the ultimate end user.

Supplier evaluation and selection is a very effective means of communication between the manufacturer/supplier/distributor/end user. Its major strengths are:

- It stresses the total quality concept in supplier performance and ties in the customer's concept of perceived quality, as well as product characteristics, in its measure of manufactured quality.
- It demands a commitment from your management to performance excellence in every area of business.
- It identifies areas in supplier performance that are below your set standards of performance.
- Corrective action is taken to completely eliminate problem areas caused by poor supplier performance.
- Recognition is given to suppliers and individuals whose levels of performance meet your set standards of excellence.
- The process of improving quality through better performance never stops; it is an iterative process that produces results year after year.

You, as purchasing manager, must take the initiative to strive for continuous improvement and a constant evolution toward supplier/customer/manufacturer/distributor excellence. By reviewing your supplier relationships, you realize that you cannot allow them to remain constant. These relationships will either improve as you implement the necessary changes for performance excellence, or they will deteriorate. In other words, if you do not manage and engineer change, change will manage you and your company.

Old habits of inertia need to be broken as your company incorporates plans for performance excellence in all areas of its business relationships. Obstacles to performance excellence cannot remain when there is an atmosphere of controlled, continuous, constructive change taking place.

CHAPTER 4

EVALUATING SUPPLIER REPRESENTATIVES AND SUPPLIER SALES ASSISTANCE

Supplier representatives and independent sales representatives play crucial roles in product and supplier acceptance at manufacturer, distribution, and end-user levels. It is the responsibility of purchasing, manufacturing, and sales groups to measure and analyze the quality and effectiveness of representation being given by these reps.

UNDERSTANDING THE SALES REP'S FUNCTION

Good supplier and independent sales reps focus on the needs of manufacturers, distributors, and end users. It is important that both supplier and independent sales reps give you concise information about the supplier or suppliers they represent and their products.

Suppliers employ two types of sales representation. They either use their own sales reps, or they contract with an independent sales firm for the sale and representation of their products. Supplier reps are employed by a single supplier and are responsible for the sale of that supplier's products in a particular geographical area. They should be loyal to the supplier that employs them and to the products they represent. An independent sales rep is either self-employed or works for an independent company that handles several major suppliers and/or manufacturers and their product lines.

There are other differences between these reps that you need to be aware of. For instance, they handle product promotions and warranties, display product knowledge, and provide product coverage in different ways:

Product promotions. Independent sales reps do a better job with the administration of product promotions. For example, suppliers require distributors to keep all accounting records for their promotions. However, the independent sales reps will generally do most of the accounting and record-keeping on the product promotions they are involved in.

Warranties. Warranties may not be handled as diligently by independent sales reps. Some suppliers net their warranty returns against sales volume, thereby reducing sales revenues for the independent sales rep.

Product knowledge. The independent sales rep's product knowledge may not be as thorough as a supplier rep's because he or she represents multiple suppliers and products.

Product training. While some independent rep firms do offer product training, for the most part they depend on the supplier's technical representative for actual product training activities.

Product coverage. The independent sales rep is able to cover a broad range of suppliers and supplier products during visits to your purchasing department or sales location. This can be advantageous for the distributor with multiple suppliers because there will be fewer reps visiting and taking up valuable time at multiple sales locations. There is also a caution here. These reps tend to concentrate on representing the products that produce the most sales revenue for themselves and the suppliers they represent. It is up to you and each branch manager to make sure they cover all of their suppliers and products that directly affect your company's volume of sales on each visit.

The rep who is supplying raw material directly to a manufacturer is doubly important to the success of the manufactured product. It is essential for this rep to be well informed about the raw material used by the manufacturer and to be well informed about the product or products the manufacturer is producing. It is most helpful for this rep to be technically oriented and capable of suggesting alternative manufacturing methods and materials that can save production time, reduce the product price, and/or improve product quality.

An effective company or independent sales rep will carefully plan the purpose and content of each visit to a manufacturing facility. He or she might have to address the manufacturer's engineering, production management, and purchasing managers on a single visit, and preparation is vital for successful visits.

There are essentially six issues that demonstrate the abilities of each supplier or independent sales rep that directly affects your company's sale or use of his or her supplier's products:

Communication. Are the sales reps doing business with your company friends or strangers? Your supervisors should be able to communicate freely with all reps about the handling, storage, or use of their products. It is also imperative for all personnel at multiple branches to know each supplier and independent sales rep and how to contact him or her when they need sales assistance. This helps improve the use of the reps' material usage, sales, or service knowledge.

Product knowledge. This is the greatest asset a sales rep possesses. All reps can describe their products and product costs. Some even know how their products function. However, those who actually have an in-depth product knowledge are assets to both you and their companies. They will not only know about the physical aspects of their products, they will know how their products relate to your needs.

Sales assistance. Supplier reps should be able to provide information to sales and purchasing on anything from better pricing, terms, and product availability to actually closing customer sales. These all come under the heading of sales assistance. Reps should be able to give information to manufacturing and engineering on anything about form, fit, or function.

Literature availability. Purchasing, sales, and marketing depend on supplier literature for product information. Therefore, all reps should keep your product literature current and provide literature for their supplier's new product lines and supplier policies.

Manufacturer/supplier/distributor/end user problem solving. The ability and willingness of supplier and independent sales reps to resolve problems of manufacturers, suppliers, distributors, and end users are a vital part of successful partnering and good customer relationships.

Training programs. It is the responsibility of reps to offer, plan, and implement product-training programs for your company's sales and service departments to help stimulate product sales. The implementation of product-training sessions (or the lack thereof) affects your customer relationships and is part of supplier and independent sales reps' performance measurement.

It is important for you to monitor and analyze all these issues because they affect your company's sales volume, profits, supplier relationships, and customer service. Your suppliers expect your company to sell or use their products, and you cannot jeopardize valuable manufacturer/supplier/distributor partnerships by allowing unacceptable supplier and product representation. You also have an obligation to supply your customers with the best value for their money. You cannot do this without everyone's assistance.

MONITORING AND ANALYZING COMMUNICATION SKILLS

Your company's sale or use of supplier products relates directly to the rep's ability and willingness to communicate. When your purchasing, sales personnel, and production managers know reps personally and know they can be depended on, they have confidence in the supplier and supplier products, which results in an increase of supplier sales.

Reps who just happen to stop by, sit around drinking coffee, then ask if there are any problems on their way out the door, are not communicating or making an effort to provide quality sales calls. They are wasting their time and your time.

On the other hand, reps who make appointments with your purchasing personnel and with key people at each of your company's sales or manufacturing locations and show up on time ready to discuss business issues are certainly appreciated. These reps will have a definite purpose for making an appointment and will be ready to do constructive business with you. These reps are communicating and are assets to the supplier and to you.

The majority of supplier and independent sales reps make calls to a distributor's primary purchasing location only. However, you should expect your reps to add two additional visits to their agendas:

- Companies with multiple sales or manufacturing locations should expect their reps to make quality calls to each location in their geographical area.
- Reps should visit all the people who deal with their products in each location. This includes visits to receiving, material control, and quality

control departments. By making visits to these departments they will know if material is being shipped properly, packaged correctly for ease in handling, storage and retrieval, and if quality standards are met on every shipment.

Monitoring the Number and Purpose of Sales Calls Made by Supplier and Independent Sales Representatives

Monitoring the number and purpose of sales calls to your company can help determine your rep's communication skills and abilities. These calls should be monitored by department managers in your purchasing, sales, production, engineering, and material control departments. In the case of multiple branches, monitoring should be done at each outside branch location by branch managers. Effective monitoring can be done by using a sign-in log and performance evaluation form.

Using a Sales Rep Sign-in Log

You will want to use a sign-in log in your purchasing department and at each manufacturing or sales location to monitor sales rep calls. The log should contain the following information for effective monitoring:

- Branch location
- Date (day/month/year)
- Rep's name
- Supplier represented
- Products represented
- Person visited
- Purpose of visit

An example of a sales rep sign-in log is illustrated in Figure 4-1. You will want to instruct all of your company's reps to complete the log every time they visit. The branch manager at each location has the responsibility of making sure the log is filled in properly and sent to your purchasing coordinator on a monthly basis for consolidation and storage. This information will be used during the grading and evaluation of your suppliers and their reps.

Figure 4-1: Rep Sign-in Log

BRANCH LOCATION: Alexandria Louisiana

DATE: 9/91

DAY	REP'S NAME	SUPPLIER	PRODUCTS	PERSON VISITED	PURPOSE OF VISIT
7/8	Sam Smith	Dupont	Refrigerant	Charles	Check Leakers
7/9	Bob Johnson	Honeywell	Thermostats	Charles, Billy,	New Products
			Air Cleaners	Sam	Price Increase
			Relays		Customer visits
					with Charles
7/10	Bill Dobson	Dobson's Rep.	Equipment	Charles & Billy	New Stocking Plans
		Agency	Switches		New Product Fliers
		a) Johnson	Sprayers		Floor Displays
		b) Warren			
		c) Smith Inc.			

Branch Manager: Charles Bell
signature

Monitoring the Quality of Rep Visits

An effective tool for monitoring the quality of your reps' visits is a sales rep performance evaluation form. This form should be designed to give you information on a rep's performance regarding:

- Contactability.
- Product literature update.
- Warranty problems and how they are handled.
- Joint calls to your customers.
- Internal plant contacts including purchasing, sales, engineering, production, and material control.
- Product knowledge including both supplier's and your company's products.
- Quality of customer assistance.
- Product training sessions—internal and external.
- Supplier product promotions.
- Overall quality of sales calls.
- Frequency of sales calls.

An example of what this form might look like for distributors is illustrated in Figure 4-2. Manufacturers are interested in different grading parameters for reps. For example, manufacturers are more interested in plant contacts to engineering and production control than distributors are. Technical knowledge about the rep's products as well as the products being manufacturered is another area that concerns manufacturers. Therefore, the form illustrated in Figure 4-3 is more appropriate for their use.

The branch manager at each location has the responsibility of making sure this form is filled in properly and sent to your purchasing coordinator on a monthly basis for consolidation and storage. This information will be used during the grading and evaluation of your suppliers and their reps.

EVALUATING THE REP'S PRODUCT KNOWLEDGE

Well-informed reps will know every aspect of the products or services they are offering. It is not unreasonable for you to expect reps to be knowledgeable in the following areas:

Figure 4-2: Rep Performance Evaluation Form—Distribution

Representative: Sam Smith **Date:** 1/22/93

Sypplier (s): Dupont **Sales Location:** Alexandria, La.

ISSUES FOR PERFORMANCE MEASUREMENT	90%-100% Excellent	80%-89% Good	65%-79% Average	Below 65% Needs Improvement	COMMENTS
Contactability	√				We are always able to get in touch with Sam.
Product literature update		√			
Warranty problems and how they are handled		√			
Joint sales calls to our customers		√			
Quality of customer assistance		√			
Involvement in product training sessions	√				Sam conducted several programs on ozone depletion.
Handling of supplier product promotions	√				
Quality of sales calls		√			
Frequency of sales calls		√			

Branch/Department Manager: Charles Bell
signature

Figure 4-3: Rep Performance Evaluation Form—Manufacturing

Representative: William Davis **Date:** 1/28/93

Sypplier (s): Benton Casting Inc. **Sales Location:** Sheridan, Ark.

ISSUES FOR PERFORMANCE MEASUREMENT	90%-100% Excellent	80%-89% Good	65%-79% Average	Below 65% Needs Improvement	COMMENTS
Contactability		√			
Communication skill			√		
Product knowledge - our products				√	Needs to understand our products better. Doesn't know how his products relate to our product.
Product knowledge - supplier products		√			
Internal plant contacts - sales, engineering, production, and material control			√		Must make sure to check with Materials Control on each visit.
Quality of customer assistance				√	Is not able to answer engineering questions about his quality control procedures.
Availability of technical data		√			
Helps resolve supplier problems			√		
Active in suggesting product improvements				√	Needs to meet with Production Control and engineering more often.
Frequency of sales calls			√		

Branch/Department Manager: Jim Phillips
signature

Material	Pricing factors
Content	Availability of alternate products or services
Weight	Shipping methods
Size	Manufacturing methods
Color	Availability parameters
Lot sizing	Competitive issues
Packaging	Ecology factors
Labeling	

Reps providing raw material or products directly to manufacturers should be educated in the following areas:

- They should know the function of the manufacturer's product in the marketplace.
- They should know the customers the manufacturer sells to at the consumer level.
- They should know how their material or services fit into the manufacturer's product.
- They should have some idea of their product's cost contribution to the manufacturer's finished product.
- Those suppliers that provide materials or services to the work-in-process flow of the manufacturer's products must understand the production flow and operations within the manufacturing facility.
- Whenever necessary, reps should be able to provide engineering information and make available appropriate technical drawings.

You should require that your suppliers suggest better methods for overall product improvement. Be sure they know your product and design engineers and quality control managers. Introduce them to receiving and warehouse managers and production supervisors. Your material control group will want to know about suppliers' product availability, lead time, and dependability of continued supply.

MONITORING AND ANALYZING THE QUALITY OF SUPPLIER SALES ASSISTANCE

Reps are your representatives to their suppliers, your advisors when manufacturing problems occur, and your extra salespeople when dealing with your customers. Their involvement in giving and getting you adequate sales assistance from their suppliers can take on many different forms. Your reps should be providing assistance in the following areas: access to toll-free communication lines, product information services, including contacts with supplier's management, and supplier advertising.

Analyzing Communication Expenses

An analysis of expenses that can be accrued by not having free access to communication lines will divulge some interesting facts. For example, look at your telephone expense. A large part of your company's long distance telephone charges accrue to the purchasing, expediting, and sales departments.

The majority of distributors use their own personnel to answer technical, engineering, and warranty questions for their customers and themselves when they should be using their supplier's personnel. You cannot expect your clerical personnel to provide adequate information regarding these issues, especially when you have multiple suppliers. Your reps can be instrumental in helping you get and maintain free access to communication lines. This opens the door for better supplier/distributor/customer communication and can make a drastic reduction in current communication expenses.

Toll-free telephone and fax numbers. Your reps play an important role in helping you get assistance in these areas:

- They can be instrumental in helping you get access to toll-free communication lines.
- They can make sure you have separate and current toll-free numbers for technical, engineering, and warranty assistance.

Electronic interface. Electronic interface is also an excellent method of communication. It can increase the ease by which you can get and give product information and help you give better customer service.

During our pilot program, one of our suppliers provided electronic computer interface for its distribution network. Its rep played an invaluable role in helping us establish and maintain communication. He trained our personnel to use the supplier's program effectively and continued to assist us until the electronic interface was fully operational.

We were assigned a code that allowed access to the supplier's product inventory and production file. We could easily check availability of product, next production cycle, and forecast date of next available inventory. Our supplier updated status every day, so we could see when our orders were completed and scheduled for shipment.

Our purchasing department also used the supplier's computer interface to place orders. The status of newly placed orders could be checked—usually within two-to-three hours—to determine current status and the expected delivery date.

This supplier also downloaded information directly to our computer, providing new production schedules for each item on order. With this information, our purchasing department was able to plan future orders using the most current information about the supplier's product availability.

The manufacturer's electronic interface program was a tremendous success with our company. Availability of parts could be checked each time an order was entered. The orders could easily be checked for completeness and for errors once they were entered, and our order entry became faster. Supplier order numbers were available the same day for editing purposes. When orders were shipped, we had the method of shipment, carrier name, quantity and departure readily available. We could give better service to our customers by being able to give them shipping dates that were realistic. Orders for this manufacturer's product increased significantly.

Our engineering department also worked on problems together with the supplier's engineering department using the same electronic interface.

Monitoring Product Information and Sales Services

The product information services you should expect from supplier and independent sales reps include:

- Updating all product and sales catalogs.
- Providing sales brochures on new and current products.
- Keeping product price lists current.
- Cataloging all engineering updates.
- Verifying all supplier and supplier rep's telephone and fax numbers.
- Reviewing product displays.

- Checking on-hand availability for their supplier's products.
- Noting product shortages.
- Encouraging and helping with the return or exchange of slow-moving items.
- Helping dispose of idle inventory by reducing sales price or providing co-op funds to assist sales.
- Issuing availability schedules for new products.
- Providing material drawings and specifications when necessary.
- Assisting in solving product-flow problems.
- Assisting in solving special material-handling or product-storage problems.
- Contacting their supplier's management to help solve major problems.

Sales assistance you should expect includes:

- Providing posters, counter displays, and rules for product promotions allowed by suppliers and approved by you.
- Quality joint sales calls with your company's sales personnel.
- Solving warranty problems.
- Expediting open product orders and customer back orders.
- Arranging product training seminars for counter and outside sales personnel and your customers.
- Providing supplier plant visits for your company's sales personnel, their customers, and upper management.
- Availability of sales and training videos for you and your customers.
- Supporting open houses by providing door prizes, assisting in preparations, and making personal appearances.
- Participation in trade shows and product fairs.
- Supporting special sales through cooperative sales prices.

The degree of product knowledge and the ability to share product information are crucial to suppliers' and distributors' sales. A representative must be able to provide *real* assistance to you and your customers. This assistance is given by implementing sales promotions, by providing technical information when necessary, and by making job site visits with marketing and sales personnel when necessary.

Availability of Product Literature

Literature availability is an important sales aid. Many companies provide literature with both sales and technical information. They generally provide this to new distributors free of charge. Other catalogs, as well as brochures, are provided as a portion of advertising allowances with each purchase of goods.

It is very time consuming for sales and purchasing employees to look up all the information they need for every product they sell. Distributors with multiple suppliers have to look through every supplier's catalog for minimum order quantities, best price buys, freight terms, and warranty information. If that information is not available on one page of a supplier's catalog, the supplier or independent sales rep should provide you with this information on easy-reference fact sheets.

It is the job of each supplier and independent sales rep to keep your literature updated. The amount of time you have to spend dispensing literature can be reduced if your suppliers and their reps do their job effectively.

Supplier literature should be concise and provide the following product information:

- Pricing
- Best product price levels
- Quantity price breaks
- Packaging
- Adequate descriptions
- Dimensions
- Functionality
- Technical issues
- Minimum order requirements
- Warranty
- Shipping methods
- Terms of sale
- Payment terms

Figure 4-4 is an example of good supplier information provided by an independent supplier rep. All of the information is given on an easy-reference fact sheet. Figure 4-5 is an example of inadequate supplier information that is of little value to you or your company. The information is general in nature and incomplete, and the manufacturer refers to other literature for additional information.

Figure 4-4: Good Product Information Provided by Reacond Associates

C & R Products Compay
1000 E. Del Amo Blvd.
Carson, Ca. 90746

Phone: 213-537-2800
Fax: 213-537-7673

Reacond Associates
1515 Royal Parkway
P.O. Box 40057
Euless, Tx. 76040

Phone: 817-267-4891
Fax: 817-267-4896

PRODUCT LINE:	URETHANE FOAM KITS (ONE AND TWO COMPONENT) SPECIALTY SEALANTS, CAULKS & ADHESIVES, FIRESTOP SYSTEM PRODUCTS, BLAZE BARRIER CLOTH, HIGH TEMP PAINT & TAPE, THERMOSTAT GUARDS, FLASHLIGHTS, ELECTRIC CORD/ADAPTERS, CONDENSATE PANS, & VARIOUS HVAC SERVICE PRODUCTS & TOOLS
MINIMUM ORDER:	$50.00 NET. (CASE QUANTITIES ONLY)
FREIGHT:	$1,250.00 NET BILLING PREPAID
ORDER FROM:	REACOND ASSOCIATES OR FACTORY
WAREHOUSED:	REACOND ASSOCIATES
SHIP FROM:	REACOND OR C & R PRODUCTS
EMERGENCY ORDERS:	RECEIVED @ REACOND BY 11:00 A.M. WILL BE SHIPPED SAME DAY WHENEVER POSSIBLE.
BACK ORDERS:	PLEASE CONTACT FACTORY
WHOLESALER NOTES:	STOCKING PROGRAM AVAILABLE
WARRANTY INFO:	C & R TO CREDIT OR REPLACE WITH NEW AT THEIR OPTION

SEE PRICE SHEET FOR COMPLETE DETAILS ON TERMS AND CONDITIONS.

IMPORTANT

DEFECTIVE MATERIAL MAY ONLY BE RETURNED WITH PRIOR AUTHORIZATION BY C & R PRODUCTS CO. RETURNS ARE TO BE SENT PREPAID AND WILL BE SUBJECT TO A 15% RE-STOCKING CHARGE. NO RETURNS WILL BE ACCEPTED AFTER THE CODE DATE. FREIGHT DAMAGE CLAIMS MUST BE SETTLED WITH THE PUBLIC CARRIER.
5/31/90

Courtesy of Reacond Associates

Figure 4-5: Inadequate Product Information

GENERAL INFORMATION

- For additional information refer to XYZs catalogs.
- This price list supersedes all previous prices and quotations. These prices are in effect from the date shown and all items will be invoiced at the time of shipment. Prices are subject to change without notice.
- Terms - net 30 days.
- All orders are subject to acceptence by XYZ. Possession of this price list does not constitute an offer to sell.
- Prices listed are FOB shipping point unless otherwise noted.
- Prices include standard warranty as described in General Conditions of Sale and Warranty.
- Minimum billing - $50.00.

XYZ can accept no responsibility for possible errors in catalogs, brochures, and other printed material. XYZ reserves the right to alter its produdts without notice. This also applies to products already on order provided that such alterations can be made without subsequential changes being necessary in specifications already agreed.

XYZ, INC.

XYZ, INC.
P.O. Box 000
Somewhere, U.S.A.

Telephone: 1/234/567/8900
Telefax:
Telex:

Printed in USA

MONITORING SUPPLIER ADVERTISING

The key to effective supplier advertising is that it reaches your customers with information that is important to them. This type of advertising is very important in "pull-through" sales. The money your suppliers spend on regional and national advertising should be recognized in your evaluation program. You need to make sure that your supplier's advertising can be seen or heard by your customers and recognizes your company as a local distributor. Your company's advertising should reference the same supplier and products.

There are basically four product/customer relationships covered through supplier advertising:

- New products to new customers
- New products to current customers
- Current products to current customers
- Current products to new customers

Supplier advertising is used to increase your company's current status between existing products and its customer base. The message tends to strengthen the relationship customers have established with your company's current product offering and stimulate sales in existing market areas.

It also introduces products to new and established customers. Supplier advertising should explain advantages of a new product over existing products and help establish different buying patterns for a new group of customers. It must communicate something "better" as an incentive for changing buying patterns.

Supplier advertising helps improve relationships with your company and its customers. It signals to customers that your company is seeking new, innovative products to help them in their businesses. Therefore, it should be consistent and informative in nature.

Good supplier advertising increases product sales, builds goodwill, and improves your company's reputation—it communicates. It is your responsibility to review the method, message, and effectiveness of supplier advertising in your market area. Look for:

Consistency. Advertising methods should be consistent with your market's habits. For example, national television advertising may have little effect on your company's product sales, but ads in local newspapers or local sales journals may be very effective. Your market may go to work early and work late, preventing your customers from seeing or reading literature containing product advertising. However, customers may listen to the radio in their vehicles, offices, or homes during the day, making radio a more effective advertising method.

Information. The message transmitted through supplier advertising must be informative to be effective. For example, it might include the following information:

- Product pricing
- Sales locations
- Form, fit, and functions of new products
- New uses for old products
- Product quality information
- Ecology information
- How a product can increase personal comfort
- What the product can do for customers.

When supplier advertising contains useful information, it helps build good will between your company and its customers.

Monitoring Your Market Area for Advertising Effectiveness

It is up to you to monitor your market area. Ask customers if they have seen or heard supplier advertising. Determine how many of your company's customers take advantage of cooperative funds for their local advertising. See if your company's sales increased as a result of the advertising programs offered by your suppliers. Review your local market journals and newspapers for supplier ads.

Here are examples of supplier advertising you will want to monitor for effectiveness:

- Stuffers for mailing advertising to selected customers
- Customized advertising such as calendars
- Spot radio or TV ads that tie you or your customers to a supplier's product
- Special sale fliers or ads in local trade journals or magazines

- Billboard ads
- Truck decals
- Uniform programs
- Giveaways (hats, cups, pens, etc.)
- Supplier product promotions
- Incentive trips.

Determine which advertising method is best for your company and its customers and relay the information to your suppliers for more effective advertising and results.

Reviewing the Availability and Purpose of Co-op Advertising Funds

Many suppliers have cooperative (co-op) funds available to you for promotion and advertising purposes. These co-op advertising funds accrue as a percentage of your purchase dollars. They may be used to offset your advertising expenses for promoting the supplier's product. There are two stipulations to these cooperative funds:

1. The advertising activity must represent the supplier's product or logo in some manner.
2. You must share in a portion of the expense for the advertising activity.

For example, a supplier might want to set up a dealer network in your area. Each dealer or contractor that participates in this network might be provided with customized uniforms or shirts with the supplier's name and logo on the back or on the pocket, or perhaps truck decals. The expense of the customized uniforms, shirts, or truck decals would be a shared expense between the supplier, distributor, and the dealer.

Manufacturers will find that co-op advertising can give an instant quality image to their distributors. For example, distributors may include the manufacturer's name or logo as well as their own on customized items used for advertising. By doing so, customers begin associating your company's name with particular manufacturers.When the shared expense is between the supplier, distributor, and the dealer, the distributor will require the dealer to make a purchase-dollar commitment of the supplier's product before making co-op funds available.

Determining the Effectiveness of Supplier Promotions

Supplier promotions are also a form of sales assistance. Often, companies utilize sales promotions to encourage sales activity. The supplier, the supplier rep, and the independent sales rep have the following responsibilities in supplier promotions:

- They should conduct most of the advertising and accounting for the activities that relate to the product promotion.
- They should solicit your advice to make sure the promotions will be effective.

It is your responsibility to make sure you have been notified about these activities in plenty of time to prepare your position. You may find that some suppliers do not allow enough preparation time for you to be able to participate in their product promotion. You may not find out about some product promotions until they are over.

CAUTION: Suppliers should *never* be allowed to run a promotion without the approval of you, upper management, marketing, and sales.

Product promotions, when properly administered, are effective sales aids. When they are mishandled, the results can be disastrous. For example, it is not uncommon for suppliers of room air-conditioning products to offer trips as an incentive to encourage product sales. These trips might be offered to sales personnel as well as customers. When this type of promotion takes place, you have a major concern: It is your job to make sure the products involved in the promotion are not sold prior to the awarding of the trips and then brought back for credit once the promotion and trip are over.

The results of mismanaged promotions can actually have suppliers and their distributors awarding prizes for *fewer* sales. An apparent increase in sales dollars can be the result of price increases instead of sales promotions. Consider two additional cautions before participating in this type of promotion:

1. Be careful in using percentages for increases as a result of these promotions. Low figures can be increased drastically with only a slight increase in unit sales.
2. Make sure that the sales of items during supplier promotions are profitable to your company. Your sales department may be able to show great

performance figures by reducing the price of the product. They can qualify for the supplier promotion and actually cost you money through lower profits at the same time.

Without these precautions, the suppliers, your sales department, and your customers win—and you lose! Therefore, you want to make sure supplier promotions are tailored to your needs to make sure you win, too.

SOLVING MANUFACTURER/SUPPLIER/ DISTRIBUTOR/END-USER PROBLEMS

When you and your suppliers, their reps, and independent sales reps develop quality partnerships that include your manufacturers and customers, the results can be amazing. For example, during the pilot program one of our suppliers suggested we do a joint survey of our market area. The object was to see what could be done to increase our business.

Our internal management and the supplier's marketing management spent several weeks determining the best method of conducting the survey and the appropriate customer-related questions. With the help of the supplier and the supplier reps, we surveyed a large geographic area by splitting it into zones to hold customer meetings. The sales managers in these zones were instructed to invite a selected number of customers and potential customers to be our guests at dinner meetings. These customers and potential customers were encouraged to ask any question or make any comments they felt were important to us, the supplier, or the rep.

One potential customer said that he required his workers to be on the job site by 8:00 a.m. every morning. Since our sales location did not open until 8:00 a.m., they did not come to our sales location for supplies. It was easier to buy their supplies from one of our competitors.

As a result of this conversation, our sales location began to open for business at 7:30 a.m., resulting in a steady increase in customers and in sales. By beginning a partnering relationship with a valued supplier and the supplier's reps, we were able to extend that partnership to include our customers. Through improved communication, we were able to find and solve unexpected problems that were costing us customers and profits.

During the same time frame, we had an opportunity to help a faucet manufacturer solve product-related problems. The manufacturer was making faucets to be used in kitchens. Unfortunately, the faucets leaked.

The manufacturer was using a unique machine designed specifically for high-pressure testing of these faucets. The unit was working properly, and all of the faucets tested were passing. However, the completed faucet units were still experiencing leak failures in the field.

The company that designed and built the high-pressure test machine invited the manufacturer's management and engineers to its plant location to study the leakage problem. They discovered that the lack of pressure in many homes was allowing a back-flow of liquid that was causing leakage. A minor design change in gaskets and the addition of a second-stage testing of low-pressure situations on the test equipment solved the problem.

This supplier was willing to help identify the cause of the leaking faucets and take corrective measures by improving the design of the pressure-testing machines it was manufacturing.

Joint ventures with quality partners helping each other can solve problems and increase sales for the manufacturer, supplier, distributor, and end user.

Determining the Importance of Engineering Assistance

You may have a customer with unique needs that can only be worked out with the assistance of your supplier's engineering department. When this happens, the supplier rep or independent sales rep should be more than willing to work with you, your customer, and the supplier's engineering department to help find a solution and to provide your company with material specifications and drawings when necessary.

When reps are willing to help you provide this type of customer assistance, they are a definite asset to your company and your company image. After all, people helping people is a prime example of what effective partnering is all about.

MONITORING SUPPLIER PARTICIPATION IN SUPPLIER TRAINING PROGRAMS

Sales and product training is another area in which suppliers should be graded. Suppliers who offer active participation in training your outside and inside sales forces and your production and material-handling groups about their products are valuable only if their reps are willing to make the extra effort to provide this service. Your company's performance will show the effect of good product training.

Carrier, a manufacturer of air-conditioning products, is a company that is committed to product-training programs for their customer network of dealers and contractors. Training is given on issues ranging from basic air-conditioning to more complex problems relating to refrigeration. Carrier's reps are a very valuable part of this program and provide special literature, training aids, and, in the case of new products, conduct the training sessions.

These training activities are extremely important to each distributor's customer base. They help customers learn about the products they sell and service. Through this type of communication, customers know they can get answers to all their questions regardless of the complexity of the problem. Carrier distributors provide product training programs to new and existing customers throughout their geographical areas.

Areas where supplier training is vital include:

- Proper material handling and storage
- Material mix
- Material identification
- Stock rotation
- Hazardous material handling and disposal
- Proper use of tools and machinery
- Methods of identifying defective material
- How to obtain proper credit for defective material from the manufacturer/supplier

You can see how supplier reps and independent sales reps play crucial roles in all the issues we have discussed. The quality of supplier sales assistance can be monitored in these areas by using the supplier performance evaluation forms previously discussed and shown in Figures 4-2 and 4-3.

REAPING THE BENEFITS OF PERFORMANCE EVALUATIONS

You are providing a great service to yourself, your suppliers, their sales representatives, and independent sales representatives by conducting supplier evaluations. The results can be unlimited. The following case example is one way performance evaluation helped our company personnel change their opinions and attitudes about a rep.

CASE EXAMPLE

A supplier representative was viewed as a pushy, arrogant person by the majority of sales personnel in our company. During a performance evaluation meeting, the evaluation team member representing sales was very outspoken and very opinionated about this particular supplier rep. One of his comments was, "I don't understand how this rep rated so high in last year's evaluation." Once the evaluation began and facts were presented, this team member's opinions based on negative feelings were set aside. As facts were presented, the team member's negative attitude toward the supplier rep changed. Here are the graded results of the supplier rep's performance based on actual data:

- Number of sales calls made to distribution and its branches during the evaluation period: 120
- The number of branch locations visited during the evaluation period: 100% (The rep covered over 40 branches in an area that stretched from the southwest border of Texas to the northeastern part of Louisiana.)
- The supplier rep conducted product shows and demonstrations in all five of distribution's territorial regions.
- The supplier's product sales doubled in one year's time.
- The supplier rep introduced new products and made sure the appropriate product information was given to distribution and its branches, helping solidify new product sales.
- Profitability on the supplier rep's line of product increased. This profitability had shown a steady increase each of the three years this rep had been servicing our company.

Yes, this supplier rep was pushy and sometimes seemed arrogant, but the bottom line was he was doing his job. In fact, he was doing his job so well that the supplier he represented was among the top ten performers when evaluation results were tallied for that year.

Once factual data were presented, the team member who disliked this rep made a remarkable change in attitude. As a result, our company personnel realized the rep's pushy nature was a reaction in part to the feelings our personnel were projecting. They began to change the way they communicated with the rep and the pushy, arrogant behavior diminished. When personality differences and feelings are set aside and facts considered, the outcome can be astounding.

There are many other benefits to performance evaluations:

- Reps know exactly what you expect of them and know they will be graded every year on their performance.
- Supplier reps use good performance measurement from the evaluation process to get increases in wages, to receive promotions, or even to get better job offers from other firms.
- Independent rep firms also benefit by an increase in their sales and profits by improving their performance to your set standards. They are also able to attract more quality suppliers to their firms.
- You get better quality performance from reps and suppliers, which results in increased sales and profits. Those who fail to reach out and meet the challenge will find themselves being replaced.

The final reward is expressed in a letter from Zachary R. Chaky, Jr., who is District Sales Manager for Honeywell Inc. (refer to Figure 4-6). During the pilot program Mr. Chaky was a supplier representative for two different suppliers over a 10-year period, Johnson Controls and Honeywell Inc. Both companies were among our top ten suppliers.

Mr. Chaky reached out and met the challenge to achieve performance excellence as did the companies he represented. As you can see by Mr. Chaky's letter, our suppliers and their representatives knew exactly what we expected from them and appreciated becoming quality partners with a distributorship dedicated to continual, controlled, constructive change.

Performance excellence means everybody involved wins!

Figure 4-6: Letter from Zachary R. Chaky, Jr., District Sales Manager for Honeywell, Inc.

March 5, 1992

Mr. Obie Ford
3814 Brook Shadow
Kingwood, Texas 77345

Subject: Pilot Vendor Program

Dear Mr. Ford,

As a factory representative I have participated in a wholesaler designed vendor evaluation program. Over the years I represented two different manufacturers, Johnson Controls and Honeywell, as a participant in the program. I found the program to be extremely rewarding for the wholesaler organization and their vendors.

On the wholesaler side they define the vendors' role and the role of each sales-related individual in their organization. The target of the program is to increase sales and provide recognition of those individuals who helped accomplish this task. On the vendor side each sales representative knows what should be done and what the wholesaler wants to accomplish. The end result is a working partnership between the supplier and the wholesaler. In the course of a year the efforts of the major suppliers' representatives are reviewed to determine the ten best suppliers, the vendor company of the year, and the vendor salesman of the year.

The evaluation encompasses product quality, packaging, technical expertise of the representative, number of calls made to all branches, in addition to price and availability. Over a year's time the efforts of the vendors cannot be masked by isolated targeted efforts. If a vendor makes a continuous effort throughout the year it is very noticeable.

I found the program very personally rewarding. While with Johnson Controls I was selected as one of the top ten vendors, and while with Honeywell I was selected as the Vendor Salesman of the Year. I don't know of very many wholesalers who take the time and expend the effort to reward vendors. In reality they do not have to; the increased sales are enough recognition. I will never forget the awards I received from my wholesaler partner. Of all the awards that I have received I value them the most. I hope this concept is adopted by other wholesalers throughout the United States.

Best Regards,

Zachary R. Chaky Jr.
District Sales Manager

CHAPTER 5

ANALYZING PRICING POLICIES

The product-pricing policies and payment terms of suppliers are two areas of major concern to manufacturers and distributors. Even so, they often fail to provide suppliers with documented information and miss the opportunity to help them make intelligent pricing and payment-terms decisions that ultimately affect their company's profits. One of the purchasing manager's major partnering jobs is to provide this information for your supplier's review.

For your company to survive in today's competitive global market, it must be able to monitor, analyze, and control the direct and indirect costs of doing business. Doing this will allow your company to maintain a fair profit and stay in business. Remember, *nothing is free!* There is a cost associated with everything.

There are two major pitfalls you need to be aware of:

1. New Products/New Customers—The Texas A & M University Industrial Distribution Program developed a cost ratio for companies selling new products to new customers. It is fifteen times greater than selling current products to current customers. It is a very expensive and hazardous proposition for companies to concentrate solely on this practice.
2. Waste—Many companies are aware of the ever-increasing cost of doing business and fail to monitor the effectiveness of their increase in cost expenditures. Figure 5-1 is a product cost analysis showing waste percentages. They are as high as 40 percent of the cost of products. This has to stop! Companies that continue to accept the status quo will find themselves out of business. According to W. Edwards Deming, this figure should never exceed 5 percent.

Before you can demand better performance in supplier pricing policies and payment terms, you need to understand the basics of price/cost relationships for your suppliers' businesses as well as your own. For example, each

Figure 5-1: Product Cost Analysis

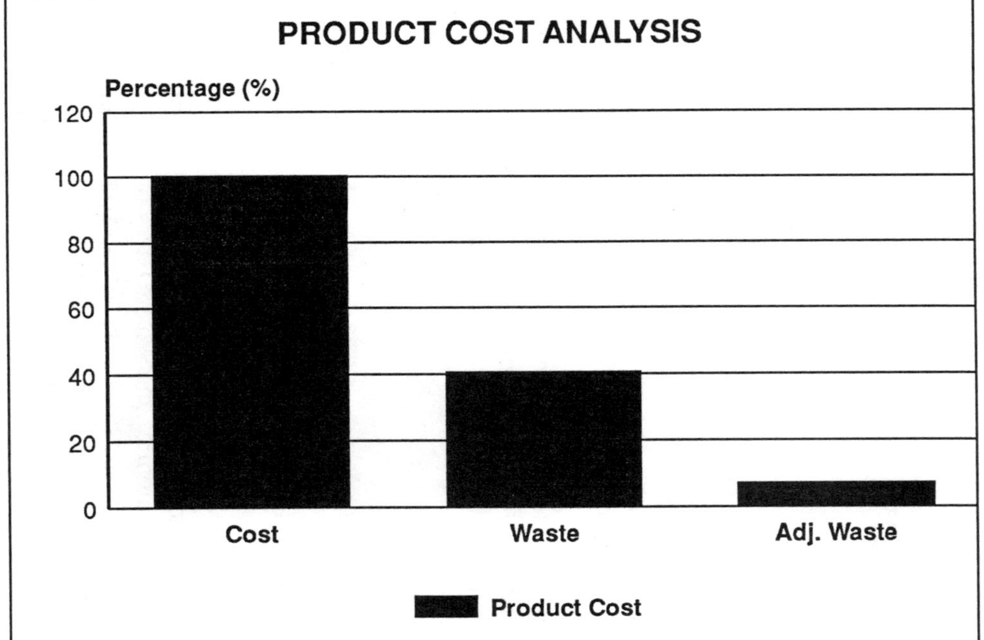

PRODUCT COST ANALYSIS

Percentage (%)

120
100
80
60
40
20
0

Cost
Waste
Adj. Waste

Product Cost

Wastes average 15-40% in product cost.
It should not exceed an adjusted waste
level of more than 5%.

level of a product's distribution chain has costs, and reasonable profits must be made at each of these levels for the suppliers to stay in business.

It is vital to the success of your company that you become aware of the following pricing drivers directly affecting product prices and your profits and how you can help your suppliers understand your standards for their performance in these areas.

FIVE PRICING STRATEGIES AND THEIR EFFECTS ON PRODUCT PRICES

You need to be aware of five pricing strategies and the effects they have on product prices:

- Competition's market share
- Measuring return on investment
- Maintaining pricing stability
- Maximizing profits
- Reducing expenses

Competition's Market Share

The corporate health of a firm can be most easily gauged by its share of the market. This is particularly true if the company has kept pace with the market size and is in tune with current market conditions. For example, one of the greatest impacts on market dynamics today is the influx of foreign competition. Manufacturers who have been complacent in their selection of supplier and distribution partners are suffering greatly. They are subjected to price squeezes from distributors who use the "ripple effect" to reduce prices. Unfortunately, this also reduces market size.

The ripple effect. The ripple effect takes place when a distributor decides to increase market share by reducing prices or by introducing lower-priced, alternate products. These actions are usually independent. That is, the primary manufacturer is not aware they are taking place.

When the ripple effect begins, other distributors either lower their prices or begin to put pressure on their manufacturers to reduce prices in an effort to keep their share of the market. When this occurs, manufacturers have two options. They can reduce distribution or reduce prices.

Manufacturers can eliminate distributors who indiscriminately reduce prices and fail to offer services, thus causing market turmoil. This is a costly, time-consuming task. Even so, manufacturers that have product recognition and can maintain demand for the product will usually take this option. It may result in a short downturn in total revenues, but the long-term result will maintain the size of the market and eventually increase it.

If price reductions are avoided, the revenue from the product will remain the same. Over a period of time demand will rebound and sales will begin to grow again. An example of this happened with one of our suppliers during the pilot program. The supplier, a large manufacturer of primary equipment for the home, selected three distributors in a specific geographical area to sell its equipment to housing contractors. Unfortunately, the manufacturer failed to do its homework beforehand. One distributor turned out to be a very poor choice, and the results were disastrous.

An overview of the inadequate supplier's business methods will help you understand some of the consequences of poor partnering:

- The distributor in question sold the manufacturer's product on the basis of price only.
- Services were not offered to customers.
- Needs were not forecast to the manufacturer.
- Inventory levels were not planned.
- Prices were reduced so low that the other two distributors could not compete and maintain a fair profit margin.
- Inventory levels could not be maintained, and the distributor could not supply the entire market area with the manufacturer's equipment.

Instead of growing, sales in the market area began to decline. The manufacturer was forced to replace the distributor that had gutted the market area with low equipment prices. It took two years for the manufacturer's equipment to regain its original status in the marketplace and to begin increasing market size.

Make sure that the partnerships you form are consistent with your company's overall goals and objectives. After all, you are joining your name and reputation to those with whom you form partnerships.

Manufacturers are often forced to reduce prices when distributors begin to sell lower-priced alternate products or when unified pricing pressure from the manufacturer's entire distribution chain occurs as a result of changed market conditions or economic environment. Price reduction is the least acceptable alternative of its far-reaching effects. It reduces the size of the market and also reduces revenue to the manufacturer. (Reduced revenue means lower wages and lower profits, which result in reduced availability of labor, land, and investors.)

Measuring Return on Investment

Many manufacturers target a level of return on investment or on net sales to set pricing strategies. This is usually a long-range objective, although short-term changes may occur. These will tend to average out since they are both based on sales volume.

The choice of partners, the exchange of information, and the measure of performance are critical factors in this pricing strategy. Along with the advent of highly leveraged buyouts in recent years, the trend has been away from managing assets to managing cash flow. This has prompted cutthroat tactics in the distribution chain in order to survive in the short run. Many manufacturers and distributors have been forced into a succession of short-range objectives and ever-changing strategies to reach cash flow goals. When this happens the distributor as well as the customer are adversely affected. Fluctuating revenues cause cutbacks in inventory that affect customer service and reduce revenue. It can become an endless circle. If it is not stopped, it eventually eliminates the companies forced to take these actions.

Maintaining Pricing Stability

Some companies attempt to keep stable pricing in their markets even though product demand may fluctuate. This generally works best when there is a clear product leader in the market area. Usually this strategy is used to maintain market share or return, which means that stable pricing is an approach to these objectives. Of course, this does not mean that everyone in a particular industry has the same price for similar products. It simply means that they maintain a constant relationship to the pricing leader. For example, companies may be higher or lower in price, or price may change from region to region, but they would rather maintain these relationships to the pricing leader than to get into an all-out pricing war.

The advent of government-supported, foreign pricing competition has created a running battle among manufacturers and distributors to maintain pricing stability. Here again, partnerships are vital in the stability of a marketplace. The manufacturers and their supplier and distribution partners that are willing and able to maintain pricing performance have a chance to maintain pricing stability in today's competitive, global marketplace.

Maximizing Profits

Maximization of profits is probably the most-followed practice in pricing. Again, this is a long-range goal and is generally practiced over an entire product offering, rather than on individual items. It means that some items may be sold at very low margins or even at short-run losses, while others maintain higher margins. The overall revenue maximizes profit when measured across the entire product line. Resources will be allocated evenly and reasonably when this is practiced over the long run. The firms that have stayed in constant contact with suppliers and customers, that have been consistent with performance standards to their suppliers, and diligent in maintaining their customer performance standards will be rewarded. Those who have been complacent with these measurement standards will disappear.

The bottom line, even in pricing goals, is that changes are inevitable. Only those companies that have continual, controlled, constructive change will survive. The key is maintaining constant performance as measured by the needs of your customers.

By reviewing the illustration in Figure 5-2, you can see how prices, added costs, and profits change at each level of a supplier's distribution chain. Every level of distribution must cover product costs and expenses and maintain a profit to survive.

Competition will not allow your prices to be unreasonable. Market dynamics will only allow a reasonable price before the customer either does without the product or uses an alternate item.

Your hedge against these actions is in the value added to the product or in increased services for which your customers will pay. You must create this value-added image in your customers' minds. This can be done by working with your suppliers to develop strategies that will maintain your image of providing fair value for the prices you charge. For example, suppose two suppliers, A and B, provide a like product to a market area. Supplier A is known for having the lowest-priced product and owns the low-end-price share of the market. Supplier B has an image of being a quality supplier, but begins to offer a "no-frills" product to penetrate the low-end-price portion of the market. In response to Supplier B's new "no-frills" product, Supplier A

Figure 5-2: Price and Cost Changes for Levels of Distribution

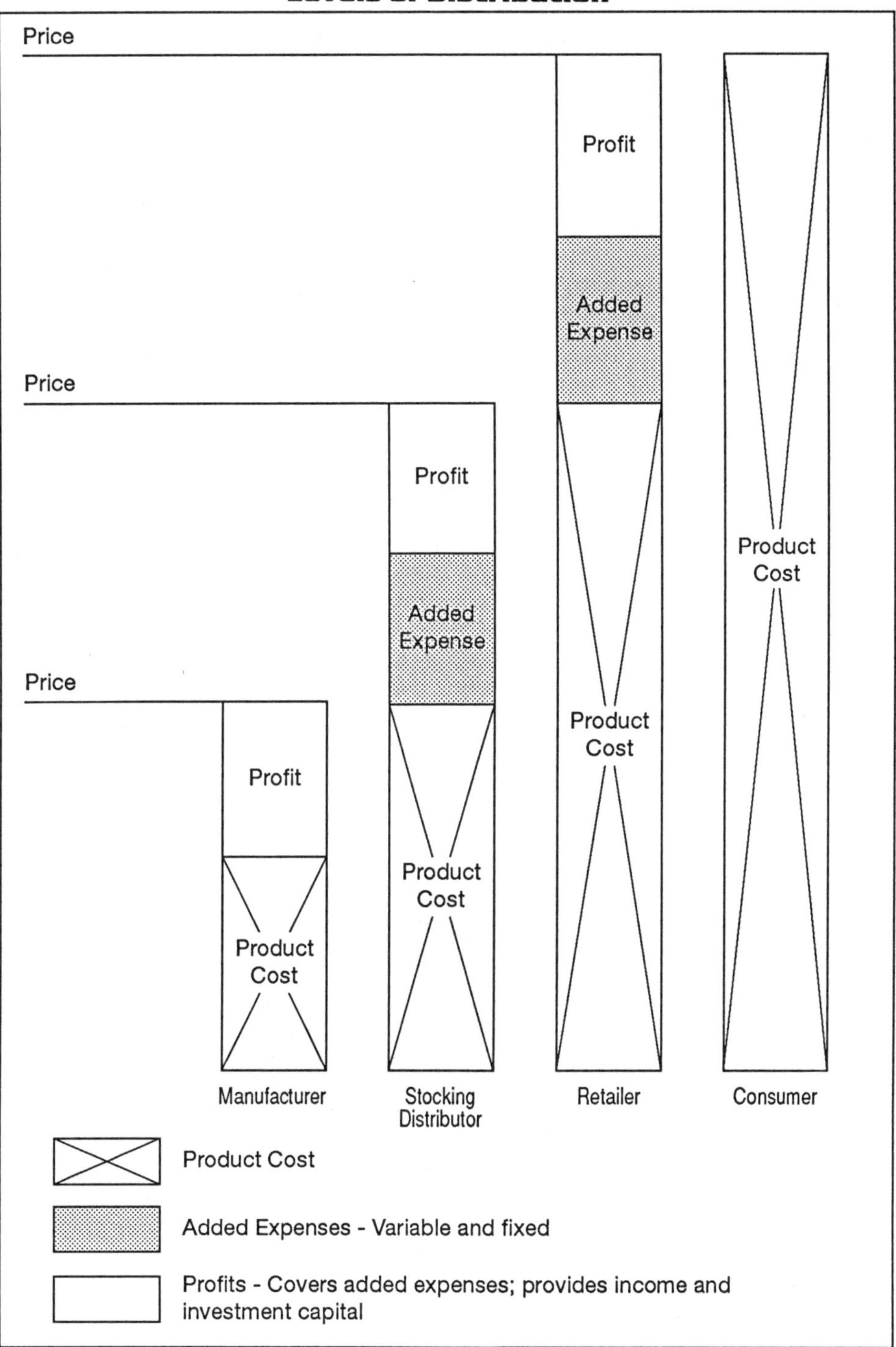

immediately begins to offer a five-year extended warranty to customers. Supplier A has an established track record in the market area and knows the exact effect Supplier B's new product will have. Supplier A has two advantages over Supplier B:

1. Supplier A knows in advance that Supplier B is targeting the low-end market area and that it will cause greater product-to-customer costs for Supplier B.
2. Supplier A has conducted a customer survey to find out exactly what customers want.

Supplier B is caught completely off guard when Supplier A begins offering the five-year extended warranty and has to rethink pricing and market strategy. Supplier B does not know how its new "no-frills" product will perform over an extended period of time. Therefore, its portion of the market will be marginal, at best, until it determines the feasibility of following Supplier A's lead and also offering an extended warranty.

Supplier A has successfully maintained its market share by maintaining product price and adding value to the product in the customers' minds. There is an added cost to Supplier A, but it is not anywhere near the loss of revenue that would have come from lowering product price.

Reducing Expenses

The reduction of expenses has a far greater effect on bottom line profits than price increases. When expenses are decreased, profits increase by the same amount. However, price increases are diluted by terms, discounts, and marketing expenses. Another danger is a loss of market share. It is up to you to encourage your suppliers and your company management to adopt an aggressive cost-reduction and expense-elimination program.

Blanket purchase orders. A manufacturing firm might use very large quantities of a supplier's product in the manufacture of a particular product. By using a blanket purchase order agreement, the manufacturer agrees to buy a certain quantity of the supplier's material within a set time period. The supplier is willing to quote the manufacturer a firm price over the set time period and to hold the material at its facility until the manufacturer requests release of the material. There are advantages for both companies:

Supplier benefits:

- The supplier has a committed purchase order for sales through a given time period.
- Production schedules may be smoothed to fill down periods.
- Economies of volume buying can be used in the purchase of material.
- Better customer service can be maintained through constant availability of product.

Manufacturer benefits:

- Pricing is constant over a given period of time and, in most instances, reduced.
- Availability of product is assured.
- Average inventory can be reduced.
- Storage space can be allocated properly (often it can be reduced).

Planning cost reductions. Planning on reducing costs is an approach that only works if a company is dedicated to cost containment. The purchasing manager should encourage all of his or her company's suppliers to practice cost containment. Supplier representatives can be questioned about their manufacturers' cost containment practices. If they do not know, they should find out and provide the answers on their next visit.

One company took this approach to cost containment:

- Every department in the manufacturing facility was given a budget to reach in cost reduction.
- The cost reduction was made a part of the annual review plan for each department. Before annual reviews were performed, the cost savings budget had to be obtained.

The cost savings ideas that were generated as a result of this plan were amazing. Of course, the plan varied according to the amount of potential cost reduction. For example, the personnel department might have had a cost reduction budget of a few thousand dollars, while the material control department had a cost reduction budget of hundreds of thousands of dollars.

Many employees were skeptical of the plan, but every department met its objective, and some even exceeded it. Savings of almost $1,000,000 were generated in the first year. This was not bad, considering that the total cost of goods produced was $18,000,000. This company's cost reduction plan netted better than 5 percent of total cost of goods produced at the company's location.

THREE PRICING LEVEL POLICIES

There are essentially three pricing level policies within each product market that manufacturers, distributors, and retailers use:

- Low pricing
- Average pricing
- High pricing

Understanding the Use of Low Pricing

Suppliers can become very aggressive in product pricing. They initiate pricing competition by refusing to be under-priced. For example, a supplier can maintain low pricing by reducing product costs or by reducing profit margins.

Product costs can be cut in several ways. For example, they can be cut by redesigning products or parts, using alternate materials and/or methods of manufacture, finding and using different material suppliers, or reducing labor costs. Reducing profit margins is the least desirable action since it reduces net revenues to the supplier's company.

Redesigning products or parts. It is not uncommon for manufacturers to reduce product cost as well as enhance the functionality and durability of their products through redesign. For example, television was originally black and white. Now, through enhanced design we have color displays, hookup to any number of TV stations, cable, and VCRs that enable us to view movies in our own homes or make our own family movies. Through continued redesign material content has been reduced and prices continue to decline.

Using alternate materials and/or methods of manufacture. The use of alternate materials can mean a substantial savings for the manufacturer. For example, the introduction of plastics in the manufacturing industry affected the design, weight, functionality, and durability of many products and reduced manufacturing costs by billions of dollars.

Plastics also affected the wholesaler, retailer, and the end user. At first, plastic products or products with plastic parts were considered to be cheap imitations of better products. However, as the strength and durability of plastics increased and cost advantages were maintained, plastic became not only acceptable, but desirable.

Using alternate materials has even affected our money! Alloy metals have replaced solid silver and copper in the minting of U.S. coins—another material-substitution, cost-saving measure.

Finding and using different material suppliers. Every manufacturer and distributor must continue to seek out new, cost-efficient material, new manufacturing methods, or new products and encourage current suppliers to update old products.

Purchasing managers can monitor this through new product analysis like the one shown in Figure 5-3. This report links past suppliers to your selection of suppliers in the current year. It shows the dollar amount of sales and purchases for each of these suppliers and allows you to compare the dollar amount of new products to the total sales or purchases of your company. This will help you determine the dollar amount of purchases or sales your company has experienced through new product sales. For example, distributors may find that new product sales account for more than 30 percent of their annual sales volume. Manufacturers will want to compare previous or current sources of material supply to new ones to recognize the saving generated through the manufacture of new products or new sources of supply.

Figure 5-4 is a New Product Analysis Report showing the comparison of purchases from the previous and current supplier (A). It also indicates that an old supplier (C) was replaced with a new one (B) and engineering approved the use of an alternate material from Supplier D. Finding new sources of supply allows the manufacturer to use low-pricing if necessary.

Reducing labor costs. The use of shop-floor control techniques can change the size and/or routing of product through different machine cost centers. Reallocating labor power may also bring about labor cost containment, another part of product costs.

The use of automated machinery and the advantages obtained in better material flow through machining operations can result in cost savings. These types of change may also improve product quality. The use of numerically controlled, multi-operation machinery can do both.

Figure 5-3: New Product Analysis—Sales

NEW PRODUCT ANALYSIS—SALES

Year Ending _____

Supplier	3 Years Ago	2 Years Ago	1 Year Ago	Total for Last Year
A	$20,000	$ 30,000	$ 50,000	
B	5,000	7,000	12,000	
C	3,000	3,000	3,500	
New Suppliers 3 years ago. Total last year.				$ 65,500
X		5,000	7,000	
Y		100,000	300,000	
Z		1,500	5,000	
New Suppliers 2 years ago. Total last year.				312,000
D			7,000	
F			25,000	
G			32,000	
New Suppliers 1 year ago. Total last year.				64,000
Total sales last year of products introduced during the last 3 years.				441,500
Total sales last year.				$2,020,000
New product sales ratio (percent of total sales)				21.7%

A local valve manufacturer produced a line of high-volume brass valves. The market was very competitive, margins were slim, and price increases were out of the question.

The valve manufacturer learned of a new machine that had the capability of changing a three-machine work center with three machine operators into a single machine center with one machine operator. This multi-stage machine was also able to produce the brass valves at a much faster pace and improve product quality as well.

When the manufacturer purchased the new machine, two-thirds of the labor power was reallocated to other positions to help manufacture other product lines. A marginally profitable product line was changed into a good profit producer by reducing labor costs and improving process flow of the product.

Figure 5-4: New Product Analysis—Costs

NEW PRODUCT ANALYSIS—COSTS

Year Ending ______

Supplier	New Cost	Old Cost	(old-new) Difference	Reason
A	$67,000	$ 75,000	$ 8,000	introduced a new line of fasteners
B	3,500	(supplier replaced supplier C)		
C		5,000	1,500	
D	70,000	100,000	30,000	alternate material proposal accepted by engineering
Total cost savings			$ 39,500	
Total cost of sales for 1992			790,000	
% of cost savings			5.0	

Reducing profit margins. A supplier whose profit margins are reduced will try to compensate by an increase in sales. The goal is to get a larger market share to offset the loss of margin revenue.

Figure 5-5 shows that a supplier with a normal 25 percent gross margin on sales that is reduced by 2 percent will need a 9 percent increase in sales to earn the same profit dollars.

A reduction of profit margins is the least advisable method for supporting low pricing. It is usually a supplier's last resort to maintain current sales volume. Furthermore, a supplier might be willing to reduce profit margins and discover that a product sales increase is not possible.

Cost reduction is the method of choice for suppliers that want to maintain low pricing. It is totally under the supplier's control and does not need product sales increases to maintain dollars of profit.

A supplier's leadership in pricing depends on pricing aggressiveness. Its pricing performance is determined by its capability and willingness to use all the factors discussed here.

Figure 5-5: Sales Increases Needed to Offset Reduced Profit Margins

Gross Profit Margins	Reduced Profit Margins	Sales Increases Needed to Maintain Dollars of Profit
25%	–2%	+9%
25%	–3%	+14%
25%	–5%	+25%
30%	–2%	+7%
30%	–3%	+11%
30%	–5%	+20%

Understanding the Use of Average Pricing

Suppliers that price their products somewhere between the lowest-priced product and the highest-priced product have average pricing. These suppliers cannot command the higher level of pricing because customers do not consider their products to be value leaders. However, they do maintain a fair price/value balance that is higher than the less expensive brands of like products. This group of suppliers will usually set prices as a percent of the higher priced product. As that product price increases, the average price will also increase. This practice, as discussed earlier, maintains margins and market share.

These suppliers are the "me too" group. They will follow the leader even though they may not have the same need or incentive to move pricing levels.

Understanding the Use of High Pricing

At the top of the pricing chain are suppliers who maintain the highest pricing levels in the industry. There are essentially four ways they can support their pricing levels:

1. Being the recognized quality leader in the field
2. Adding value to an existing product

3. Adding additional customer services
4. Manufacturing a priority product

Being recognized as quality leaders. Suppliers who are recognized as being quality leaders in their field produce a superior product. For example, their products might be made from better materials with workmanship that extends the product life. Their products command a higher price in the marketplace than those of competitors manufacturing a similar product.

Adding value to an existing product. The supplier's distribution chain might add to the product value as it moves from level to level. For example, distributors might:

- Repackage a supplier's product for ease of handling.
- Assemble products that are received unassembled.
- Provide additional product promotions and advertising for a supplier's products.

Contractors and installers might offer quality installations to support higher prices. A manufacturer may "finish" a product or may use an existing product as part of another product.

Providing additional customer services. Additional customer services are provided at each level of the supplier's distribution chain. There is an array of additional services that can be offered, such as:

- Product delivery
- Product training
- Technical sales assistance
- Better product availability
- Additional product coverage in the marketplace by having multiple sales locations.

Offering priority products. A supplier might offer a priority or patented product. When this happens, the supplier will charge what the market will pay for the product. If the product price seems unreasonable to customers, they will do without the product or purchase a substitute. For example, this has happened in the medical industry. Laboratories have developed new, more effective medicines and priority products for combating infections and diseases. The results of their research are patented medicines with extremely high price tags. In some cases would-be users have found alternate means of obtaining effective substitute medicines through the use of generics. Customers should strive to obtain alternate products when prices are unreasonable.

ANALYZING SPECIAL PRICING

Many suppliers offer special pricing to entice manufacturers and distributors to purchase large quantities of their products at a reduced cost. These programs do not always provide a savings to the customer. There are essentially three types of special pricing suppliers can offer. They are volume pricing, quotation pricing, and preseason pricing.

Five Considerations in Volume Pricing

Suppliers offering volume pricing bring five factors into their pricing:

1. Economy of scale in production
2. Carton quantities
3. Bulk quantities
4. Packaging and labeling
5. Minimum orders

Economy of scale. Economy of scale is the ability of a supplier to make large production runs of a product. It is less expensive to produce an item in larger quantities. When customers are willing to purchase large product quantities, the supplier can make a larger production run and manufacture and sell the products at a savings to the supplier, manufacturer, and distributor.

Carton quantities. Suppliers often sell products in master carton quantities only. Factors such as handling, storage, and protection are studied before making the decision to sell in master carton quantities. For example, a supplier's price sheet for master carton quantities might look like the one illustrated in Figure 5-6.

Figure 5-6: Price Sheet for Master Carton Quantities

Product: KYZ Widget

Catalog Number	Suggested List Price	Carton Quantity	Distributor Pricing Net Each 1-10	11-100	101-up
12345	$15.00	10	$ 7.50	$ 7.13	$ 6.77
11237	25.00	12	12.50	11.88	11.28

Carton Quantities: All orders for broken carton quantities will be shipped and invoiced at the next highest standard carton quantity.

Many suppliers do not allow purchases less than their master carton quantities. For example, ABC, Inc., sells thermostats in master carton quantities consisting of twenty-four thermostats each. If you have a customer who wants to purchase eighteen thermostats from you, you must be willing to purchase the master carton quantity of twenty-four from the supplier and keep the six remaining thermostats in stock until someone else has a need for them. You have to absorb the cost of the six remaining thermostats or pass it on to your customer. An alternative is to convince your customer to accept an alternate brand of thermostat that is readily available and does not have to be purchased in master carton quantities.

There are two major pitfalls to this type of transaction:

1. The costs of purchasing master carton quantities might be more than you care to invest.
2. Suppliers might lose your business.

These problems need to be shared with your suppliers through supplier performance evaluations. Suppliers can benefit by making changes in master carton quantity policies. Otherwise, a good product or feature may be doomed to failure simply because the supplier has a packaging problem.

Bulk quantities. Another negotiation point for the manufacturer is that of buying in bulk quantities. Instead of each piece being individually boxed, an entire lot may be purchased and packaged as a single lot in master cartons only.

Packaging and labeling. Often, the same item sold to the consumer is also an integral part of a larger manufactured unit. The supplier, by using different packaging and labeling, can offer the material to the manufacturer at a lower cost.

Minimum orders. Suppliers who set minimum prices or quantities on their orders have determined how much it costs for them to process an order. They want the costs involved in order processing to be covered in their minimum order price. This practice actually discourages manufacturers and distributors from placing small orders. For example, a supplier might stipulate that a minimum order for its product is $100. If you purchase one item that costs $52, you will receive an invoice for $100. Your evaluation of these suppliers should reflect the need for change.

Acquiring Better Product Pricing by Getting Special Quotations

Another area of pricing consideration is special quotations. When customers need extra large quantities of a product, suppliers may be willing to quote prices lower than those in their published price sheets. For example, a plumbing distributor might have a customer with a contract to construct government-subsidized housing nationwide. The expectation of extra-large volumes of some products over an extended period might cause a supplier to quote lower prices. A special price quotation might look like the one illustrated in Figure 5-7.

When quotations are made by a supplier, the pricing is also made available to other distributors of the product that are bidding on the same job or those reaching the same quantity level.

Understanding preseason pricing

Preseason pricing is offered to many companies prior to a supplier's busy season each year. There are two objectives in preseason pricing:

1. The supplier wants customers to purchase enough product during the supplier's slow season to keep the work force intact.
2. The surge of product demand that occurs during the supplier's high selling season can be evened out.

Figure 5-7: Special Price Quotation

Job Name: Lake Front Subdivision

Builder Name: Better Homes

Project Size: 1,500 Homes (There are 10 widgets per home.)

Competition: American Widget, Fast Way Widget

Product: XYZ Widget

Catalog Number	Normal Best Price 101-up	15,000 pieces
12345	$6.77 Each	$6.00 Each

The supplier's sales force is given a package of incentives to offer customers. For example, ABC, Inc., manufacturers of room air conditioners, has a peak selling season from May through mid-August. Its lowest selling period is from December through February. Its preseason offer is issued on November 1, one month before the low selling period. A preseason price break is offered to distributors placing large orders between November 15 and December 15. The preseason program might look like the example in Figure 5-8.

While preseason ordering looks promising to customers, there are risks that need to be considered before ordering. For example, forecasting errors, problems in logistics, and poor turns of inventory can cause havoc in your company.

Forecasting errors. Forecasting out for extended periods can result in buying the wrong mix of product and mistakes in order quantities.

Problems in logistics. Problems in logistics can occur when multiple locations are involved. This results in additional handling and shipping costs. Also, the danger of damage increases each time material is handled.

Poor turns of inventory. The results of bringing in product all at one time are poor turns of inventory. It is bad business practice to tie up a company's available funds just to accommodate suppliers.

Figure 5-8: Preseason Pricing Program

Plan 1

- Order 500 units for delivery before March 15, 1993, and receive 1992 pricing.
- Freight is prepaid to one location.
- You will receive the best pricing for all of 1993 at 1992 pricing levels on fill-in orders.
- You will receive delayed payment terms:

⅓ of payment is due March 25, 1993
⅓ of payment is due April 25, 1993
⅓ of payment is due May 25, 1993

Plan 2

- Order 1000 units with two possible shipping dates: one shipment by March 15, 1993, and the second shipment by June 15, 1993. You will receive 5% off 1992 prices.
- Freight is prepaid on a full truckload shipment, and one drop-off is allowed.
- You will receive the best pricing for all your 1993 fill-in orders at 1992 prices.
- You will receive a 1% cash discount if your invoice for each shipment is payed by the 10th prox or a 30-60-90-day delayed billing on both shipments.

Plan 3

- Order 2000 units with three possible shipments: one by March 15, 1993, the second by June 15, 1993, and the third shipment by August 15, 1993. You will receive 8% off 1992 prices.
- Freight is prepaid on a full truckload shipment. Each shipment can have two drop-offs without penalty.
- You will receive the best pricing for all your 1993 fill-in orders at 1992 prices.
- You will receive a 2% discount if the invoices for each order are paid by the 10th prox, or 30-60-90-day delayed billing.
- An additional 2% discount is allowed for advertising or promotion activities on a co-op basis.

The supplier offers three plans to provide incentives for preseason buying for distributors of different sizes. Each plan is important. However, Plan 3 offers more incentives.

When participation in supplier preseason programs is mandatory for best pricing, distributors can lose considerable amounts of money. These programs are a definite negative in supplier performance.

ANALYZING PRICING CHANGES—THE "ME TOO" SYNDROME

All suppliers do not actively engage in cost reduction activities and frequently raise prices with little, if any, explanation. Requiring your suppliers to justify the need for price increases is important to your company, your customers, and our economy. It is a crucial part of your supplier performance evaluation.

The "me too" syndrome is too common in industry today. Simply stated, if an industry leader decides to announce a price increase, other companies follow suit, whether they need an increase or not. Those companies that hold prices firm must be recognized as pricing leaders in your performance evaluation. Unfortunately, industry must go through economic recession to learn the hard lesson of cost containment and expense reduction. For an example of the relationship of cost and expense reduction to price increases, refer to Figure 5-9.

You can see by examining Figure 5-9 that it is much more profitable to work on cost and expenses. The companies that are able to hold the line on prices and reject the "me too" syndrome deserve recognition for their efforts.

Examining Legitimate Reasons for Price Increases

Some legitimate reasons for price increases might be: material costs, labor costs, packaging costs, transportation costs, supplier taxes, additional advertising, promotions, or training programs. Increases in these areas do not have a one-to-one relationship to product cost. For example, a 3 percent increase in material cost to a supplier should not mean a 3 percent price increase in the cost of the finished product. Only that portion of the total cost affected by increased prices should be increased. For example:

Labor Cost	=	$ .40
Material Cost	=	.60
Total Item Cost	=	1.00

Figure 5-9: Relationship of Cost and Expense Reductions to Price Increases

XYZ Company

Gross Profit is 30%

Earnings before taxes is 5%

Sales = $100 Million

Sales = $100
Cost of sales = 70
Gross profit = 30
Expenses = 25
Earnings before taxes = $ 5 = 5% of sales

If we reduce cost by 4%:

Sales = $100
Cost of sales = 67
Gross profit = 33 = 33%
Expenses = 25
Earnings before taxes = $ 8 = 8% of sales

What sales price increase would give us the same results as a 4% cost reduction?

Sales = $110
Cost of sales = 77
Gross profit = 33 = 30%
Expenses = 25
Earnings before taxes = $ 8 = 7.3% of sales

In this example a price increase of 10% is needed to give the same results as a 4% reduction in costs. The EBT went from $5 to $8—an increase of 60% in earnings before taxes!

Now look at the effect of reducing expenses by the same 4%, using the same starting point.

Sales = $100
Cost of sales = 70
Gross profit = 30 = 30%
Expenses = 25 = 25%
Earnings before taxes = 5 = 5%

With a 4% reduction in expenses the number would look like this:

Sales = $100
Cost of sales = 70

Gross profit = 30 = 30%
Expenses = 24 = 24%
Earnings before taxes = 6 = 6%

What price volume increase is needed to produce the same results if our expenses stay at the 25% of sales rate?

Sales = $120
Cost of sales = 84
Gross profit = 36 = 30%
Expenses = 30 = 25%
Earnings before taxes = 6 = 5%

A 20% price increase in sales would be necessary to achieve the same effect as a 4% reduction in expenses.

Suppose a supplier signs a new labor contract that gives a 5 percent increase in employee wages. Then costs would be affected this way:

Labor Cost .40 × 1.05 = $ .42
Material Cost = .60 (no increase)
Total Item Cost = 1.02

The result is a 2 percent increase in total cost of the product. All too often, the full 5 percent is passed along as a price increase of the total product cost.

These factors all play a critical role in the overall performance of suppliers' pricing. They have to be addressed before the purchasing manager can understand the true needs of a supplier's complete distribution chain and the needs and expectations of the final consumer.

You need to continually monitor and measure the pricing structure and proposed price changes of your suppliers. Your current and new suppliers need to realize that you review the total price/value relationship of their products. It is important for you to make a practice of requiring price increase justifications from your suppliers. Do not let the "me too" syndrome settle into your suppliers' methods of price controls. Become familiar with your suppliers' products and be aware of pricing pressures and pricing policies suppliers use to establish pricing levels. Help your suppliers understand that you require performance excellence from them in the important factor of pricing. Supplier evaluation and selection can help you achieve continual, controlled, constructive change in supplier pricing methods.

PART TWO

MEASURING SUPPLIER PERFORMANCE

Setting Performance Standards and Conducting Supplier Evaluations—Who Makes the Grade?

CHAPTER 6

MONITORING KEY TECHNICAL ISSUES THAT AFFECT OVERALL SUPPLIER PERFORMANCE

Lead-time predictability, back orders and overshipments, inventory rebalancing, warranty procedures, payment terms, packaging and labeling, and emergency needs are key technical issues that affect overall supplier performance. Manufacturers, distributors, and their suppliers need to understand the requirements of each issue and how to take full advantage of existing supplier policies, improving them when they can. Supplier dedication to performance in these areas is a vital part of effective partnering and the team approach to supplier/customer/manufacturer/distributor communication.

DETERMINING LEAD-TIME PREDICTABILITY

Lead-time predictability is a term that is often misunderstood by suppliers, their representatives, and even purchasing professionals. The question is not how *often*, but how *consistently* suppliers can deliver product within their own stated lead time. The critical issue is the ability of suppliers to *always* deliver in the time frame they specify. It is unacceptable for a supplier to give a two-week delivery time for a product on one order and to vary the delivery time from four to six weeks on additional orders for the same product.

Using an average lead time as an evaluation standard is useless because it denotes a varying length of time for delivery of goods. A consistent length of time, be it one week or six weeks, can be covered by the size of the order point. The order point is the amount of product on hand when an additional order is placed for that product. However, if the supplier's inability to be predictable in lead time must be covered by using safety stock, the customer is forced to make "guesstimates" as to the length of time it has to maintain additional product in inventory to meet its customers' demands. This increases average inventory substantially. A company can maintain inventory at a much lower level and meet customer demands with fewer outages by eliminating the guesswork in its suppliers' stated delivery times.

It is a simple task to use a computer to store supplier lead times and then continually project receipt dates of material ordered. The purchasing manager then compares the actual receipt of goods on every order placed to each supplier's planned receipt date by looking at the computer report that lists both dates for each order. At year end, the purchasing manager can determine suppliers' performance on lead-time predictability by analyzing actual data.

Figure 6-1 illustrates what a computerized Lead-Time Analysis Report might look like. The columns should be completed as follows:

P.O. #. The purchase order number that appears on the form used to order an item or items.

Supplier. The name of the company an item or items are ordered from.

Item. Ordering company's internal part number(s) for the item or items being ordered.

Quantity. The amount of each item being ordered.

Required delivery date. The required delivery date can be calculated by computer or by manual input as an override to the computer date. An override date is used when the supplier sends a formal notice that lead time has been extended. When an override date becomes permanent, computer records should be changed to reflect the new date. Never allow purchasing agents to put ASAP (as soon as possible) on purchase orders—it is not a measure of time!

Date received. The date material orders are actually received at a company's location. Do not allow order processing time to become part of the supplier's calculations for lead time. It is a part of total lead time, but should not be a part of a supplier's performance analysis.

Quantity received. The actual amount of material received on a particular purchase order number. (Companies that continually place items on back order should be reviewed. Better service might be available elsewhere.)

Partial/complete. An indication of whether the order received by a company was a complete order, a partial shipment of the quantity of an item or items ordered, or a completion of a previous back order.

You can quickly measure the performance of your suppliers on lead-time predictability by summarizing information (required delivery dates vs. actual delivery dates) from the Lead-Time Analysis Report. This can be done by sorting the report by supplier, your company's required delivery dates, and the actual delivery dates. An easy measure of the total number of orders you place with a supplier in relation to the number of completed and backorders the supplier ships to your company can be made by sorting the report by purchase order number within each supplier.

Your objective in the area of lead-time predictability is to help your suppliers reach a 95 percent level of accuracy for on-time deliveries. (You can use other levels of accuracy for on-time deliveries.) The key to their improvement is your ability to present them with data showing that their lead-time performance does not measure up to their own stated standards in this area.

Figure 6-1: Lead-Time Analysis Report

Lead-Time Analysis Report							
P.O. #	Supplier	Item	Quantity	Required Delivery Date	Date Received	Quantity Received	Partial/ Complete

MONITORING BACK ORDERS AND OVERSHIPMENTS (SHIPPING ERRORS)

Back orders and overshipments cause imbalances in inventory, job delays, and customer service problems and create monumental problems in receiving and accounting departments.

Many manufacturers and distributors will not tolerate back orders because they create inventory imbalances. For example, when contractors place orders with manufacturers or distributors, they usually need all the items being ordered to complete specific jobs. If all of the items ordered are shipped except one and that item is a vital part of the contractor's installation project, the total shipment becomes ineffective. When this happens, manufacturers and distributors have to put the received goods into their inventories until back orders are received. This increases their inventories significantly, but their product sales remain the same. They also have to deal with disgruntled customers.

The amount of time a company spends in monitoring back orders, overshipments, and correcting shipping and receiving errors can be multiplied by each level of management that becomes involved in solving these problems. When errors are not detected until invoicing occurs, and the original invoice does not match the receiving document, it takes twice the number of people to correct the problem and costs five to ten times more than problems that are resolved at time of receipt.

Inventory receiving time more than doubles on back orders and requires an increase in labor hours for the paperwork alone. Some computer systems are designed to accommodate total receipt of orders very easily. A person simply accesses the receiving log of the purchase order, hits the correct key indicating total receipt, and the receiving process is complete. However, if several items are back ordered or partially shipped, all received items must be entered individually. For a purchase order of 200 items with five items on back order, the receiving clerk has to enter 195 items instead of one to complete the receiving transaction. Unfortunately, not many systems accommodate partial shipments easily.

Back orders also cause multiple receipts, which increase the possibility of receiving mistakes. Orders with multiple receipts can be received more than once and are difficult to identify correctly. Confusion results in receiving delays that can be extended for days or even weeks and involve many people.

We had one extreme case of back orders and multiple receipts involving a grille and register manufacturer that got into the practice of shipping orders in many installments. Some orders would have as many as 20 shipments before completion. In some instances, receipts would occur on a daily basis for several weeks. Receiving errors soared, and receipt time was completely unreasonable. The company cost to correct these errors resulted in lost profits and poor customer service. The manufacturer made the company appear unreliable. Not surprisingly, we selected another manufacturer to supply this product.

When shipping errors are made by suppliers, the consequences can be very costly for those involved in correcting the errors. Shipping errors have a negative effect on manufacturer/distributor/end-user relationships.

During the pilot program we ordered a large rooftop air-conditioning unit for a contractor to install in a new building. The unit ordered was not a standard product because the customer specified a specific voltage. The order was placed, acknowledged by the supplier, expedited, and shipped on an emergency basis. We notified the customer that the equipment would be delivered the next day, and the contractor made arrangements for a crane to be on site to lift the equipment into place for installation. The product was received as scheduled at the job site. When the contractor tried to install the piece of equipment, he discovered the voltage was incorrect. The container labeling indicated that the item was the correct voltage, but the product shipped was not the product designated by the label.

We were notified about the error and, in turn, contacted the manufacturer. A search at the manufacturer's facility revealed that the correct piece of equipment was still sitting in shipping, unboxed. Both pieces of equipment looked the same except for a small metal tag that indicated the voltage. The material handler who packaged and shipped the first item was a new employee and had not read the metal tag. Our customer was furious. His expenses for the crane, extra work force, and scheduling of his best contractor had been wasted, and customer relationships were ruined.

The solution was very costly to the manufacturer and to us. The manufacturer air freighted the correct piece of equipment to the job site the next day and paid for the crane and the work force. We were left with two receipts, the expense of making two trips to the job site, and the chore of picking up the wrong equipment, repacking it, and arranging for its return to the manufacturer. That was not the end of the story. Our accounting department received two invoices for the same piece of equipment. The manufacturer had not tied the return of the wrong piece of equipment to the first shipment. It took several labor hours to correct the billing problem. Receiving, inventory, purchasing, and accounts payable personnel were needed to resolve the situation.

A larger tag indicating the voltage, placed conspicuously on the equipment, might have averted the problem in this case, if the new material handler had been trained to look for it. The manufacturer unreasonably expected the new, untrained material handler to deal with the emergency situation and make the right product selection. Many companies use entry-level people in this type of position with minimal training. If they show promise, they are moved quickly to other positions in the company. The result can be a steady stream of untrained, entry-level people in critical positions. Supplier evaluation will help you and your supplier pinpoint these problem areas and bring about constructive change.

EVALUATING INVENTORY REBALANCING POLICIES (RETURN POLICIES)

The importance you place on evaluating your supplier's inventory rebalancing policies tells suppliers that this is a vital part of your expectations for quality supplier performance.

Inventory rebalancing (return policies) is usually stated in the terms and allowances section of supplier purchasing literature. These policies state that material can be returned to the supplier if it is in salable condition and within the manufacturer's date codes. Literature may further stipulate that restocking and freight charges will be levied for material returned. The supplier also reserves the right to approve items before they can be returned.

Returning an excess supply of goods will help you three ways:

1. It will help you avoid the problem of obsolete material.
2. You can reduce your average inventory investment by improving turns of inventory.
3. You can give new products a fair test of marketability without fear of being stuck with too much inventory or having the wrong mix of product to satisfy customer service.

Eliminating Obsolescence Problems

Obsolescence is a problem throughout distribution chains. It causes manufacturers and distributors to have millions of dollars tied up in unusable products.

There are essentially three reasons for having obsolete or non-moving merchandise: (1) new product design, (2) poor judgment in product sales, and (3) lack of communication.

New product design. The redesign of products is often needed and implemented by manufacturers during product life cycles (the time a product is usually in demand) to maintain product sales.

Major problems arise when the manufacturer fails to include in the new design planning process all groups that will be directly affected by the product's new form, fit, or function. It is not uncommon for manufacturer's management to decree that a product newly designed by the engineering department be ready for sale immediately. When this happens, literally thousands of dollars can be wasted, particularly if the redesigned product does not contain the same raw material the old product did. The manufacturer is then "stuck" with a large supply of obsolete raw material. However, when engineering plans and coordinates the redesign of a product with management, materials control (including purchasing), production control, quality control, sales, and marketing, this kind of waste can be avoided.

CASE EXAMPLE

A manufacturer planned to redesign a product to accommodate automated manufacturing techniques. While the new design was planned and engineered, the manufacturer purchased the new machinery and raw material needed for the new design.

A prototype of the new product was produced, and the manufacturer's distributors were invited to see the redesigned product. They were asked to evaluate the product and make comments.

One of the distributors pointed out potential problems with a motor mounting and the location of a flow control valve. He suggested that a contractor be consulted about the functionality of the new product design. However, pride of ownership prevented the manufacturer from following the distributor's suggestion.

When the manufacturer put the product on the market, sales were good. However, when contractors began to install the newly designed units two major flaws were noted:

- The motor mounts were not sturdy, making it almost impossible for motor replacement.
- Improper location of the valve that regulated inlet flow prevented contractors from making the inlet connection that was necessary to install the units.

Had the manufacturer heeded the distributor's suggestions and consulted a contractor when the prototype was introduced, these problems could have been averted. As it was, the units were rejected by contractors because of faulty design. The results were disastrous for the manufacturer and distributor:

- The manufacturer's new units became obsolete overnight.
- The manufacturer had to put the units on hold, and engineering had to change the product design—again.
- Enormous amounts of money were tied up in units that would not sell, and massive rework expenditures were needed.
- Distributors with an ample supply of the manufacturer's old product in stock found themselves stuck with obsolete merchandise when the manufacturer's newly redesigned product hit the market.
- When the newly redesigned product was found faulty by contractors, distributors were stuck again.

There are basically three points to check before putting new products into your inventory: forecasting, customer demand patterns, and communication. They can help companies avoid obsolescence.

Forecasting. Purchasing and inventory control should never make forecasts on new items. Sales and marketing should project demand. Formal monthly forecasts should be projected by sales or marketing and supported by sales or marketing management before new material is ever put into stock. When a distributor's sales group tells purchasing it can sell a particular item in large quantities, needs to justify what it is saying with more than an educated guess. If sales do not happen as "guesstimated," the distributor will have large quantities of a product in inventory with no product movement.

Customer demand patterns. Many manufacturers and distributors will not stock new material or products when more than 10 percent of demand is sold to any one customer. When this customer stops using the material or products or decides to purchase them from other companies, the original stocker is stuck with slow-moving and eventually obsolete material.

A well-known manufacturer that I work with requires that each item without demand be supported by a monthly sales forecast, by item, by month. The marketing manager must formally sign off on the forecast before manufacturing will put any material into stock. There is also a kicker—when sales do not occur, any loss of funds due to obsolescence or lack of movement is charged against the marketing department's next year's budget for sales incentives.

This may seem stiff, but sales and marketing should not be making guesses. They should research each new product and have more than a hunch before requesting that new items be put in stock.

Communication. Engineering, materials control, production, and purchasing should be in constant contact with each other. All too often, product changes occur without everyone involved with the products being aware of the change. Surprise changes can cause enormous problems.

CASE EXAMPLE

A valve manufacturer had a very large contract to supply equipment for a power plant. The approved bills of material included specific material in the construction of the valves. The manufacturer owned the foundry that provided the specified material to the production facility. The production manager and the manager of the foundry decided it would be easier to use an alternate material in the valve construction. The substitute material was stronger, easier to pour in the foundry, and easier to machine at the manufacturing facility.

Everything was fine until the customer's inspector discovered the material substitution in a finished valve. The valve was rejected, as were the valves containing the substitute material that were already installed in the power plant. All the valves had to be removed and returned to the manufacturer—at the manufacturer's expense.

It did not matter that the substitute material was of superior quality. The problem was that the material was not the material stipulated in the original bill of material that had been approved by the customer and various government agencies. It was impossible for the manufacturer to change the bill of material; therefore, the valves in question had to be put in stock, and replacement valves manufactured using the correct material.

Seasonal or prepricing buys occur when suppliers offer price incentives to their customers for preseason buying. They may also offer their customers the opportunity to save money by allowing them to buy before price increases. Both are acceptable practices if everyone involved is aware of the circumstances under which the offer or offers are being made. However, a lack of communication can cause problems related to obsolescence:

- The engineering department should be consulted to make sure a design change is not imminent for the product in question.

- Items purchased to cover seasonal increases or to avoid price increases should be items with stable demand patterns for the periods covered by the buy. Make sure item forecasts are checked before making purchases.
- Material control and manufacturing should be aware of the anticipated buy. They may want to make changes in production runs. Receiving must be notified, and warehousing must be able to provide storage space for additional material.
- Sales and marketing must be aware that material is being made available to cover the seasonal period or that a pending price increase has been delayed because of quantity purchases. Sales might have switched customers to another product line. This would cause demand for the previous item to drop drastically.

Using an Obsolete/Slow-Moving Analysis Report

It is important to establish a way of identifying obsolete or slow-moving items in your data base. For example, you might elect to run a selection report (a selection report simply lists all items having a zero demand in a selected time frame) and then manually mark the items that need to be eliminated, such as new items with no established demand pattern or items used specifically for warranty purposes.

Seasonal items might not have demand during your designated slow-moving period. Therefore, you should make the designated period for slow-moving merchandise long enough to cover any possible seasonal demand functions.

The use of an Obsolete/Slow-Moving Analysis Report like the one in Figure 6-2 can help you eliminate present obsolescence problems. Items on the report are identified as slow-moving or obsolete. Slow-moving means items that have not had demand in 12 months. Obsolete means items that have not had demand in 24 months.

The report includes the following information:

- A list of all obsolete and slow-moving material.
- Warehouse location—The warehouse location is important to inventory control and sales. They must be able to identify storage areas to find products.
- Part numbers—Part numbers are important for product and supplier identification.

Figure 6-2: Obsolete/Slow-Moving Analysis Report

Obsolete/Slow-Moving Analysis Report

Warehouse Location: ____________________

Part #	Item Description	Qty	Unit Cost	Total Cost	Cum Cost	*Status
24325	¾" moly bolt	500	$ 3	$ 1,500	$ —	O
79844	side panel	3	500	1,500	3,000	S
37983	old unit	1	5,000	5,000	8,000	O
99766	7" S.S. gear	80	100	8,000	16,000	O
Total				$300,000		

Total obsolete material = $185,000 (61.7%)

Total slow-moving material = $115,000 (38.3%)

*O = Obsolete Items (no demand in 24 months)
S = Slow-Moving Items (no demand in 12 months)

- Product descriptions—Good product descriptions aid product identification.
- Quantity—An accurate count of material is important to inventory and sales.
- Unit cost—The unit cost of each item is important to purchasing, sales, and accounting. (Do not let your computer system automatically increase the cost of your obsolete goods. You want to reflect the cost you actually paid for the obsolete or slow-moving parts.)
- Total cost—The total cost is the extended unit cost times the quantity on hand.
- Cumulative cost— Cumulative cost is a running sum of all items. This allows you to measure the effect of each item on the total cost of obsolete material.
- Status— Buying systems will often identify any item with a zero on-hand balance. Be sure these items are identified as being obsolete (O) or slow-moving (S), or you may find that as soon as the items are sold the computer system may attempt to order the same parts again.

The first run of this report should be for the total company. Subsequent runs should list material by the warehouse in which it is kept.

Sorting by part number will usually separate the items into supplier categories. You might include subtotals by supplier. This will give you information to talk to your suppliers about all the obsolete material in their product lines.

Sorting by item description will place like items in groups. (Standard descriptions should be in place before using this option.) This sort will allow your company's sales force to make options available to potential customers.

Sorting by total cost within each major sort category will allow you to identify and concentrate your efforts on the items with the largest dollar impact.

Everyone in your organization must be aware of the purpose and content of your Obsolete/Slow-Moving Analysis Report. You want them to know the magnitude and scope of the problem you are dealing with. It is helpful for engineering, manufacturing, material control, sales, and marketing to receive copies of the report. Also, send it to all of your company's locations—especially when multiple warehouse locations are involved—because they are potential disposition spots.

You can suggest several methods of disposing of the obsolete/slow-moving material to the appropriate department heads. For example, sales and marketing can help you in price reductions and special sales incentives:

- Price reductions—Reduced prices entice your customers to save money by purchasing products at lowered prices.
- Special sales—Having a special sale will also bring your customers' attention to obsolete or slow-moving products. For example, a firm I was working with decided to have a "Special Season Sale" to eliminate as many items as possible from its obsolete list. It offered one of the most common items in its particular industry to the public at cost value (loss leader concept).

The amount of the product each person could purchase was limited and stipulated as "in-store purchases only." All obsolete and slow-moving material was prominently located throughout the distributor's sales area marked with "special unit pricing" and "special quantity prices." Inside and outside salespersons were located in strategic areas to conduct "special" tours for customers as they arrived for the special sale.

The one-day special sale was considered a great success. The distributor's obsolete and slow-moving items were reduced 50 percent.

- Substituting parts—Engineering may be able to utilize some items by suggesting substitution of parts during the manufacturing process. However, some cost value may be lost if the item being substituted is more costly than the item it is replacing or if the material has to be shipped to a different location. Even so, this use is better than distressed pricing or losing the full cost of the items when they are scrapped.

Negotiating for Product Return

Purchasing can negotiate for product return to the supplier, for sales to other manufacturers or distributors, or for scrap.

Product return. Purchasing is always involved in the disposition of obsolete and slow- moving merchandise. You will want to contact every supplier involved with the merchandise to ask for their assistance in disposal. When these suppliers allow return of the material, they usually have stipulations attached to the offer. For example, they may charge a restocking fee or require a replacement order of other goods.

Sales to other manufacturers or distributors. You also have the option of selling obsolete and slow-moving items to manufacturers or distributors other than the one you purchased the merchandise from. The original supplier will be able to suggest additional companies that might be willing to purchase the product(s) in question. A good partnership supplier will make contacts for you and arrange all the details for transfer of goods.

Sales to distress merchandise companies. Another option is to sell the obsolete or slow-moving merchandise to companies that deal with distress merchandise. You will want to clear the selling price with upper management and accounting before making final arrangements for the sale.

Scrap. Naturally, the last resort to get rid of obsolete or slow-moving items is simply to scrap the stuff. It is important not to let scrap material stay in your inventory for indefinite periods of time. It ties up inventory funds and overstates the worth of your asset base.

The following is an example of what one company did to reduce its inventory of obsolete/slow-moving material. The following guidelines were used to identify obsolete and slow-moving material:

- Obsolete—no use in two years.
- Slow-moving—no use in one year.

- The true cost of each item was identified.
- The material was then classified, codes were applied to all items in a given level, and the warehouse location was identified for ease in handling.
- Guidelines for material disposal were set. All material identified as obsolete could be sold for any portion of costs. Slow-moving items were categorized by item for sales potential and divided into three categories:
  - Items that could be sold at cost
  - Items that could be sold at 50 percent of cost
  - Items that could be sold for any portion of cost

A monthly Obsolete/Slow-Moving Sales Analysis Report was prepared listing every item and its special coding by warehouse location. Figure 6-3 is an illustration of what this report looked like. The report contains the following information:

- Warehouse location—The location(s) where obsolete/slow-moving merchandise is stored.
- Date— This report is produced at the end of each month so the figures represent balances at the end of each monthly period.
- Part number and description—The part number is the internal company designation of the part with its associated description.
- Designation codes—These codes apply to obsolete and slow-moving material and set limits on unit sales prices.
- On-hand (O.H.) quantities—The amount of on-hand merchandise at the beginning of the time period covered by the report.
- Unit cost—The actual cost of items, the amount paid for the material.
- Total cost—The on-hand quantity times the unit cost of the merchandise.
- Unit sales—The number of pieces of the items sold over a 30-day period.
- Unit sale price—The unit price of the items sold.
- Amount returned—The difference between unit cost and sales price times the number of pieces sold (cost – sales price × quantity sold). This total amount is added to the location revenue for the month. This assures revenues are not reduced for selling obsolete material.
- New quantity on-hand—The amount of obsolete items on hand at each branch location at the end of the sales period.
- Total returned—The total of the amounts added to location revenues to compensate for items sold below cost.

Figure 6-3: Obsolete/Slow-Moving Monthly Sales Analysis

Obsolete/Slow-Moving Monthly Sales Analysis

Warehouse Location: ____________________ **Date:** __________

Part #	Item Description	*Code	O.H. Qty	Unit Cost	Total Cost	Unit Sales	Unit Sales Price	Amt Rt'd	New O.H. Qty
24325	¾" moly bolt	Y	500	$ 3	$1,500	50	$ 2.50	$ 25	450
79844	side panel	J	3	500	1,500	1	500	—	2
99766	7" S.S. gear	K	80	100	8,000	10	85	150	70
Total Returned							$175		

Code Totals = Beginning $ Value	*Code	Sales	Ending $ Value
$ 1,500	Y	$ 150	$1,360
1,500	J	500	1,000
8,000	K	1,000	7,000
Total $11,000		$1,650	$9,350

*Codes = Y—items can be sold for any factor of costs
J—unit sales price must not be less than unit costs
K—unit sales price must be equal to or greater than 50% of unit cost

- Code totals—This column gives a recap of the activity within each special code designation. Notice that sales are figured at unit cost.
- Total—The summation of all code totals.

Management allocated special funds to each warehouse location to bring revenues back to cost for each item disposed of properly. That meant that each location could dispose of obsolete and slow-moving items without losing revenue. The only stipulation was that disposition had to be according to the special classifications given to the items in question.

A special bonus of $50 (net) was offered to every employee in each location when the location's reduction goal was met. On the other hand, any material that had to be written off at the end of the year resulted in a dollar-for-dollar reduction to the location's operating revenue.

The final results of this program were outstanding. The dollar value of the material was reduced from $496,000 to $17,000. Obsolete inventory was completely eliminated. Non-producing assets of $479,000 were turned into a cash flow of available funds. Slow-moving inventory was reduced to $17,000, every person in the company received a $50 bonus, and a small profit on these goods was realized by the company as a whole.

Using Card Systems for Disposition of Obsolete Material

A card system may also be used for disposition of obsolete material. Figure 6-4 illustrates what the card might look like.

Purchasing can send a group of obsolete material disposition cards and an obsolete material list to each department. Purchasing should ask department managers to encourage employees to write suggestions for material disposition on the cards and return them. It is the purchasing department's responsibility to review and circulate each card to engineering, materials control, manufacturing, accounting, and sales for final approvals before material disposition is physically made.

Regardless of the approach you choose for handling the disposition of present obsolete material, the key to the entire operation is for you to be personally involved.

The challenge to your suppliers becomes evident when you communicate your company's position through the supplier evaluation and selection processes. You want suppliers to realize that their companies and yours cannot tolerate practices resulting in obsolete material. The same message must be communicated throughout your company and vigorously supported by management.

Calculating Turns of Inventory

A good supplier realizes that funds tied up in obsolete or slow-moving material are idle. This affects your company's ability to purchase additional inventory from his or her company. Suppliers have a vested interest in making sure your company has good, usable, salable products. The strength of supplier partnerships through supplier evaluations makes inventory reduction a joint venture.

The "earn and turn" concept is a tool that will help you measure the effect inventory rebalancing has on your company's sales and net profit.

Figure 6-4: Obsolete Material Disposition Card

Obsolete Material Disposition Card

Warehouse Location: _________ **Date:** _________

Part #	Item Description	Qty	Disposition	Initiator
45879	8" S.S. gear	70	Substitute for 8" carbon steel gear—part # 97643	WOF

Department Approvals (please initial):

Engineering ______ Manufacturing ______
Materials Control ______ Accounting ______
Purchasing ______ Sales ______

Instructions:

- Use one card per item to be altered.
- Engineering—Approval by Engineering is necessary before substitutions can be made.
- Materials control—Materials Control is responsible for all changes in inventory records.
- Purchasing—Purchasing is responsible for making any corresponding changes in outstanding purchase orders for the item being substituted.
- Manufacturing—Manufacturing is responsible for accepting substitutions based on approval from Engineering.
- Accounting—Accounting is responsible for making adjustments in the cost difference between the item in question and the item being substituted.

(The disposition may vary, but all departments must be fully aware of the changes being made and that all transactions are completed correctly.)

You can communicate the importance of inventory rebalancing policies to your suppliers by understanding the "turn and earn" concept: the more you turn your inventory, the more your earned profits increase. In other words, it is imperative for you to keep your average inventory level as low as possible to increase your turn rate of inventory. The results are higher profits for you and your suppliers. Figure 6-5 shows how to calculate the number of times your inventory turns in one year.

Figure 6-5: Calculating Average Inventory and the Number of Inventory Turns

Time	Jan.	Feb.	Mar.	April	May	June
Ending Cost of Inventory	3,700	3,500	3,200	3,000	3,500	3,200
Time	**July**	**Aug.**	**Sept.**	**Oct.**	**Nov.**	**Dec.**
Ending Cost of Inventory	3,700	3,500	4,000	4,000	3,500	3,200

Average inventory is the sum of all these values divided by 12, or $3,500. The next number needed for our example is the total cost of sales for this same period of time:

Sales = $10,000
Profit from sales = 3,000
Cost of sales = 7,000

Now that we have these numbers we can calculate turns of inventory.

Cost of Sales/Average Inventory = Turns of Inventory

$7,000/$3,500 = 2 turns of inventory.

Calculating Gross Margin Return on Inventory Investment

The importance of the "turn and earn" concept is illustrated by looking at gross margin dollars generated by inventory investments. The old rule of thumb stated that every dollar invested in inventory should earn one dollar a year in gross margin dollars. The new rule states that every dollar invested in inventory must earn between $1.40 and $1.50 in gross margin dollars to show a reasonable return on investment. Figure 6-6 illustrates how to calculate gross margin return on inventory investment.

Figure 6-6: Calculating Gross Margin Return on Inventory Investment

Calculating Gross Margin Return on Inventory Investment (GMROI)

GMROI (Gross Margin Return on Inventory Investment)
= inventory turn × percent GM/1–GM

Let's look at a calculation of GMROI:

Investment in inventory turns 1.5 times and yields 30 percent gross margin.

GMROI = 1.5 × .3/.7
GMROI = .64 = A very poor return!

By doing a little math, you will see that in this example, the GM or Gross Margin percent has to be 50 percent in order to maintain a gross margin return on inventory (GMROI) of1.25 if inventory turns only 1.5 times. Stated another way: The turn and earn concept measures the gross margin earned for the dollars invested in inventory.

Negotiating Supplier Return Policies to Increase Inventory Turns and Profits

Many distributors and manufacturers are beginning to realize the importance of balancing their mix of inventories. Evaluating your suppliers on this issue is critical to your success in maintaining control of your inventory. Keeping a broad mix of products in your inventory is not the answer to increasing sales and profits. The truth is, you need to keep larger quantities of the items that sell well in stock to increase sales and profits. It is depth, not breadth, that makes the difference.

It is hard to estimate correctly the mix and quantity of new products that will sell. Therefore, the right to return items that do not have demand by the end of a reasonable trial period is very important to your company. That trial period should never last beyond one year. If your suppliers understand the benefits of inventory rebalancing, they will actually want you to return slow-moving items. Why? Because it will free up your inventory dollars to buy more of their products that are selling well.

If you buy more products with high demand, your sales and your supplier's sales will increase, and your customers will be happy because you are meeting their immediate needs. The bottom line in inventory rebalancing is: The more turns of inventory your company experiences, the greater the volume of sales and increase in profits for everyone involved.

The following case is a good example of how supplier evaluation and selection can increase communications and profits.

CASE EXAMPLE

One of our major suppliers with high product quality and customer recognition through extensive advertising took the position that inventories at distributor locations were not its problem.

In 1980-81, this supplier did not have an inventory rebalancing policy and would not allow distributors to return goods under any circumstances. It took an "act of Congress" to return material to the supplier. During this time, many of our sales personnel regarded the supplier as a necessary evil. Given the opportunity, they would no longer have stocked the line of products. Our inventory mix of this supplier's products was terrible, obsolete material was too high, and customer service was poor because our sales personnel did not actively try to sell the products. In fact, they would switch customers to other product brands whenever possible.

When our first Supplier Evaluation and Selection Report was received in 1980 by the supplier's top management, changes came quickly. By the end of 1981, the supplier's middle management was instructed to work closely with distribution's management to improve relationships. The supplier changed local representation and began taking an active role in all levels of our company's sales and purchasing management. One of the first issues was obsolete and slow-moving items. The supplier began to change its no-return policy. Products that were not suitable for our customer base were moved to other areas of the country where they could be readily used.

Not only was product returned, but warranties were processed in a timely manner and product training increased. In a matter of one year, the image of this supplier changed dramatically in the eyes of our sales personnel. They became confident in the supplier's new dedication to making changes that would help them at local levels. Sales in the supplier's products increased sharply and by the end of 1984, the supplier's local representative was selected as Supplier Representative of the Year.

MEASURING THE EFFECTIVENESS OF A MANUFACTURER'S PRODUCT WARRANTIES

A warranty is a written guaranty to the purchaser of a product's integrity and of the manufacturer's responsibility to the customer for product repair or replacement of defective parts.

Measuring warranty effectiveness is critical to you and your suppliers and to the well-being of your customers. Inadequate warranties can play havoc throughout a distribution chain. Inadequate suppliers' warranties can cause confusion in your quality control/service departments, the loss of customers and company profits, numerous accounting nightmares, imbalance in inventory, and lengthy processing times.

Dealing with Warranty Confusion in Your Quality Control/Service Department

There are warranties on almost every product or service you can think of, and they vary in degrees of complexity from "no warranty" to "satisfaction guaranteed or your money back." Some suppliers offer *no hassle* warranties on their products, which means that if you return a defective product during the life of the product warranty, it will be replaced immediately. Figure 6-7 is a No Hassle Warranty provided by Robinair. The company has an excellent warranty statement that is easy to understand and easy to process.

Translating warranties and warranty procedures can be very difficult as they are written from a legal perspective. It is not unusual for companies to spend time and money translating product warranty procedures into language their sales personnel can recognize. Reacond Associates, one of Robinair's independent representatives in the Southwest, has translated Robinair's warranty procedures in even more concise terms. Figure 6-8 is Reacond's restatement of Robinair's No Hassle Warranty statement.

Distributors also are required to follow the supplier's procedures in the administration of warranty recovery for every product line they carry. This results in employee training nightmares and can mean the loss of warranty monies. Warranty problems can go unrecognized until a physical inventory is taken. Even then, if careful documentation of warranty exchanges are not provided by a warranty service department, warranty problems will still not be recognized.

Figure 6-7: Robinair's "No Hassle" Warranty

ROBINAIR'S *No Hassle* WARRANTY

We're so convinced Robinair vacuum pumps and test instruments are the finest available that we back them with our exclusive one year "No Hassle" warranty. If your Robinair pump fails, you can return it for an immediate over-the-counter replacement within one year of date of purchase. Just take the product covered by this warranty — along with proof of purchase — to your Robinair dealer and you'll get a new unit.

No waiting. No complicated forms. No hassles.

All Authorized Robinair Wholesalers can provide you with a new, identical piece of equipment in exchange for a malfunctioning one as long as you have proof of purchase and the conditions listed below are met.

Vacuum Pumps — All direct drive Rotary Vane Pumps are covered by the "No Hassle" replacement policy for 12 full months provided . . .

A. The date of claim does not exceed one year from date of purchase by the user or 18 months from the wholesaler's original date of purchase as determined by the manufacturing date code.

B. The pump is found to be mechanically defective and is returned with a full description of the defect. Defects obviously due to abuse, mishandling, or accidental damage are not covered by this warranty.

Remember that contaminated vacuum pump oil or improper oil levels adversely affect pump operation; you should eliminate these possibilities before making a replacement claim.

C. The pump must have been purchased new.

Robinair RVP pumps covered by this warranty are:

15100 1.2 CFM, single stage pump
15101B 5 CFM, two stage pump
15102B 3 CFM, two stage pump
15120 10 CFM, two stage pump

Test Instruments — The following conditions must be met for an over-the-counter exchange:

A. The date of claim does not exceed one year from date of purchase by the user or 18 months from wholesaler's original date of purchase as determined by the manufactured date code which appears in the battery storage cavity.
Example: a code of 158 means the unit was manufactured in the fifteenth week of 1988.

B. The instrument is found to be mechanically defective in materials or workmanship. Defects due to obvious mishandling, misuse or accidental damage are not covered by this warranty.

C. The instrument must have been purchased new.

Models which are covered by this special exchange policy are:

14830A Thermistor Vacuum Gauge
14840 Analog Temperature Tester
14945 Electronic Charging Scale
17002 Digital Thermometer
17017 Digital Clip-On Meter
17024 Digital Multimeter
17030 Digital Thermometer
17060 Refrigerant Leak Detector
17075 Digital Multimeter

General Warranty — All Robinair products are covered for one full year from date of purchase by a limited warranty on parts and workmanship — see the back of this page for complete details.

Our liberal warranty coverage is further assurance that you've made a smart choice when you picked Robinair. Our products are designed and built for consistent, trouble-free use. But if something should go wrong, we stand behind them with the best warranty in the industry!

ROBINAIR

General Warranty

All Robinair products are warranted to be free from defects in material and workmanship under normal use and service for a period of one year after the sale of the product by Robinair Division. Exceptions to this policy will be individually identified. Robinair's sole obligation under this Warranty shall be to repair or replace any defective product or parts thereof, which are returned to Seller's factory, transportation charged pre-paid within the period mentioned above, and which upon examination are proved to Seller's satisfaction to be defective. The Warranty shall not apply to any product or part which has been subject to misuse, negligence or accident. The Seller shall not be responsible for any special or consequential damages and the Warranty as set forth is in lieu of all other warranties either expressed or implied. However, Seller makes no warranty of merchantability in respect to any Robinair products for any particular purpose other than that stated in this literature and any applicable manufacturer's shop or service manuals referred to therein, including any subsequent service bulletins.

FACTORY AUTHORIZED SERVICE/REPAIR FACILITIES

East	Central	West
Chuck's Equipment Corp. 515 Beach 72nd Street Rockaway Beach, NY 11692 (718) 474-7467	Robinair Division Robinair Way Montpelier, OH 43543 (419) 485-5561 (800) 822-5561	Vernon Electric Company 233 West Jefferson Blvd. Los Angeles, CA 90007 (213) 747-7491

Replacement and Service parts may be ordered direct from the factory in Montpelier, Ohio. Address all orders and correspondence to — Attention: Service Department.

General Warranty — Any product requiring in-warranty repair service should be sent to the Robinair factory or to the nearest authorized repair center. Be sure to include proof of purchase. Repair shipments may be made by either the wholesaler or by the user.

No Hassle Warranty — A credit for the full value of any product covered by this warranty will be issued to the wholesaler's account when the defective unit is received at our factory in Montpelier, Ohio. Send all over-the-counter exchange units along with supporting documentation to the attention of the Service Repair Department.

Call our toll-free Service Line for help in using and servicing Robinair equipment. Call 1-800-822-5561 in the continental U.S. In Ohio call 419-485-5561.

Terms and conditions of the "No Hassle" warranty are subject to change without notice.

All shipments should be made to repair centers with transportation paid. Out-of-warranty items may be returned by a wholesaler or directly by the user. There will be a charge for repair of out-of-warranty items.

SPX — *Robinair Division SPX Corporation*

ROBINAIR — *Robinair Way, Montpelier, OH 43543-0193, Phone 419-485-5561, TWX 810-490-2544, FAX 419-485-8300*

Form SA 313 (4/89)

Figure 6-8: Restatement of Robinair's "No Hassle" Warranty

ROBINAIR DIVISION SPX CORPORATION ROBINAIR WAY MONTPELIER, OH. 43543	REACOND ASSOCIATES 1515 ROYAL PARKWAY P.O. BOX 400457 EULESS, TX. 76040
PHONE: 419-485-5561 FAX ORDERS: 800-322-2890 TECHNICAL HELP: 800-822-5561	PHONE: 817-267-4891 FAX: 817-267-4896

PRODUCT LINE:	HIGH VACUUM PUMPS, OIL, MANIFOLDS, VACUUM VALVES ASSEMBLIES, CHARGING HOSES, CHARGING CYLINDERS, CHARGING SCALES, CHARGING STATIONS, LEAK DETECTORS, FITTINGS & VALVES, TEST EQPT., TUBE WORKING TOOLS, CAPILLARY TUBING, GENERAL TOOLS, APPLIANCE TOOLS & REFRIGERANT RECOVERY EQUIPMENT.
MINIMUM ORDER:	$50.00
FREIGHT:	$1,250.00 PREPAID
ORDER FROM:	ROBINAIR @ FAX 1-800-322-2890
WAREHOUSED:	REACOND ASSOCIATES- SPECIFIED PART #'S CONSULT PRICE SHEET FOR RW DESIGNATION
SHIP FROM:	ROBINAIR OR REACOND ALL B/O FROM FACTORY
EMERGENCY ORDERS:	RECEIVED @ REACOND BY 11:00 A.M. WILL BE SHIPPED SAME DAY WHENEVER POSSIBLE
BACK ORDERS:	FAX OR CALL ROBINAIR
WHOLESALER NOTES:	SPRING STOCKING QUALIFYING DEC 15 TO MAR 1
WARRANTY INFO:	NO HASSLE ON PUMPS & INSTRUMENTS, 1 YR FROM DATE OF SALE, RETURN FRT PPD TO ROBINAIR "INDICATE IN WRTG - ISSUE CREDIT ONLY!" GENERAL WARRANTY-LESS THAN $25 HOLD FOR REACOND TO FIELD SCRAP. oVER $25 RETURN FRT PPD TO ROBINAIR TO REPAIR OR REPLACE

SEE PRICE SHEET FOR COMPLETE DETAILS ON TERMS AND CONDITIONS

IMPORTANT

REPAIR OR REPLACEMENT items in or out of warranty must be returned to factory, transportation charges prepaid. PLEASE TAG EACH ITEM STATING CAUSE OF FAILURE. pLEASE DO NOT WRITE DEFECTIVE! Items returned for CREDIT without written authorization will be refused. DO NOT SEND any returns to reacond. REACOND has no facilities for repair and items returned to them delay repair, replacement, or issuance of credit.
6/5/90

Courtsey of Reacond Associates

In the manufacturing quality control department the problems are the same. The majority of suppliers have different quality standards and different procedures for the disposition of defective goods. Quality control should give purchasing a report on each shipment received from each supplier of goods. Purchasing should negotiate a credit on every purchase made to coincide with the supplier's stated defective rate. That is, if the supplier indicates that its product experiences a 1 percent defective rate, then the supplier should allow a 1 percent discount on the total amount of each invoice. When an arrangement like this is negotiated, defective parts can be reduced to scrap.

Training Employees to Handle Warranties from Many Suppliers

Many distributors buy products from multiple suppliers. Each of these suppliers writes its warranty policies to satisfy its own internal material movement needs. As a result, distributors find it difficult for all of their sales personnel to know and understand all the warranty procedures and paperwork. Distributors have to provide some type of warranty training for these employees. This can be a nightmare—especially if you are dealing with 100 suppliers.

During the pilot program discussed at the begining of this book, supplier evaluation allowed us to describe this monumental problem to our suppliers. They, in turn, agreed to allow our company to use our own return material form for the return of defective material. The fact that our personnel knew how to use our form and understood our internal paper flow cut our inventory loss due to defective material by 40 percent.

Losing Customers and Profits

When poor quality products leave a manufacturing plant and eventually fail in warranty, the results can be far more costly than just the product cost. Property damage, bodily injury, and the ultimate loss of customers can mean enormous costs to manufacturers and distributors that have to satisfy their customers.

It is not uncommon for management to tell employees to take defective products back in exchange for new ones just to keep customers satisfied.This generally does placate customers, but what about the costs to your company? Defective products that are not properly accounted for can cost your company thousands of dollars in lost revenues, as well as inventory shrinkage.

Identifying Accounting and Inventory Problems Caused by Defective Material

Defective material disposition can result in extreme problems for accounting. Three areas hit very hard are sales, inventory values, and supplier credit. All of these are important to the accounting department:

Impact on sales. Defective goods become net deductions to sales dollars. When they are not accounted for properly, they also reduce product demand. The reduction to product demand causes problems for purchasing because forecasting for future demand can be altered significantly by warranty returns. This can cause poor availability of product in the future. Furthermore, the reduction of sales dollars adversely affects cash flow, sales forecasts, and profit generation, where accounting needs data for its projections of earnings and cash flow.

Inventory values. Warranties have the potential to affect inventory adversely in planning and control. Many inventory systems do not adequately provide for the return of defective material. Items returned for warranty generally do not have a separate part number designation. Therefore, the return will act as a net deduction to demand usage. In other words, the use of an item for warranty purposes is not included as demand for forecasting purposes. Figure 6-9 is an illustration of this.

This is also a serious problem for manufacturers who use Material Requirements Planning (MRP) or the Just-In-Time (JIT) concept of material procurement. If component parts for warranty purposes are not factored into product demand, there will always be a shortage of component parts. Normally, the bill of material for an item is reduced to its component parts, then extended for the number of pieces per assembly, and that is what is manufactured or purchased. The amount of safety stock factored into these quantities is to cover the variability of the demand for the end product. If items are also used to satisfy warranty replacements of items already in the marketplace, the component stores will always be short of those items.

Figure 6-9: Quantifying Problems Warranties Cause in Inventory Planning

Quantifying the Problems Warranties Cause in Inventory Planning

Sales of item X = 50 pieces
Usage for warranty = 10 pieces
Returned in warranty = {10} pieces
Net usage = 50 pieces

In formulating demand for future periods the count of 50 pieces was actually used. This accounting of demand causes a shortage of material in future periods because the pieces used for warranty replacement are not being counted as demand usage. In reality, 60 pieces were used; the ten returned were not reused. As long as this situation is not corrected, shortages in inventory will continue to occur.

In some systems this problem is compounded. Where the warranty item is not separated by a different part number or by an altered return procedure, it is added back to inventory on hand. The returns inflate the numbers, which indicate more inventory available for sale. For example:

Pieces available for sale = 100
Sales of item = 50 (subtract from pieces available)
Usage for warranty = 10 (subtract from pieces available)
Returned in warranty = {10} (These will be added back to pieces available for sale.)

After all transactions have taken place, pieces available for sale will look like this:

Beginning available = 100
Sales = {50}
Usage for warranty = {10}
Returned in warranty = 10

Available for sale after transaction = 50 pieces

Of course, we realize there are only 40 pieces available for sale. The ten pieces returned for warranty purposes are defective and are not available for sale.

Handling Problems Caused by Supplier Warranty Policies

Corrections for accounting and inventory problems caused by inadequate supplier warranty policies can be handled by using additional part numbers and by recording warranty returns to sales figures:

Use additional part numbers. Using different part numbers for warranty-returned items is a cumbersome approach to settling the problem. Every item must have a good part number and one that is used for warranty purposes. Inventory file size grows greatly, and proper accounting is difficult.

Record warranty returns to sales figures. Record warranty returns to sales figures only in the accounting unit that records sales. Place piece demand in a holding branch or account designated for warranty return activity. This method allows for the correct deduction to sales dollars and avoids the problems of affecting demand usage, on-hand availability, and inventory.

Establish a warranty department. A warranty department that is responsible for the physical disposition of warranty materials can greatly increase the probability that warranty material is handled properly and in a timely manner.

Processing Supplier Credits or Allowances for Warranty Material

Supplier credits or allowances for warranty material are based on three factors:

1. Legitimate warranty causes—All suppliers clearly state product failures that are covered by their warranty policy. Warranty credits are not issued for customer abuse of products or faulty installation.
2. Proper identification of product failures—Inadequate identification of product failures can result in the denial of warranty credit.

3. Timely processing of warranty material, including paperwork—This is usually stated in a supplier warranty policy. The lack of discipline in processing warranty material within a stated time period can cause an item to be refused warranty credit.

It is your company's responsibility to make sure warranty information is properly gathered and processed within the guidelines stipulated by each supplier.

ANALYZING PAYMENT TERMS

Payment terms are incentives offered by many suppliers to promote fast payment of invoices. Terms are stated as discount percentages given to customers if their invoices are paid in a specific time period set by the seller. For example, a supplier might offer the following payment terms:

2% tenth prox. net 30 days

This payment term stipulates that if a customer pays an invoice by the tenth of the month after the invoice is received it will earn a 2 percent discount off the total invoice amount. Figure 6-10 shows the calculation of the effective annual percentage earned by taking discounts.

Through supplier evaluation, you can analyze payment terms offered by suppliers and compare supplier performances in this area. Understanding the facts and being able to measure payment terms will help you begin negotiating more favorable payment terms with your suppliers.

Terms can also be expressed as time. For example, the term for time might be stated as "Payments may be made ⅓ 30 days, ⅓ 60 days, and ⅓ 90 days." This type of term extends the distributor's payments over a 90-day time period. The examples given in Chapter 5 for preseason pricing show this type of payment schedule.

There are additional uses of payment terms:

- Some distributors will use the terms extended to them by their suppliers as incentives to their customers by offering them the same form of cash discounts or delayed payments.
- Companies that compete on a price basis only will use terms to reduce product costs.

Figure 6-10: Calculating Effective Annual Percentage

Calculating Effective Annual Percentage

You can calculate effective annual percentage in this way:

$$\text{Effective annual percentage cost} = \frac{\text{\% of discount}}{(100\%\text{-discount})} \times \frac{365}{\text{(credit period-discount period}}$$

$$\text{In this example, effective annual percentage cost} = \frac{2}{(100 - 2)} \times \frac{365}{(30 - 10)}$$

$$= \frac{2}{98} \times \frac{365}{20}$$

$$= 37.2\%$$

In this example, the annualized cost of not taking the discount can be costly for your company.

The use of terms as incentives or price concessions is a marginal practice because it puts pressure on the accounts payable department. Bills must be paid in the stated discount period, or the incentives or lowered cost will be a net loss of profits.

EVALUATING YOUR SUPPLIER'S PACKAGING AND LABELING

Effective Packaging

The size and strength of product cartons must be properly engineered by manufacturers for adequate product protection. Other major considerations of carton design are storage, type of material to be boxed, and product identification of items to be packed in master and individual cartons.

- Storage instructions include information such as, "This side up," "Only stack three high," "This product guaranteed fresh if used before May 26," "Store in a cool, dry area," etc.
- Material handling instructions will include, "Use only squeeze trucks," "Lift from other side," "Use pallet jacks only," etc.
- Product identification gives the number of items in a container, size, weight, color, and the name of the material.

Master cartons are designed by the supplier to protect the contents from being damaged during shipping and handling. Master cartons can contain several individual cartons of products.

Product packaging should also provide a degree of protection to the ultimate end-user. One of the greatest changes in individual product packaging was caused by the poison problem in over-the-counter medicines. Food containers went through a similar change for consumer protection.

All of these features must be evaluated in relation to customer needs. If containers do not provide the functions needed in your industry, suppliers need to know the specific problems that occur as the result of poor carton design.

Palletizing and Shrink-Wrapping

Many suppliers provide special product-packaging features designed to assist distribution in the marketing chain of a product. Two of these special features are palletizing and shrink-wrap:

- Palletizing is done by placing products (master cartons and individual cartons) on skids.
- Shrink-wrap is a thin sheet of plastic material that is placed around products or skids of products.

Both these features are important in providing convenience and cost savings to the distribution effort. They provide product protection and ease in handling, transportation and storage.

CASE EXAMPLE

A major supplier produced several hundred different sizes and types of a product. A truckload of the product averaged about 15,000 pieces. The supplier did not palletize his product and loaded and stacked a 40-foot trailer so that the load would not shift. When this product was received at our location, it took two people all day to unload, identify, count, and stack the unpalletized products. Material was damaged, and it was extremely hard to identify and receive the products properly. The results were costly.

Evaluation of the supplier showed the magnitude of this problem. Proper documentation of the problem helped the supplier make much-needed changes in product protection in shipping and handling. The supplier agreed to palletize future shipments and to shrink-wrap each skid. The 16 labor hours that had been needed to unload a truckload of products was reduced to less than 4 labor hours. Product identification was much easier; total receipt of each shipment was reduced to one day, with errors almost eliminated. The supplier did charge extra for this service, but that charge was more than offset by expense reduction at the receiving location.

Other benefits of palletizing and shrink-wrapping are:

- Identification of products is more accurate.
- Storage space is used more effectively.
- Shrink-wrapping discourages theft. Enclosed containers or skids make it more difficult to remove packages or parts without detection.
- Point-of-purchase sales are assisted by shrink-wrap packaging of individual parts, which allows the material to be displayed more attractively to stimulate impulse buying.

Labeling

Proper labeling on master and individual cartons is vital in all phases of a product cycle. Manufacturers, distributors, and end users depend on labels to supply information about products such as descriptions, package quantity, methods for proper handling, position for proper storage, date codes, warnings, etc. Labels have to be legible on all cartons and products to be effective. Information that may be easily read at ground level may be completely unreadable when the container or product is at the top of a ten-foot rack.

Labels on master and individual cartons should always show the weight of the container and proper method of storage such as, "THIS END UP." When necessary, labels must indicate the proper material handling equipment, such as "USE ONLY SQUEEZE TRUCKS," and the suggested stack height of material.

Suppliers can provide customer protection by adding warnings on packaging and labeling when the contents are hazardous materials or when caution is needed in shipping and handling. Other forms of customer protection are date codes, tamper-proof containers, and ecology protection.

When containers and products are not labeled properly, it can be very costly to manufacturers, distributors, and end users. For example, improper labeling causes receiving errors, storage problems, retrieval errors, inaccurate inventory records, confusion at branch sales locations and to customers, and accounting mix-ups. Inadequate product labeling wastes hundreds of labor hours while manufacturers and distributors remedy problems and, ultimately, affects bottom line profit.

Bar Coding

The use of bar coding for better product identification, reduction of product loss, and lower costs is becoming more prevalent. Bar coding is gaining popularity because it is a better way to collect information for the computer, and it is highly efficient.

The majority of today's computerized manufacturing industries are using bar coding in warehousing, inventory control, product packaging and identification, sales, and accounting. Bar coding can result in many economies for suppliers, manufacturers, and distributors in these areas even when not everyone is participating. Despite its potential, relatively few distributors use bar codes.

In the future distributors will carry 15 percent less inventory, but will have 20 percent more SKU's (stock keeping units). Bar coding is the only answer to managing this increase in the need for information. Data from the Industry Bar Code Alliance indicate that by 1995, 49 percent of products received and 62 percent of products shipped will be processed by scanning equipment reading bar codes.

The use of bar coding in pricing and in the sale of material can insure the correct accounting for products throughout your company. One of the major concerns a distributor has is the unit sale of items that have been received in bulk form. A master chart showing the correct bar code for the item being sold is a solution to this problem. For example, suppose you purchase and distribute many small items that are received in bulk quantities— items such as fittings, nuts, bolts, washers, etc. Bar codes on the master containers of these items definitely aid in identification at receipt. However, when these items are sold by the piece, proper identification can be a major issue. You can eliminate this problem by using laminated cards with the item description, a picture, and the bar code and placing them at the point of sale. When items are matched to their picture and description, the corresponding bar code can be scanned to complete the correct identification, price, and cost of the product.

Manufacturers using bar coding on their packaging and labeling earn a plus from distributors at evaluation time.

PROVIDING EMERGENCY SERVICES

Customers expect you to *always* provide on-time deliveries and to fill stock orders on a regular basis. When you cannot meet their expectations by supplying standard products when they are wanted, you create an unfavorable image in customers' eyes. They expect you to perform 100 percent of the time. Remember, when you perform 100 percent of the time, you are only meeting your customers' expectations. On the other hand, if you can supply a customer's emergency needs one time, you establish a positive image that won't be forgotten. Supplier evaluation will help you set guidelines for your expectations of supplier performance in emergency situations.

Many suppliers offer emergency service at an increased cost. It usually is well worth the added cost, and customers are more than willing to pay the price. Always give suppliers credit during the evaluation process by adding additional points to their grade for providing this service and for being able to perform to their own standards.

It is not uncommon for suppliers to give lip service only to your customer's emergency needs and charge additional money for emergency services they cannot and do not provide. If these added costs are unreasonable or if suppliers cannot perform emergency services within the time frame given, it is you who pays the consequences. Suppliers that can meet the emergency needs of their customers are very important.

CHAPTER 7

ESTABLISHING STANDARDS AND GRADING PROCEDURES FOR MEASURING SUPPLIER PERFORMANCE

Setting effective measurement standards and grading procedures is a vital part of a supplier evaluation and selection program. These standards and procedures become measuring sticks or report cards for manufacturers and distributors to use in identifying needed change in supplier performance.

Learning to set measurement standards includes ranking suppliers, determining the relative importance of ten parameters, and adding weight factors—all of which become a permanent part of your grading procedures.

ESTABLISHING STANDARDS FOR MEASURING SUPPLIER PERFORMANCE

Four Keys to Setting Effective Measurement Standards

Every supplier should be informed ahead of time that an evaluation is taking place and should understand that the same standards are used for each supplier being evaluated. Therefore, simplicity, reasonability, consistency, and factuality are the keys to establishing standards for measuring supplier performance.

Simplicity. Evaluation cannot be so technical that no one understands the method used. A common sense technique for setting measurement standards that clearly communicates the grading method used is vital to every effective supplier evaluation and selection program.

Reasonability. The measurement standards set for each category being evaluated must be attainable by suppliers and their representatives.

Consistency. Consistency gives credibility. Continued alterations of measurement standards will nullify evaluation effectiveness and indicate an inability to identify key issues. Consistency also insures each supplier and representative being evaluated of receiving honest evaluations.

Factuality. Suppliers and their representatives value the grading results of the evaluation process and will make changes in their performance based on facts that are supported by documentation. Suppliers and their representatives cannot be successfully evaluated using only feelings or vague, nondescript terms.

Using Objective Vs. Subjective Measurements

Objective measurement is the measurement of data based on observation, documentation, and analysis. Suppliers set performance levels for themselves in areas such as lead-time predictability, emergency situations, payment terms, pricing, warranties, etc., and print them in their product literature. Objective measurement means actually measuring suppliers' levels of compliance to your established standards. For example, Figure 7-1 is an example of Malco Products, Inc.'s product literature containing its written policies. Malco's payment terms are net 30 days from invoice date F.O.B. Annandale, Minnesota. This statement is the performance Malco has set for itself. If you have determined that the standard for your industry is 2% tenth prox—net 30, then Malco's evaluation grade in this parameter is sub-standard.

Another example is lead-time predictability. Your standard in this case reflects the supplier's ability to perform within its own guideline. Therefore, you are actually measuring the supplier's compliance to its own written or stated standards.

Figure 7-1: Malco Products, Inc.'s Product Literature Showing Its Written Policy Statements

MALCO PRODUCTS, INC.
Annandale, Minnesota 55302-9135 U.S.A.

Manufacturing UPC ID #86406

SPECIAL FREIGHT ALLOWANCE AND VOLUME DISCOUNT SCHEDULE		
Order Total	Shipping	Volume Discount
Under $50.00	$5 Handling Chg.	None
$950.	Full Freight	None
$1,500.	Full Freight	1%
$2,000.	Full Freight	2%
$3,000.	Full Freight	3%
$4,000	Full Freight	4%

POLICIES · Effective January 14, 1991

GENERAL POLICIES
Distributors prices shown are before volume discounts.

Orders for less than standard package quantity shown in price sheet will be automatically increased to the standard package quantity.

We reserve the right to make changes in design, material, or finish in an effort to improve our products without special notification.

All purchase orders submitted by our distributors are assumed as accepting our general terms as stated herein, any conflicting terms stated on the Purchase Order cannot supersede our terms.

PRICING
Malco offers a volume discount based on the total dollar value of an order. All invoices will be priced at printed price shown in the Confidential Distributor Book. If a blanket order is in effect at the time of the order receipt, the price of fasteners will be the blanket order quantity price. The volume discount applicable to the order will be deducted on the invoice and be reflected in the invoice total. **See schedule above for volume discounts.**

To take advantage of the volume discounts, orders from multiple locations may be combined if the following conditions are met:

- ✓ All orders must be under one primary purchase order number.
- ✓ All billing must be to one location (address).
- ✓ All orders must be received together and processed at one time.
- ✓ If purchaser elects to have shipments made to multiple locations each shipment will stand along for freight. $950.00 orders (priced at printed Distributor Prices) are required for full freight allowance (prepaid freight).

Prices are subject to change without notice. Prices prevailing at the time the order is received will apply.

PAYMENT TERMS
Terms are net 30 days from invoice date F.O.B. Annandale, Minnesota.

SMALL ORDER HANDLING FEE
Malco has no minimum order size. A handling fee of $5.00 will be added to all orders for less than $50.00 net. Repairs and non-cataloged Repair Parts are excluded.

SHIPPING TERMS
Prices are F.O.B. Malco's Shipping Dock, Annandale, Minnesota. Title passes directly to you at the moment we place the merchandise into the hands of the carrier.

Freight will be prepaid and allowed via cheapest way to a single destination within the continental limits of the U.S.A. on orders (printed price) of $950.00 or more (Alaska and Hawaii $1500.00). Freight differential due to more expensive routing specified will be charged to customer.

LOSS OR DAMAGE
You must immediately, upon receipt of merchandise, report all claims for losses or damage in shipment directly to the delivering carrier. Any delay may cause you a loss. All merchandise is shipped F.O.B. Malco's Shipping Dock. Therefore, the carrier is legally responsible only to you for any losses arising out of shipment. Although our responsibility for product ends upon receipt by the carrier, we will gladly extend whatever assistance is required.

Do not deduct the price of the damaged or lost items from your Malco invoice. Pay your invoice price in full and submit your claim to the carrier for your losses.

SHORTAGES
Any shortages on your shipment must be reported within thirty days of the shipping date for proper verification and possible adjustment. All packages are sealed when they leave the factory. If seal is broken when received, submit your claim directly to the delivering carrier for your losses.

ADDITIONS
There is no handling fee for additions. Additions to the original order placed same day will qualify for the same freight and volume discount schedule. We do not accept additions to back orders.

BACK ORDERS
Back orders will be shipped as soon as possible. All back orders will be shipped freight prepaid.

MALCO GUARANTEES THE SALE OF ALL CURRENT PRODUCTS
If you decide that any current Malco items are not moving fast enough to satisfy you, you may return them to Malco for a full credit of your purchase price. (NOTE: unless copies of the appropriate Malco invoices are included with the returned merchandise, purchase price is considered to be the price prevailing in the price sheet immediately preceeding current prices).

No restocking charge - no special permission required when returning merchandise. Simply enclose a note stating that it is overstock merchandise and prepay shipment to our factory in Annandale. It is IMPORTANT to pack carefully and securely because merchandise not received in good enough condition to be put directly onto our shelves must be repackaged at your expense.

BLANKET FASTENER ORDERS
A distributor can qualify for additional discounts without taking delivery of these fasteners in one shipment, provided a fastener blanket order has been established. To establish a fastener blanket, a distributor must submit a regular purchase order signed and dated which states: **"Blanket order for "X" million fasteners to be released within the next 12 months."** All bulk and packaged quantities of Nylon Ties, Rivets and Sheet Metal Screws (including Zip-in™ and Bit-Tip®) may be combined into one fastener blanket. (Machine screws and nuts are excluded). In establishing a blanket order, it is not necessary for the distributor to commit himself to what size or types of fasteners he will be ordering.

Each release order must state **"These fasteners to be released from our blanket P.O. #____________".** The minimum release is 25M fasteners from any blanket order. Orders for release of less than 25M fasteners will be billed at BASE price but will be considered as released against the blanket. Each release stands alone for freight.

Malco will automatically reinstate fastener blanket orders for subsequent 12 month periods, provided the requirements are met each year. Blanket size will be automatically increased if justified by purchases reaching the next higher level, or automatically decreased if purchases do not meet the existing blanket size.

Request Fastener Blanket Fact Sheet SL3351C for full details concerning this program.

BLADE DISCOUNT PROGRAM
Extra volume discounts, based on total number of pieces per order, are available at various quantity levels. Reciprocating Saw Blades are priced out as a separate category immediately following the alphanumeric section of this book.

EXTRA 10% ON SCHOOL ORDERS
All Malco items that you sell for use by students will be invoiced at printed price less 10%, provided we receive a copy of the school's purchase order. Any volume discounts will then be applied. We expect schools to be sold at Trade Price less 10%.

WARRANTY
All Malco Tools and Accessories are warranted for the life of the product to be free from faulty workmanship or materials.

Our obligation assumed under this limited warranty is to make a replacement of any part or parts that our examination determines as being defective. Parts which have been worn out from normal use, misuse, or improperly handled will not be covered under warranty. Malco assumes no responsibility for any consequential damages related to the malfunction of one of our products.

RETURNS AND REPAIRS
When returning products to Malco for repair, warranty claims, or overstock, they must be returned prepaid to our factory in Annandale, Minnesota. When Malco sends the warranty replacements or warranty repaired tools back to you, the freight will be prepaid.

For your safety and to reduce shipping costs, remove attachments and personal effects before shipping. We reserve the right to decline responsibility when repairs have been made or attempted by others.

Tape rule blades or blade end hooks, are not guaranteed against breakage. A missing bolt or nut, a broken crimper blade, etc., will not be considered reason for whole tool replacement.

Our most popular repair and replacement parts are in our price sheet. If you need current pricing on a part not listed, please contact the factory.

ADVERTISING
Free sales aids, including display materials, counter literature, stuffers, catalogs and price sheets are available in quantities upon request.

Our policy does not allow us to underwrite any portion of the cost of publishing distributor catalogs. However, our advertising department is readily available for assistance. We cannot give advertising allowances.

Subjective measurement bases judgments on observations such as consumer preference in quality that is based on price as a perceived value. It is continuous and documented.

Both objective and subjective measurements are used in the grading process, with the major emphasis on objective grading. Remember, you will earn the respect of suppliers and their representatives by producing hard data based on continuous observation, documentation, and analysis.

There are seven parameters that require objective measurements: lead-time predictability, emergency services, product pricing, shipping and receiving, return policies (inventory rebalancing), payment terms, and warranty procedures.

Lead-time predictability. Suppliers give specific dates for product delivery when your purchasing department places orders. You can measure their compliance to their stated delivery dates by comparing the dates goods are received with the anticipated delivery dates generated when the orders were placed.

Emergency services. You can find suppliers' policies for emergency service in their product literature. Therefore, you can measure suppliers' performance in emergency situations against their written emergency service procedures.

Product pricing. Supplier product-pricing literature contains product-pricing information. You can measure the levels of quantity pricing and the supplier's aggressiveness in product pricing against its written pricing policies and other pricing concessions that can be negotiated.

Shipping and receiving. Your material handling department can identify and document shipping and receiving problems, such as back orders, overshipments, poor loading procedures, etc., when goods are received.

Return policies (inventory rebalancing). Suppliers' return policies are included in their product literature. These statements cover the amount of material that can be returned, the time involved, and the penalty charged for product return. You can evaluate your suppliers by how closely they comply with their own written return policies.

Payment terms (billing policies). Terms also are supplied in product literature. Your accounts payable department can supply information covering a supplier's willingness to resolve billing problems.

Warranty procedures. Written warranty statements of supplier products are also addressed in supplier product literature. Warranty occurrences and your supplier's compliance to its own warranty statements are documented by your warranty department.

Product quality is the only parameter in distribution where subjective measurements are used. Product quality is a perceived value. Your sales and marketing group can measure product quality in relation to your customer's perception of value received for price paid.

Product quality in manufacturing uses objective measurements. The manufacturer's quality control department can supply all the quality standards information needed for each supplier's evaluation. The department will also be able to provide information about each supplier's performance to its own set standards of quality by actual measurement.

Finally, there are two parameters that use both objective and subjective measurements: sales/production aids and packaging and labeling.

Sales/production aids. Supplier advertising, product promotions, and product-training programs for manufacturers, distributors, and end users are keys to successful product production and marketing when they are provided. Subjective input from your engineering, production, materials control, sales, and marketing departments determine their effectiveness.

Packaging/labeling. The protection afforded a product by its packaging and the product information included on the product package label are measured objectively. However, the effectiveness of supplier packaging and labeling in situations such as storage, retrieval, identification, and sales is tempered by subjective input from your material handling, production, and sales departments.

Quantifying objective and subjective measurements is discussed later in this chapter when we describe how to develop a point system for evaluating each item.

ESTABLISHING PARAMETER RANKING AND WEIGHT FACTORS

Ranking evaluation parameters is determining the relative importance of each parameter in your evaluation process and rearranging them in order of importance. Adding weight factors to each parameter is assigning numerical values to your parameters. By doing so, you can establish the degree of importance of the first parameter in relation to the last or least important parameter in the ranking.

You will set parameter rankings and weight factors at the beginning of your supplier evaluation and selection program that will not change. This is vital to the consistency and acceptability of your program. To ensure complete agreement on the parameter rankings and weight factors in your evaluation program, it is advisable to enlist the help of your company president and other department managers including marketing, production, sales, distribution, material control, and accounting in this process. Call for a meeting and get a consensus of those present.

Three Steps to Ranking Parameters

In previous chapters the following parameters were chosen as important to distribution and manufacturing in a supplier evaluation and selection program:

Quality
Sales/Production Aids
Lead-Time Predictability
Warranty Procedures
Product Pricing
Back Orders/Overshipments
Emergency Services
Inventory Rebalancing
Packaging/Labeling
Terms (Billing Policies)

You will determine the importance of these parameters in relation to each other in a three-step, iterative process.

Step 1: List All Parameters for Ranking

Make a list of all parameters to be ranked by your company president and department managers. Use a chalk board to simplify the process.

Step 2: Determine the Relative Importance of Your Parameters

Begin parameter ranking with quality. Ask for input on the relative importance of quality to the next parameter, sales/production aids. A simple majority vote will determine which is more important—quality or sales/production aids. If the majority agrees that quality is more important than sales/production aids, quality will get one vote. Continue comparing quality with the remaining eight parameters. In the example in Figure 7-2, the majority agreed that quality was more important than all other parameters, so the total votes for quality as the number one parameter is nine.

Figure 7-2: Determining the Relative Importance of Parameters

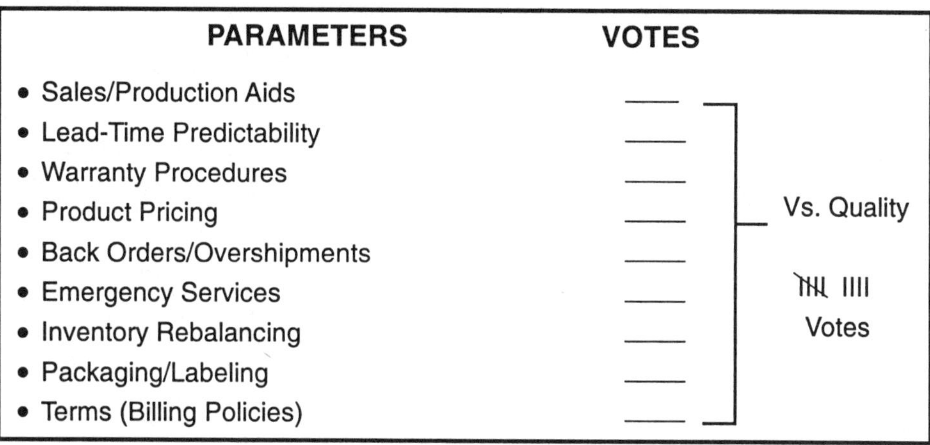

PARAMETERS	VOTES	
• Sales/Production Aids	____	
• Lead-Time Predictability	____	
• Warranty Procedures	____	
• Product Pricing	____	Vs. Quality
• Back Orders/Overshipments	____	
• Emergency Services	____	~~IIII~~ IIII
• Inventory Rebalancing	____	Votes
• Packaging/Labeling	____	
• Terms (Billing Policies)	____	

Step 3: Continue This Ranking Process for the Remaining Nine Parameters

The total number of votes for quality is entered under the heading Final Tally. Sales/production aids is moved to the right of the remaining eight parameters. Figure 7-3 indicates that sales/production aids is more important than seven of the remaining eight categories. Product pricing was judged more important than sales/production aids and received one vote.

This process is continued for each of the remaining parameters. The result of this exercise is a numerical ranking of all parameters in order of their importance to your company. The final parameter ranking becomes a permanent part of your Supplier Grading Report.

Determining the Importance of Each Parameter

During the actual grading process a supplier's performance rating on both quality and sales/production aids could be five. When this happens, you can express their relative importance by using weight factors. There are two steps in determining the weight of importance of each parameter.

Step 1: Set the Limits for Your Range of Values

Setting the outside limits for your range of values is the first step in determining weight factors for each parameter. Take care not to set weight factors so far apart that they are not numerically reasonable. By using too wide

Figure 7-3: Continuation of the Ranking Process

PARAMETERS	VOTES	FINAL TALLY
• Lead-Time Predictability	___	Quality 9 votes
• Warranty Procedures	___	
• Product Pricing	I	Vs. 2. Sales/ Production Aids
• Back Orders/Overshipments	___	
• Emergency Services	___	𝍸 II Votes
• Inventory Rebalancing	___	
• Packaging/Labeling	___	
• Terms (Billing Policies)	___	

a numerical spread you make it possible for suppliers to achieve an overall high grade for performance by scoring well on selected issues.

For example, suppose you set quality as the number 1 or most important of 10 parameters and emergency services as being the least significant. Determine whether quality is 50%, 70%, 80%, or 200% more important to your company than emergency services.

Your management team will discuss and vote on the numerical value for quality in relation to emergency services, thus setting the extreme limits for the range of values to be used in the grading process. If they agree that quality is 70% more important than emergency services, the extreme limits for your weight factors will be 70% (1.7) for quality (the highest range) and 0% (1.0) for emergency services (the lowest range). If there is a disagreement, a majority vote will decide the issue.

Use the ranking of parameters 1 through 10 shown in Figure 7-4 as your revised weighted-parameter rankings.

Step 2: Add the Weight Factors to the Parameter Ranking

Weight factors for parameters 2 through 9 will be set between the extreme values, 1.7 and 1.0. You will notice in Figure 7-5 that packaging and labeling have the same weight factor as emergency services, 1.0. This means they had an equal number of votes for rank of importance. The established weight factors become a permanent part of the Supplier Grading Report illustrated in Figure 7-6.

Figure 7-4: Setting Extreme Limits for Range of Values

PARAMETER RANKING	WEIGHT		
• Quality	1.7	(70%)	high
• Sales/Production Aids			
• Product Pricing			
• Lead-Time Predictability			
• Back Orders/Overshipments			degree of importance
• Return Policies			
• Warranty Procedures			
• Terms (Billing Policies)			
• Packaging/Labeling			
• Emergency Service	1.0	(0%)	low

Figure 7-5: Adjusted Parameter Ranking Showing the Addition of Weight Factors

PARAMETER RANKING	WEIGHT
• Quality	1.7
• Sales/Production Aids	1.6
• Product Pricing	1.5
• Lead-Time Predictability	1.5
• Back Orders/Overshipments	1.4
• Return Policies	1.3
• Warranty Policies	1.2
• Terms (Billing Policies)	1.1
• Packaging/Labeling	1.0
• Emergency Shipments	1.0

Figure 7-6: Supplier Grading Report

SUPPLIER GRADING REPORT

Grading Scale
1 = Very poor
5 = Average
10 = Excellent

Supplier: A

Date: 2/92

PARAMATERS	WEIGHT FACTOR	(times)	PERFORMANCE GRADE	(equals)	TOTAL POINTS
QUALITY	1.7	X	8.0	=	13.6
SALES/PRODUCTION AIDS	1.6	X	6.0	=	9.6
PRODUCT PRICING	1.5	X	4.0	=	6.0
LEAD-TIME PREDICTABILITY	1.5	X	7.5	=	11.25
BACK ORDERS/OVERSHIPMENTS	1.4	X	5.5	=	7.70
RETURN POLICIES	1.3	X	9.0	=	11.7
WARRANTY PROCEDURES	1.2	X	6.0	=	7.2
TERMS (Billing Policies)	1.1	X	7.0	=	7.7
PACKAGING and LABELING	1.0	X	7.5	=	7.5
EMERGENCY SERVICE	1.0	X	8.0	=	8.0
			PARAMETER GRADE TOTAL		90.25

SUPPLIER REPRESENTATIVE: Mr. Bob Smith

VISITS: Total number of sales locations: 25
Total number of visits made by rep: 21
Total number of sales locations visited: 16
60 %

COMMENTS: More visits to sales locations are needed. Bob needs to improve product knowledge and customer skills.

ADDITIONAL COMMENTS: Quality - New design award of one point included in perf. grade. Sales Aids - Promotions were not effective. Results were negative. Production Aids - Reps did not exhibit good product knowledge. Did not schedule visits.

GRADING HISTORY	1992	1993	1994	1995	1996
PARAMETER GRADE TOTALS	90.25				
YEARLY RANKINGS					

MAILING INFORMATION:
President or V.P. of Marketing
Supplier's Name
Address
City, State, Zip

CC: Supplier or Independent Sales Rep
Supplier or Independent Company
Address
City, State, Zip
President of Distribution or Manufacturing
Other: ______________
____
____

ESTABLISHING A GRADING SCALE AND APPLYING IT TO EACH EVALUATION PARAMETER

Establishing a grading scale for the supplier evaluation process is done by setting a grading scale range of 0 to 10 for all parameters. Zero is the lowest grade a supplier can receive for poor performance, and 10 is the highest grade attainable, given for excellent supplier performance. Five is the average (midpoint) value.

Setting grade standards from 0 to 10 means that a supplier receiving a grade of 10 on the parameter of greatest importance to you—quality—will accrue 17 points:

10 (points) × 1.7 (weight factor) = 17 points

The same supplier receiving a grade of 10 for emergency services will accrue 10 points:

10 (points) × 1.0 (weight factor) = 10 points

Therefore, multiplying the weight factor of each parameter by the supplier performance grades gives the total performance grade for each parameter. An example of this grading method is shown in the Supplier Grading Report.

Establishing a Grading Procedure for Evaluating Supplier Quality

The method of evaluating the quality parameter is different for distribution and manufacturing. We will set the measurement standards for both.

Setting Quality Measurement Standards for Distribution

The distributor can establish subjective measurement standards for quality in four steps.

Step 1: Set a Grading Scale for the Parameter of Quality

First, set the average grade, or your midpoint value at 5. This will apply to products that neither add nor detract from their competitive position because of quality.

Step 2: Set the Highest Value for Quality

The next value to set is 10. There is always one supplier in every product category considered to be "the best." This supplier's product is preferred by customers for its perceived quality and reputation. It demands and is sold at a higher price. Grade 10 is used for the product that is the acknowledged industry leader in quality because 10 is the highest grade possible.

Your quality ranking should now look like this:

Supplier Quality	Point Value
The acknowledged industry leader in quality.	10
Products whose quality does not add or detract from their market competitiveness.	5 (midpoint value)

Step 3: Add Grades 6 Through 9 to Your Grading Scale

These grades will cover products with a competitive edge because of your customers' perception of quality. These products command higher prices in the marketplace. Scores will be based on input from the field.

Your quality ranking should now look like this:

Supplier Quality	Point Value
The supplier's products are the acknowledged industry leader in quality and price.	10
The supplier's products have competitive advantages because of the customer's perception of quality, and they can command higher prices in the marketplace.	6–9
Products whose quality and price do not add or detract from the supplier's market competitiveness.	5 (midpoint value)

Step 4: Add Grades 0 to 4 to the Grading Scale for Quality.

Products with below-average quality are graded in the 0 to 4 range. These are low-cost products that cannot compete or maintain average competitiveness when judged for quality.

Your quality ranking should now look like this:

Supplier Quality	Point Value
The supplier is the acknowledged industry leader in quality and price.	10
The supplier's products have competitive advantages because of customers' perception of quality. They can command higher prices in the marketplace.	6–9
The supplier's products are average. The quality and price do not add or detract in the supplier's market competitiveness.	5 (midpoint value)
The supplier's products are below-average in quality and pricing. They cannot compete on these characteristics.	0–4

Now we have completed the subjective grading structure for quality.

Setting Quality Measurement Standards for Manufacturing

Manufacturers will want to establish an objective grading structure for the parameter of quality. This can be done in two steps.

Step 1: Set the Highest Value (10) for your Material Rejection Rate

Your quality ranking should look like this:

Quality Standards for Manufacturing

Supplier Quality	Point Value
The supplier does not have material or service failures. The material or service supplied is always correct.	10

Step 2: Add the Remaining Grades to Your Grading Scale for Quality

Any supplier having a rejection rate from quality control of 3% or higher due to material failure will grade at zero for quality. These scores will be based on input from the manufacturer's quality control department.

The quality ranking should now look like this:

Supplier Quality	Point Value
The supplier does not have a record of material or service failures. The material or service supplied is always correct.	10
The supplier's material meets or exceeds specifications. However, rejections have occurred during the past year.	

Material Rejection Rate	Point Value
< .005	9
< .010	8
< .0125	7
< .015	6
< .020	5
< .025	4
< .026	3
≥ .03	0

Material rejection ranges should be supplied by quality control. The step increments may or may not be consistent.

Now we have completed the objective grading structure for quality.

Establishing a Grading Procedure for Evaluating Supplier Sales/Production Aids

Distributors and manufacturers will use different grading procedures for this parameter also. Distributors will be measuring the effectiveness and performance of their suppliers in providing them with sales aids. Manufacturers will measure performance of their suppliers in providing them with production aids.

Setting Sales Aids Measurement Standards for Distribution

To evaluate supplier sales aids, you need to evaluate the activities of suppliers and their sales representatives. You will score primarily on their field activities. Calls made by supplier representatives to your central purchasing are considered a "given" and should not be factored into grading unless you feel grading in that area is important or you do not have multiple locations to be serviced. Points are earned for the number of location calls made to a manufacturer or distribution company with multiple locations and reflect the number of calls made to each location. This is important when your company's multiple locations cover large geographical areas. This gives suppliers and their sales representatives a clear message to call on as many of your locations as possible.

For example, you must determine what is a reasonable number of sales calls for a representative to make on each of your locations during a one-year period. If your company has 26 locations, is it reasonable for you to expect a rep to visit each location at least twice a year? If so, 52 calls becomes your stated average for performance, and a rep can earn one point by meeting that standard.

Additional points are given to reps who exceed stated average performance in sales calls. If a rep makes 3 calls to each of your 26 locations during a one-year period, or 78 calls in all, the rep would earn 2 points because performance is above the stated average number of calls expected.

Points will also be given for purchasing assistance, advertising, product training, promotions, and the availability of toll-free telephone numbers for production, sales, or technical assistance.

Sales aids grading includes services provided by the supplier and services provided by the supplier's rep.

Supplier's Sales Aids	Point Value
Supplier advertising is done on a local and/or national level.	1
Product training sessions are initiated and supported by the supplier.	1
Supplier promotions are easy to administer and effective.	1
Toll-free telephone and fax numbers are made available by the supplier for sales and technical assistance.	1
The supplier rep is willing to give quality assistance to purchasing.	1
You must specify the number of sales calls a rep must make to your branches during the year being evaluated to obtain points.	1–2
How well does your rep perform his or her duties of product representation?	1–2
If you have multiple locations, specify the location and number of visits a rep needs to make to accomplish reasonable territory coverage.	1

The total possible grade for sales aids will add to a sum of 10 points because your established grading scale is 0 to 10.

Setting Production Aids Measurement Standards for Manufacturing

Manufacturers will want to establish the following grading structure for production aids. This parameter includes the supplier's ability and willingness to provide production aids and the effectiveness of supplier representation.

Supplier Production Aids	Point Value
You must specify the number of sales calls a supplier must make to your locations during the year to obtain points. This includes visits to production, engineering, material control, and management.	1-2

The supplier rep gives quality assistance to department managers according to their needs.	2
Training sessions are initiated and conducted by the supplier.	2
Engineering information is available from the supplier. The supplier works closely with your engineering and material control managers to insure correct usage of material or services.	2
Toll-free telephone and fax numbers are available for use by engineering, purchasing, production, and material control.	2

Establishing a Grading Structure for Evaluating a Supplier's Packaging and Labeling

The grading standards for packaging and labeling consist of earned points in areas such as product protection and identification for the distributor and manufacturer.

Packaging—Master Cartons	Point Value
Master cartons are well marked and give information for product identification and handling instructions.	1
Master cartons give adequate product protection.	1
Product quantities in each master carton are consistent.	1
Packaging—Individual Cartons	
Individual cartons give adequate product protection.	1
Product quantities in individual cartons are consistent.	1
Labeling	
Labels identify contents of master cartons and are easy to read.	1
Labels identify contents of individual cartons and are easy to read.	1
Bar coding is used on master and individual cartons and labels.	1

Products are palletized by the supplier for shipment.	1
The supplier uses shrink-wrapping for better product protection.	1

Establishing a Grading Structure for Lead-Time Predictability

Parameters that are calculated values, such as lead-time predictability and warranties, use objective measurements. In most cases, you can grade suppliers by the degree to which they comply with their own written performance statements.

Grading lead-time predictability is done by calculating the percentage of orders delivered to you by each supplier within the supplier's own stated lead time. For example, if the total number of orders delivered is 10 and the number of on-time deliveries is 7, the on-time ratio is 7, and the number of points earned is 7.

This is a ratio measuring method. The greatest number of points awarded is 10. However, the ratio used to determine the points comes from the total shipments made by the supplier during the evaluation period.

You can "build in" manufacturers' stated lead times for all the products you handle if you have a computerized system. This simplifies your product-tracking process. When you receive a shipment, the computer automatically compares planned receipt date to actual receive date and the product quantity ordered against the quantity received on a line-item basis. The number of units back ordered is multiplied by the number of *days out,* or days past the stated lead-time to get a weighted *days late* number.

The basis for your supplier's grade in this area is calculated by dividing the sum of all weighted days late by the total number of pieces ordered. The result is the number of days late weighted average for pieces delivered. See Figure 7-7.

Establishing a Grading Structure for Evaluating Supplier Warranties

In a standard warranty a product is guaranteed free from defect for a period of one year from the date of purchase. Your suppliers can earn an average

Figure 7-7: Calculating Days Late and Performance to Stated Lead Times on a Weighted Basis Stated Lead Times

Calculating Days Late

Total pieces ordered = 100
90 pieces were received 1 day late = 90 (90 pieces × 1 day)
7 pieces were received 5 days late = 35 (7 pieces × 5 days)
3 pieces were received 20 days late = 60 (3 pieces × 20 days)

$$\frac{\text{Total } 185}{100 \text{ pieces}} = 1.85 \text{ days late weighted average for pieces delivered.}$$

Calculating Lead Time to Stated Standards

The lead time to stated standards is calculated as follows:

$$1 - \frac{\text{weighted days late}}{\text{stated lead times}}$$

If the stated lead time is 30 days, the results would be:

$$1 - \frac{1.85}{30} = 1 - .06 =$$ .94, or 94% performance to stated lead times on a weighted basis.

---

starting grade of 5 for a standard warranty. For example, if the majority of suppliers have a warranty policy giving a one-year, limited-parts warranty, with defective items having to be returned, then all products with the same warranty are graded 5, the midpoint value.

Variations from the midpoint value are graded as additions or deductions. Additions are additional points given for warranty statements that make processing warranty material easier for your company and its customers. Deductions are points subtracted from the midpoint value of 5 for warranty statements that make processing warranty material more difficult for your company and its customers.

An above-average warranty policy might state that defective products will be replaced over the counter and credit will be issued to the distributor. This type of warranty earns the highest grade possible, 10, in your warranty grading.

Your warranty ranking might look like this:

Warranty Policies	Point Value
Defective products can be replaced over-the-counter and credit issued to the distributor without having to return warranty items to the supplier.	10
A one-year, limited-parts warranty with defective parts return is an average warranty and also the midpoint value for grading.	5 (midpoint value)
The supplier does not have a warranty policy.	0
ADDITIONS (points that can be added to the midpoint value)	
The supplier has a stated warranty policy printed in product literature.	+ 1
Defective parts do not have to be returned to the manufacturer.	+ 1
Replacement of defective products is repair and return or credit given, based on the customer's request.	+ 1
Over-the-counter replacement of a defective product is allowed by the supplier.	+ 1
DEDUCTIONS (points subtracted from the midpoint value)	
The supplier refuses to comply with its stated warranty policies.	– 3

Establishing a Grading Structure for Product Pricing

The midpoint, or a grade of 5, for product pricing is a comparative process. Similar products are compared and a median price established and assigned for the midpoint. Other points may be added or subtracted from it.

Your ranking for product pricing might look like this:

Pricing Terms	Point Value
The supplier is the pricing leader in its industry, with the lowest-priced product.	6
The supplier's product is not competitively priced.	0–4

The supplier's product price is competitive. Pricing is in line with the pricing of the majority of competitors.	5 (midpoint value)
ADDITIONS (+)	
The supplier initiates pricing competition and is always the first to adjust pricing to stimulate sales.	+ 1
Product pricing literature is correct and is distributed to purchasing in a timely manner	+ 1
Volume price breaks are offered by the supplier. Blanket purchase orders are used and special quotations are furnished.	+ 1
The supplier's product pricing has been consistent during the last twelve months.	+ 1
DEDUCTIONS (–)	
The supplier extends its best pricing only through preseason programs.	– 1
When the supplier increases product prices notices of these increases are always late.	– 1
The supplier cannot or will not supply justification for price increases.	– 1

Establishing a Grading Structure for Back Orders/Overshipments

The grading structure for back orders and overshipments is based on the percent of the total annual orders placed that were back ordered or overshipped. The percentage of incomplete orders is calculated and given points from your grading scale of 0 to 10. For example, your ranking might look like this:

Percent of Back Orders/Overshipments	Point Value
0% (Every order received from a supplier was shipped complete.)	10
10%	9
20%	8
30%	7
40%	6

50%	5
60%	4
70%	3
80%	2
90%	1
100% (Every order received from a supplier had shipping problems.)	0

Establishing a Grading Structure for Inventory Rebalancing

Many suppliers have written policy statements that make allowances for the return of purchased products. A typical policy allows for the return of products with authorization from the supplier and includes a 15 percent restocking charge. As the norm, this type of policy would receive a midpoint value grade of 5.

A more aggressive supplier might allow you to return a designated number of *slow moving* products each year without charge. The supplier's representatives might also help you identify such items. This supplier will earn additional points for special allowances made to you. Suppliers that allow unconditional return of inventory at any time will receive a top grade of 10.

Your ranking might look like this:

Rebalancing Policies (returns)	**Point Value**
Inventory can be returned to the supplier at any time.	10
Inventory can be returned to the supplier with prior authorization and includes a 15% restocking charge.	5 (midpoint value)
The supplier will not allow inventory rebalancing.	0
ADDITIONS (points that can be added to midpoint value)	
The supplier has a restocking charge of 10% for the return of inventory items.	+ 1
Restocking charges are not required by the supplier when items are returned.	+ 2
Supplier representatives assist you in identifying slow-moving items for return.	+ 2

DEDUCTIONS
(points that can be deducted from the midpoint value)

The supplier's restocking charge is 20%.	– 1
The supplier's restocking charge is 25%.	– 2

Establishing a Grading Structure for Payment Terms (Billing Policies)

The first step is to review your supplier's payment requirements. If the majority of your suppliers state *2% ten days net 30* for their payment terms, you will set these terms as your midpoint value of 5. The remaining payment terms will be determined from your midpoint value. Your ranking for payment terms might look like this:

Payment Terms	Point Value
5% tenth Prox. net 30 or 180 days net	10
4% tenth Prox. net 30 or 150 days net	9
3% tenth Prox. net 30 or 120 days net	8
2% tenth Prox. net 30 or 90 days net	7
1% tenth Prox. net 30 or 60 days net	6
2% ten days net 30	5 (midpoint value)
1% ten days net 30	4
Net 60 days	3
Net 45 days	2
Net 30 days	1
Less than 30 days net	0

This range for terms exists in some industries. It tends to have a statistical pattern with the extremes set for point values on both ends.

Establishing a Grading Structure for Emergency Needs

The standard for emergency services is based on a supplier with an emergency need statement written in its product literature. This becomes your midpoint value and will give 5 points to the supplier. Additional points are added or deducted to the midpoint value.

Emergency Needs is an area where the complexity of a product is taken into consideration. Companies that supply a wide range of engineered products invest more to supply emergency service to you than do suppliers with a narrow range of product offerings.

Your ranking might look like this:

Supplier Policies for Emergency Needs	Point Value
The supplier always supplies products and correct information when you have to handle an emergency situation for a customer.	10
An emergency service statement is written in the supplier's product literature.	5 (midpoint value)
The supplier refuses to provide emergency services.	0
ADDITIONS (points that can be added to the midpoint value)	
Complexity and Range of Product Offerings:	
commodity products	+ 1
complex products	+ 2
Effectiveness of the supplier's emergency services policy: (reasonable charges, minimum quantities are waived, etc.)	+ 1
The supplier's performance complies to its written statement for emergency service:	
95% to 100% performance	+ 2
90% to 95% performance	+ 1
DEDUCTIONS (points that can be deducted from the midpoint value)	
The supplier's emergency service charges are unreasonable and discourage the use of emergency services.	– 1
The supplier does not comply to its written emergency service statements and cannot perform to a 90% level of completion of your emergency needs.	–1

INFORMING SUPPLIERS OF YOUR SUPPLIER PERFORMANCE MEASUREMENT STANDARDS AND HOW THEY ARE USED

Informing your suppliers of the standards your company will be using in its performance evaluation is important. An explanation of the standards opens the door for better communication between you and your suppliers. It is important for them to know what your expectations of supplier performance are, and it also guards against misinterpretation.

Figure 7-8 is a letter introducing your supplier evaluation program to your suppliers. A summary of your Supplier Performance Measurement Standards to send with your introductory letter is in the appendix at the back of the book. You can use the examples in Figure 7-8 and the summary to introduce suppliers to your supplier evaluation program and explain your measurement standards to them. This letter and the supplier performance measurement standards should be sent to everyone participating in your program at the beginning of your evaluation program and every year thereafter.

Figure 7-8: Letter of Introduction for a Supplier Evaluation Program

DATE: February 2, 19XX

William Rogers, President
Rogers Supply Co., Inc.
1776 Travis St.
Houston, Texas 77002

Re: Supplier Evaluation Program and Supplier Performance Measurement Standards.

Dear William:

We will be conducting a supplier evaluation program this year in an effort to improve communication among ourselves, our suppliers and our customers. This program is part of our total quality process and our commitment to excellence. It is designed to identify needed change and to eliminate performance inefficiencies.

A high standard of ethics is a vital part of this program. It insures you and your representatives of receiving fair performance evaluations.

Our measurement standards are simple, reasonable, consistent, and factual. They are designed to be primarily objective in nature, thus providing you with a "measuring stick" leading to improved performance in 10 parameters important to our company.

Please review the enclosed descriptions of the Supplier Performance Measurements Standards we will be using in our evaluation process. If you have questions feel free to call.

Sincerely,

THE VERY BEST DISTRIBUTORS

Catherine Hollingsworth,
President

jlf/CH

CC: Supplier Representatioves

Enclosure

CHAPTER 8

SELECTING SUPPLIERS TO BE EVALUATED

Selecting suppliers to participate in your performance evaluation is important. Therefore, you will want to enlist the assistance of your company president or the person he or she designates to make supplier selection. Two simple, effective criteria for determining the suppliers to include in your evaluation program are volume of sales and distribution by value.

DETERMINING VOLUME OF SALES

Determining the volume of supplier sales is the first method you can use in selecting suppliers for performance grading. This is the only area in your evaluation and selection program where volume of sales is taken into consideration. Use the following guidelines in making this determination.

- List all your suppliers in descending order of their total sales volume to your company or the amount of sales you obtain from their products and the percent of accumulated total sales. Figure 8-1 is an example of what your list might look like.
- Determine who your major suppliers are by reviewing their total sales volume and each supplier's percentage of your company's total sales. Your major suppliers will represent the majority of your total product purchases or product sales. You will want to make sure they are all included in the evaluation process.
- Determine the dollar level of supplier product sales you and your company president want to cover in your evaluation process. Usually this dollar level will cover all your major suppliers. For example, a company with

Figure 8-1: Supplier Sales Analysis

This report is sorted to list all your suppliers in descending order of their total sales volume to your company. Total company sales is $30,000,000. Cumulative percentages are relative to total company sales.

$$\left(\frac{\text{Supplier} \times \text{Sales}}{\$30{,}000{,}000} = 3.3\%\right)$$

SUPPLIER SELECTION SALES ANALYSIS

Total Company Sales = $30,000,000

SUPPLIER	TOTAL SALES VOLUME	CUMULATIVE SALES	CUMULATIVE PERCENT OF TOTAL SALES
SUPPLIER X	$1,000,000	$ 1,000,000	3.3%
SUPPLIER C	750,000	1,750,000	5.8%
SUPPLIER A	700,000	2,450,000	8.2%
SUPPLIER D	600,000	3,050,000	10.2%
•	•	•	•
SUPPLIER W	2,000	30,000,000	100.0%

annual sales volume of $50,000,000 and 300 suppliers will evaluate about 100 suppliers. These suppliers should represent about 80 percent of the company's sales volume.

- If you have multiple suppliers, you might not want to include those with an extremely low sales volume. For example, you might have made one purchase of $1,000 from a supplier during the evaluation year. Since this was a one-time purchase with a relatively low dollar amount, it's a waste of time to include the supplier in your evaluation process.

COUNTING THE COSTS OF DOING BUSINESS WITH SUPPLIERS OF INDIRECT PRODUCTS OR SERVICES

Manufacturers will want to consider the costs of doing business with suppliers of indirect products or services. These suppliers should be selected carefully, especially if the manufacturer uses the product or services on a continuing basis. For example, suppliers who provide materials to tool and die makers are critical to the manufacture of a specific product. Poor supplier performance here can stop the manufacturing process just as quickly as being out of parts and can be very costly. Here are some suggestions to make selection easier:

- Review areas such as machine tools, maintenance and material handling, and freight expenses, and evaluate the performance of companies supplying these materials and services.
- Ask your accounting department to prepare a list of indirect expenditures. Indirect expenditures are costs that are not included in the direct labor or material cost of a product. These costs must be covered through product sales.

You will want accounting to list each supplier, the amount paid to the supplier, and the department in your company that received the goods or services. This list should be computerized for best results. Figure 8-2 is an example of an Indirect Products or Services List. You also want to sort the data into two lists that will aid you in calculating use of indirect products and services:

- The first list should be organized by departments, with subtotals. Department managers can use the data to analyze department expenditures.
- A second list should be done by supplier, with subtotals of dollars spent by your company. This will help you measure costs of indirect products or services.

Once these lists are prepared, ask the department managers who use indirect suppliers to confirm the list. They can provide information that will be important to the supplier selection process. For example, they might want to eliminate suppliers that are no longer used on a regular basis or add new suppliers that have taken their place. Their input will make the selection process meaningful and solidify their support for the program.

Sister companies should be included in your list of indirect products or services. They often play important roles in supplying indirect products or services to the manufacturing section of many companies. For example, a manufacturer might be part of a larger corporation with a transportation division that supplies a means of transporting goods for several of its manufacturing companies and also contracts for transportation of goods to other companies. The transportation division must be evaluated for performance like any other outside firm. Lack of performance excellence on its part can be disastrous to the companies using its transportation services. Documentation and evaluation of performance in these instances is critical.

Figure 8-2: Indirect Products or Services

INDIRECT PRODUCTS OR SERVICES LIST
SUPPLIER SELECTION

DATE: ________

TIME PERIOD: ________

Supplier	Dollar Amount	Product/ Services	Using Department	Manager	Comments
ABC Chemical	$ 50,000	product	production	Bob Smith	Product delivery needs improvement.
Sam's Grinding	25,534	service	production	Sam Jones	Late on deliveries.
Exact Engineers	75,325	service	Mfg. & Eng.	Amy Lee	Product quality is excellent.
Best Way Truck	125,139	service	Mtrl. Control	Jim Phillip	Deliveries are always on time. Quantities are correct.

DISTRIBUTION BY VALUE

Distribution by value, or the 80/20 approach, is also a good guide for determining which suppliers to include in the evaluation process. It is similar in concept to determining the volume of sales. This approach holds that 20 percent of the items you sell represents 80 percent of total sales dollars, or 20 percent of your suppliers represents 80 percent of your sales volume during the year. To identify the 20 percent of suppliers, list all your suppliers, their accumulated sales, and what percentage their sales are in relation to your company's total sales (similar to Figure 8-1).

- The first supplier listed should be the one with the largest dollar amount of your total sales volume.

- Continue the list in descending order so that it will end with the supplier having the least amount of the total sales.
- With the aid of your company president, determine what percent of your company's total sales you want to include in your supplier evaluation program.

The suppliers representing 80 percent of your total sales are to be included in your supplier evaluation process. This should comprise 20 percent of all your suppliers. Figure 8-3 is a graph illustrating distribution by value. In this case, 60 suppliers are 20 percent of a total of 300 suppliers and account for 83 percent of the total sales of the distributor.

Reviewing the Supplier's Length of Participation

Always review your list of selected suppliers for length of participation as well as sales volume. You might not have enough performance data available to support the evaluation of a relatively new major supplier, but its sales

Figure 8-3: Supplier Distribution by Value

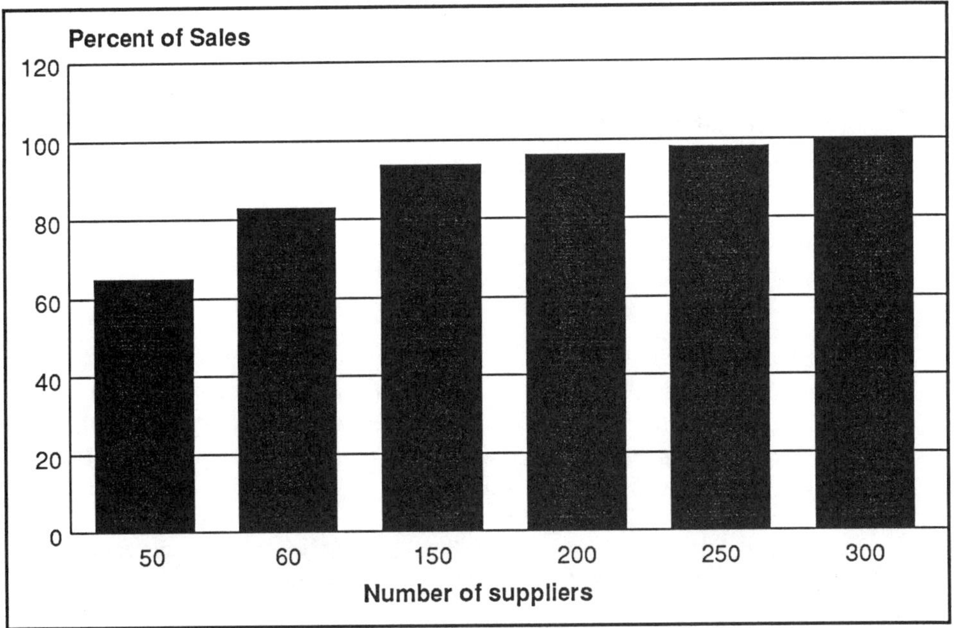

volume alone might justify inclusion. This is a decision that must be made by you and your company president.

During our pilot program, a major supplier was added in the tenth month of an evaluating year and produced sales high enough to be included in supplier evaluation. However, we had measurement of performance data for only a two-month period. There was insufficient information to grade this supplier's performance for that year. The performance data for a supplier should represent a full test of its capabilities.

NOTIFYING YOUR SUPPLIERS AND REPRESENTATIVES OF THEIR INCLUSION IN YOUR SUPPLIER EVALUATION PROGRAM

At the beginning of each year being evaluated you will want to insure that proper notification is given to the suppliers, supplier representatives, and independent sales representatives you will be evaluating. They are your partners. Therefore, you need to communicate the following information for their benefit:

- The purpose of your supplier evaluation and selection program
- Why they are being included
- Your expectations of quality suppliers
- Your expectations of quality representatives
- How grading is determined for suppliers
- How grading is determined for representatives
- When the grading process takes place
- Who does the actual grading.

Send a notification letter to each supplier representative and independent sales representative. Include an invitation to meet with the reps to explain the purpose of the program. Review each segment of the program that directly affects them and allow time for discussion at this meeting. Make sure they understand the program and your company's expectations of their performance. A sample notification letter is given in Figure 8-4. Enclose copies of your Rep Sign-in Log (Figure 4-1) and the Rep Performance Evaluation Form (Figure 4-2 or 4-3) for their information.

Figure 8-4: Notification Letter to Supplier Reps of Their Inclusion in Your Supplier Evaluation and Selection Program—Distribution or Manufacturing

Date: Jan. 5, 1993

Isaac Wilshon, Sales Representative

Pinson Iron Works

Steelville, Missouri 65585

Dear Isaac:

Our company is beginning a Supplier Evaluation and Selection Program on January 12, 1993. Each evaluation period will consist of 12 months. The program is designed to strengthen and improve our partnership relations and communications with you, your company, and our customers.

You have been chosen for participation in our program because you represent one of our major suppliers, and we want to continue striving with you, on a partnership basis, to achieve performance excellence in all areas of our businesses. As you will be personally involved in the overall grading of your supplier's performance, we would like to invite you to a meeting on Tuesday, January 12, 1993, at 6:30 P.M. We will review the Supplier Evaluation and Selection Program with you and answer any questions you might have about our expectations of supplier representative and independent sales representative performance.

A copy of a Sign-in Log is enclosed for your review. Effective beginning January12,1993, we would like you to begin using the log to sign in when you visit our sales locations. This is our way of monitoring the number and quality of your visits.

Also enclosed is a copy of our Performance Evaluation Form. This is an annual report that our branch managers will be required to fill out and send to our Purchasing Coordinator, Brittany Lynn. It will be used to monitor issues important to performance excellence. If you have any questions about our program that you would like to discuss with me, please feel free to call me at 1-800/766-7777. I am looking forward to meeting with you.

Best regards,

THE VERY BEST DISTRIBUTORS

Catherine Hollingsworth

President

cc: Henry Pinson, Sales Representative
Pleasant A. Lane, Purchasing Manager

Enclosures (2)

CHAPTER 9

SELECTING MEMBERS OF THE EVALUATION TEAM

The success of your supplier performance evaluation depends upon the competence and credibility of the evaluating team you choose. You and your suppliers need assurance that grading is done by qualified, highly knowledgeable people who are capable of presenting documented information on supplier performance. Their firsthand knowledge of supplier products and performance together with the analysis of the data compiled over the year will provide the credibility needed for acceptance by participating suppliers. Your team members anchor your program.

There are six factors to consider when selecting an evaluation team:

1. Department representation. Your evaluation team members will represent management, purchasing, materials control, accounting, sales and marketing, manufacturing, engineering, receiving, warehousing, and distribution. These key areas in your company are directly affected by supplier performance.
2. Evaluation team size. Depending on the number of suppliers to be graded, the evaluation process can be lengthy. You must keep the number of people on your evaluation team at a minimum to facilitate the discussions. Your evaluation team should consist of an odd number of members to insure that majority decisions can always be made.
3. Ethics. Take precautions to prevent undue influence from suppliers and their representatives. Use a yearly rotation process when choosing your team members.
4. Team responsibilities and duties. Evaluating team members represent management in their assigned areas of responsibility. They will provide

documented data and maintain consistent standards of measurement for each supplier being graded.

5. Availability of consultants. When your evaluation team wants additional information in specific areas vital to a supplier's overall performance grade, you have the option of asking department managers to participate in the grading process on a consulting basis only.
6. Support from upper management. Support from upper management insures that top priority and assistance is given to you and your team members throughout your company.

OBTAINING DEPARTMENT REPRESENTATION

Supplier performance affects every department in your company, including upper management. Your evaluation team members will become representatives for each of these areas:

Management representation. Management representation is part of the evaluation team's job. Your company's overall objectives of sales, customer service, profits, and return on investment must be represented during the grading process. One of the main objectives of your evaluation program is to be constructive and helpful to your suppliers. You are building a bridge to better communication with them. The evaluation decisions made and the manner in which information is distributed to your suppliers will reflect the integrity of your entire company.

Purchasing. Purchasing has a vested interest in the improvement of supplier performance. This department is charged with obtaining the best material at the lowest price and insuring the availability of product when it is needed. It has the responsibility of selecting quality suppliers, and improving supplier relationships.

Materials control. Materials control handles the physical receipt, movement, storage, and distribution of supplier products. Improvement in areas such as packaging, product identification, warehousing, storage, product availability, and lead-time predictability have great potential to reduce your company's material control costs. Therefore, it is essential for this group to have input to and representation in supplier evaluation.

Accounting. Accounting can measure the effects of improved supplier performance by measuring dollars of savings. It accounts for pricing variations, long-term discounts given by suppliers, inventory discrepancies, and problems in accounts payable and accounts receivable.

Sales and marketing. Input and representation by this group are needed for sound supplier/distributor/end-user relationships. Quality products and the customer's perception of product value are monitored in these departments. Improvements in supplier sales aids, such as advertising, promotions, product training, and information, are important for these departments in relating product awareness to the end user.

Receiving. Information about suppliers' shipping processes are important to the evaluation process. The manager of this area has information about transportation, receiving quantities, condition of material, and the availability of paperwork for the evaluation team.

Warehousing and distribution. This group has information on product packaging and labeling, palletizing and shrink-wrap, storage information, and product durability that will be used in evaluation.

Manufacturers will need representation through two additional departments.

Manufacturing/quality control. Input from these areas is necessary to manufacturers that want to monitor issues such as product quality, product availability, product training, and supplier representation. Manufacturing and quality control are affected by all these issues on a daily basis. Therefore, they are aware of problems that can be caused by fluctuating supplier lead times, poor product quality, and the lack of product training for the work force. Manufacturing and quality control are also able to monitor the amount and quality of help supplier representatives give in providing proper product information and support in the resolution of supplier quality problems.

Engineering. It is important for the manufacturer's engineering department to monitor the quality and amount of technical assistance received from supplier reps. It is imperative for supplier reps to be able to give assistance and make suggestions regarding product design changes, product manufacturing flow, and new products and to make technical product drawings available to engineering.

DETERMINING THE SIZE OF YOUR EVALUATION TEAM

You and your team members will be required to set aside your normal workday procedures and give all your time and attention to the evaluation and grading process. Therefore, you want the entire process to be completed as quickly and efficiently as possible.

There are two factors that will help you determine the size of your evaluation team:

1. The length of time it will take to complete the evaluation and grading process for all your suppliers.
2. The ability of your evaluation team members to make majority decisions on each criterion being graded and on any major issues being presented for discussion.

During the original pilot program, an evaluation team of five team members became the standard. A team of this size is capable of evaluating the performance of 30 to 40 suppliers in one day. Therefore, if you are planning to evaluate the performance of 80 to 100 suppliers you will need to allow approximately three days for your team to complete the evaluation process.

Keep in mind that a team of five can make quick, factual decisions when dealing with controversial matters and help keep your grading sessions to a reasonable length of time. If you increase the size of your evaluation team, your evaluation process will slow down as discussions become more lengthy. Each team member has a voice in the grading and evaluation process and will vote on every criterion and major issue being presented for each supplier.

Another important factor is the ability to make majority decisions. A team consisting of an odd number of members will ensure that majority decisions can always be made.

ENSURING ETHICAL EVALUATIONS BY TEAM MEMBERS

Precautionary measures are necessary when you choose evaluation team members to avoid the possibility of special treatment or catering from suppliers and their representatives. Two effective safeguards are the timing of the team selection and using a yearly rotation basis.

Timing of team selection. The timing of your team selection is very important. Individual team members need enough time before the actual grading session to gather the data and documentation they will use during the performance grading process. However, the data-gathering period must also be short enough so that supplier representatives do not have an opportunity to attempt to influence team members. A rule of thumb is to notify each evaluation team member of his or her inclusion in the program six weeks before the evaluation process.

Rotating team members. The rotation of four team members in a five-member team every year eliminates the possibility of suppliers giving special treatment to evaluation team members.

Figure 9-1 is a chart showing the evaluation team makeup for a distributor and a manufacturer. It shows team make-up from different departments and which members rotate from year to year.

DETERMINING QUALIFICATIONS FOR TEAM LEADERSHIP

As purchasing is responsible for coordinating evaluation activities and maintaining all the information pertaining to the evaluation, it is natural for you, the purchasing manager, to be the evaluation team leader. You are the management representative for your company and the only permanent or constant member of the evaluation team. You provide consistency of purpose from evaluation to evaluation. You may also represent material control, if that function is under your direction. You have more direct contact with suppliers, their representatives, and the manufacturing facilities they represent—qualities necessary for an evaluation team leader. Your major functions include:

- Choosing evaluation team members
- Delegating responsibilities to your team members
- Supervising grading sessions
- Monitoring all data used in the grading process
- Calling in consultants to clarify issues pertaining to a supplier's grade
- Preparing and delivering the team's final report to your company's president
- Dealing with the suppliers evaluated and their representatives.

Figure 9-2 is a sample form that describes the responsibilities of the evaluation team leader for distribution and manufacturing.

Figure 9-1: Evaluation Team Makeup—Distribution and Manufacturing

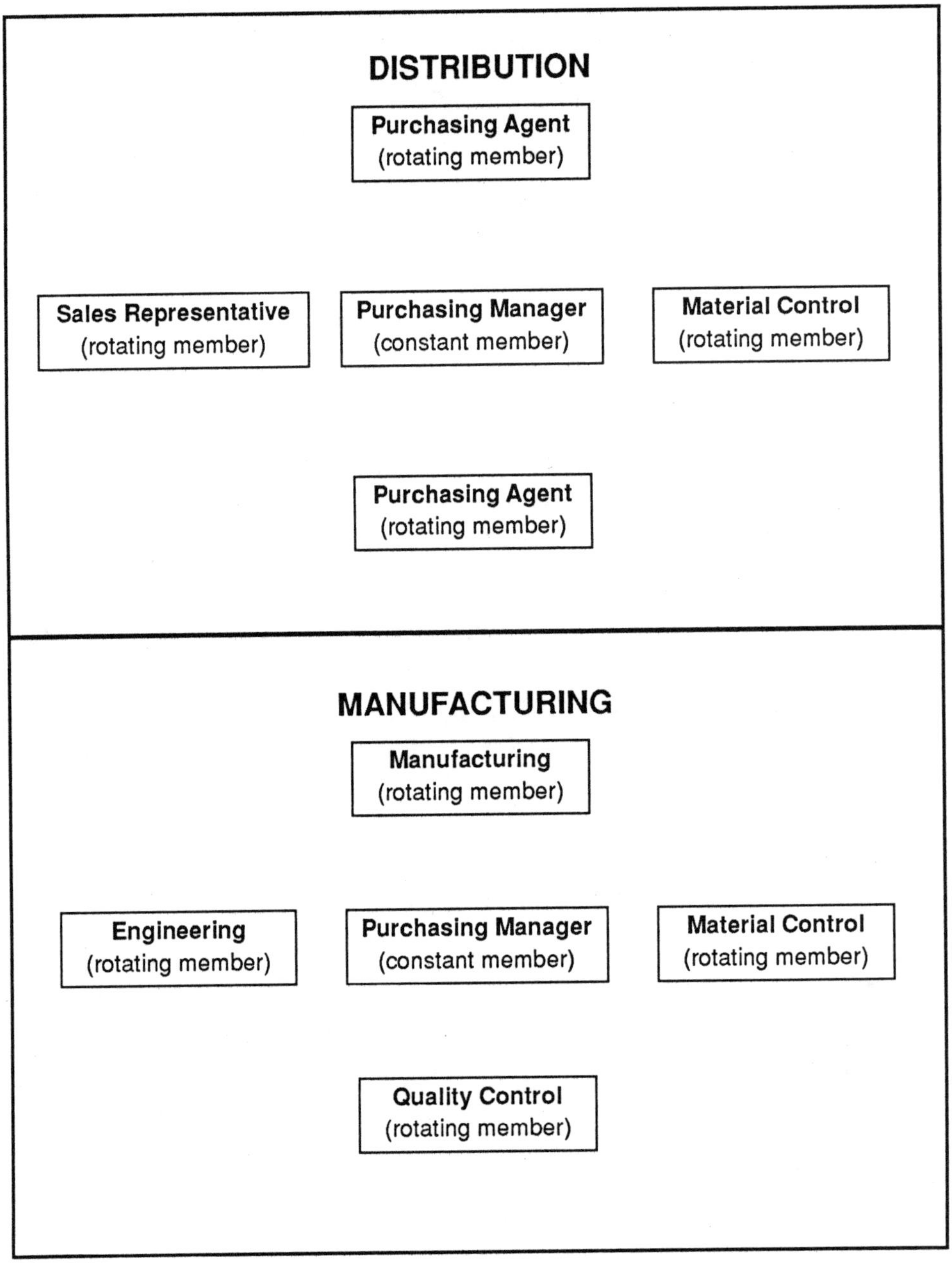

Figure 9-2: Responsibilities for an Evaluation Team Leader—Distribution or Manufacturing

NAME OF EMPLOYEE: ______________________________

DEPARTMENT: ______________________________

SUPERVISOR: ______________________________

JOB TITLE: Evaluation Team Leader

This team member is the selected constant team member. Possible candidates for this position are:

- Purchasing manager
- Owner or president of your company
- Materials control manager.

POSITION QUALIFICATIONS:

- Five years' experience in a manufacturing/distribution/purchasing management environment is the minimal requirement.
- A college degree is preferred.
- Direct contact with suppliers, their representatives, the manufacturing facilities they represent, and familiarity with all supplier products is vital to this position.

ESSENTIAL CHARACTERISTICS:

- Decision-making abilities
- An even temperament
- The ability to work with people with varying backgrounds and educations
- Creativity
- Open-mindedness.

POSITION FUNCTIONS AND RESPONSIBILITIES:

This position's primary functions include:

- The development and implementation of a supplier evaluation and selection program
- Selecting criteria to be monitored
- Setting grading standards for each criterion
- Selecting suppliers to be included in the evaluation process.

Additional functions are:

- Selecting evaluation team members
- Delegating individual duties to team members
- Supervising supplier grading sessions
- Monitoring data used in the evaluation process insuring consistent and accurate documentation of all suppliers' performance
- Presenting final evaluation grades to the company president for review
- Answering questions pertaining to supplier performance grades
- Organizing a yearly program for supplier and supplier representative recognition.

Choosing Evaluation Team Members

The selection of evaluation team members is an area where you will want to enlist the assistance of your company president. By doing so, you add to the credibility you need for your selection process and assure the cooperation of the entire company in the evaluation process. Other benefits are:

- You both have the opportunity to solidify the team mix.
- A review of the overall objectives for the evaluation process can be made.
- Special emphasis on the evaluation and grading process can be added to overall long-term company objectives.

Team members will be chosen from your company's department managers, senior purchasing agents, regional sales managers, sales personnel and/or production control, manufacturing and engineering managers. The Evaluation Team Selection Chart in Figure 9-3 lists team members, the areas of your company they will represent, their duties, length of service, and possible candidates (job titles) for each position. These people have a working knowledge of your suppliers and their representatives. For example, they are familiar with:

- Supplier sales representatives
- Supplier product offerings
- Supplier product quality
- Supplier promotion and training activities

Figure 9-3: Evaluation Team Selection Chart

Evaluation Team Selection Chart				
Position	**Department Representation**	**Responsibilities**	**Length of Service**	**Possible Candidates in Order of Preference**
Team Leader	• Management • Purchasing • Materials control • Accounting	• Supervisor • Team selection • Maintain consistency of evaluation process • Present information to team members • Evaluate suppliers	permanent	• Purchasing manager • Owner/president • Materials control manager
Team Member 1	• Purchasing • Accounts payable • Receiving	• Gather supplier information relating to product availability, payment terms, inventory rebalancing, lead-time predictablity and warranty statements • Present information to team members • Evaluate suppliers	1 session	• Purchasing agent • Materials coordinator
Distribution's Team Member 2	• Marketing • Sales • Customer service	• Gather product information on retailing to customer preference, and supplier Sales assistance • Present information to team members • Evaluate suppliers	1 session	• Regional sales manager • Outside sales person • Counter sales person • Sales analyst
Manufacturing's Team Member 2	• Manufacturing • Quality control • Engineering	• Gather information relating to quality control, availability of product-training and technical information • Present information to team members • Evaluate suppliers	1 session	• Quality control manager • Manufacturing superintendent • Engineering manager
Distribution's Team Member 3	• Marketing • Sales • Customer service	• Gather information relating to price analysis, and supplier performance in Emergency situations • Present information to team members • Evaluate suppliers	1 session	• Regional sales manager • Outside sales person • Counter sales person • Sales analyst
Manufacturing's Team Member 3	• Manufacturing • Quality control • Engineering	• same as above	1 session	• Quality control manager • Manufacturing • Superintendent • Engineering manager
Team Member 4	• Materials control • Shipping • Warehouse • Distribution	• Gather product information relating to packaging and labeling, material handling and storage, and back orders/overshipments • Present information to team members • Evaluate suppliers	1 session	• Materials manager • Warehouse manager • Distribution manager

- Supplier technical production activities
- Supplier advertising policies.

They also are familiar with your company policies as they relate to the following criteria:

- Payment terms
- Product availability (lead-time predictability)
- Warranties
- Back orders
- Special shipments
- The manufacturing process.

In short, these people are familiar with all the issues that are addressed in supplier evaluation and have special knowledge about their specific areas of responsibility.

Remember, team members are chosen on a rotating basis. For example, your marketing department might consist of four marketing managers. Therefore, you have four potential team members in this area.

When your selection of team members is complete, you will want to send them letters of notification about their roles in the evaluation process. A sample notification letter is provided in Figure 9-4. Be sure to enclose the following information for their review:

- A list of responsibilities
- A list of the suppliers chosen for participation in your performance evaluation process
- A copy of the Supplier Performance Measurement Standards (Figure 7-9)
- A copy of the Data Flow Chart (Figure 10-2).

Delegating Team Responsibilities and Duties

Your team members have specific team assignments. While assignments are basically the same for each team member, the information they are dealing with covers many different areas of your company. These responsibilities can be divided into two parts—pre-meeting activities and activities pertaining to the actual evaluation of suppliers.

Figure 9-4: Notification Letter to Selected Evaluation Team Members—Distribution or Manufacturing

January 25, 1993

Dustin Schmitt
Director of Sales—Region 5
Successful Inc.
777 Money Street
Atlanta, Georgia 30542

Dear Dustin:

You have been selected to assist in supplier performance evaluation for 1992. This is a very important activity to our company and to our suppliers, and your full cooperation is appreciated.

Please make plans to be in Houston on Monday afternoon, March 8. Evaluation will begin at 8:00 A.M. on March 9, in the East Conference Room, and will continue until all suppliers have been evaluated. We anticipate completion of this activity by Thursday afternoon, March 11. My secretary, Amy Lee, will be happy to assist you in making travel arrangements and hotel accommodations.

Attached is a list of the suppliers you will be evaluating and a job description outlining your responsibilities before and during the evaluation process. If you have any questions, contact Brandon Stepp, Manager of Purchasing.

You are invited to have dinner with me and the other members of the evaluation team on Monday evening, March 8 at 7:30 P.M. at the Stables Steak House. I am looking forward to seeing you there.

Yours truly,

Joshua Miller

President, Successful Inc.

jlf/JM
Enclosures:

- A list of responsibilities
- A list of the suppliers participating in the performance evaluation process
- Supplier Performance Measurement Standards
- Evaluation Data Flow Process Chart

Premeeting Activities

Before the evaluation process can begin, your team members are responsible for gathering documented data for each supplier being evaluated pertaining to the specific departments they represent. For example, Team Member 1 represents management in the following departments:

- Purchasing
- Accounts payable
- Receiving.

Therefore, this team member must have the ability to evaluate payment terms as they relate to your company and understand the importance of inventory rebalancing and how it affects your inventory levels. Possible candidates for this are senior purchasing agents or the materials coordinator.

Before the actual grading process can begin, this team member will have to gather data to present during the grading sessions. For example, Team Member 1 is responsible for information on the following subjects:

- The supplier's own written policy statements
- The lead-time predictability report
- Reports on back orders and overshipments.

Figure 9-5 is a sample list of responsibilities for Team Member 1.

Team Member 2 and Team Member 3 represent distribution's management in marketing, sales, and customer service. They represent manufacturing's management in production control, manufacturing, and engineering. Possible candidates for distribution can be chosen from regional sales managers, outside salespersons, counter salespersons, or sales analysts. They must be able to understand competitive issues such as pricing, customer preferences, advertising, etc., and convey this information to other team members during the supplier grading process.

Team members for manufacturing must understand the design and function of their products and understand the complete manufacturing process, including material flow and machining and assembly operations. Manufacturing can choose candidates from the production control manager, manufacturing superintendent, quality control manager, or engineering manager. Although both of these team members represent management in the same departments, they each will be gathering data for different parameters.

Figure 9-5: Responsibilities for Evaluation Team Member 1—Distribution or Manufacturing

NAME OF EMPLOYEE: ______________________________

DEPARTMENT: ______________________________

SUPERVISOR: ______________________________

JOB TITLE: Evaluation Team Member 1

This is a rotating position. The team member will be required to serve on the evaluation team for approximately ten days in any given evaluation year. This includes pre-meeting activities as well as actual supplier evaluation grading meetings. Possible candidates for this position are:

- Senior purchasing agents
- Material coordinator

POSITION QUALIFICATIONS:

- Five years' experience in a manufacturing/distribution environment is the minimal requirement.
- A college degree is preferred.
- This person must have direct contact with suppliers and their representatives.
- Knowledge of supplier manufacturing facilities and procedures is helpful.
- Familiarity with all supplier products used by our company is vital to this position.
- A good understanding of the grading process and the supplier evaluation and selection program is important.
- It is essential for this person to have the ability to make unbiased decisions based on facts.

OTHER CHARACTERISTICS:

- An even temperament
- The ability to work with people with varying backgrounds and educations
- Creativity
- Open-mindedness

POSITION FUNCTIONS AND RESPONSIBILITIES:
This position's primary functions include:

- Representing management for the following departments during the evaluation process:

- Purchasing
- Accounts receivable
- Accounts payable.

Pre-meeting activities are:

- The gathering of documentation relating to supplier performance in the following areas:
- Supplier's written policies
  - Payment terms
  - Warranty issues
  - Inventory rebalancing
  - Lead-time predictability
  - Back orders and overshipments.

Evaluation activities are to:

- Present data for each supplier during the evaluation process
- Grade each criterion for each supplier
- Record supplier grades.

Team Member 2 is responsible for information about supplier and independent sales representative performance, customer's perception of supplier product quality, and the effectiveness of supplier sales aids for distribution. Responsibilities for manufacturing include supplier and independent sales representative performance, quality control reports, product training from suppliers, availability of technical information, product quality, and supplier performance. Figures 9-6 and 9-7 are sample lists of responsibilities for Team Member 2.

Team Member 3 is responsible for information on pricing and the supplier's performance in emergency situations for distribution or manufacturing. Figures 9-8 and 9-9 are sample lists of responsibilities for Team Member 3.

Team Member 4 represents management of distribution or manufacturing in material control, shipping, warehousing, and distribution. This person should be familiar with supplier products, product reliability, and durability with regard to handling and storage issues. This team member is also responsible for gathering and presenting data for distribution or manufacturing in packaging and labeling and material handling. Possible candidates for this position are the material manager, distribution manager, or the warehouse manager. Figure 9-10 is a sample list of responsibilities for Team Member 4.

Figure 9-6: Responsibilities for Evaluation Team Member 2—Distribution

NAME OF EMPLOYEE: ________________________________

DEPARTMENT: ________________________________

SUPERVISOR: ________________________________

JOB TITLE: Team Member 2

This is a rotating position. The team member will be required to serve on the evaluation team for approximately ten days in any given evaluation year. Possible candidates for this position are:

- Regional sales managers
- Outside salespersons
- Counter salespersons
- Sales analysts.

POSITION QUALIFICATIONS:

- Five years' experience in marketing, sales, or customer service is the minimal requirement.
- A college degree is preferred.
- This person must be well grounded in customer relations and know and service customers in our specific market area.
- Direct contact with suppliers and their representatives is required.
- Knowledge of supplier manufacturing facilities is helpful.
- Familiarity with all supplier products and supplier product promotions is vital to this position.
- A good understanding of the grading process and the supplier evaluation and selection program is important.
- It is essential for this person to have the ability to make unbiased decisions based on facts.

OTHER CHARACTERISTICS:

- Decision-making abilities
- An even temperament
- The ability to work with people with varying backgrounds and educations
- Creativity
- Open-mindedness

POSITION FUNCTIONS AND RESPONSIBILITIES:

This position's specific functions include:

- Representing management for the following departments during the evaluation process:
- Marketing
- Sales
- Customer service.

Pre-meeting activities are:

- The gathering of documentation relating to supplier performance in the following areas:
- Supplier representative and independent sales representative performance
- Customer's perception of supplier products
- Supplier sales aids.

Evaluation activities are to:

- Present data for each supplier during the evaluation process
- Grade each criterion for each supplier
- Record supplier grades.

Figure 9-7: Responsibilities for Evaluation Team Member 2—Manufacturing

NAME OF EMPLOYEE: ____________________

DEPARTMENT: ____________________

SUPERVISOR: ____________________

JOB TITLE: Team Member 2

This is a rotating position. The team member will be required to serve on the evaluation team for approximately ten days in any given evaluation year. Possible candidates for this position are:

- Production manager
- Manufacturing superintendent
- Quality control manager
- Engineering manager.

POSITION QUALIFICATIONS:

- Five years' management-level experience in production operations, quality control or engineering is the minimal requirement.
- A college degree is preferred.
- This person must be knowledgeable about company products, the manufacturing process, and the relationship outside suppliers have with company products and processes.
- Direct contact with suppliers and their representatives is required.
- Knowledge of supplier manufacturing facilities and its procedures is a must.
- Familiarity with all supplier products and supplier product promotions is vital to this position.
- A good understanding of the grading process and the supplier evaluation and selection program is important.
- It is essential for this person to have the ability to make unbiased decisions based on facts.

OTHER CHARACTERISTICS:

- Decision-making abilities
- An even temperament
- The ability to work with people with varying backgrounds and educations

- Creativity
- Open-mindedness

POSITION FUNCTIONS AND RESPONSIBILITIES:

This position's specific functions include:

- Representing management for the following departments during the evaluation process:
- Manufacturing
- Quality control
- Engineering

Pre-meeting activities are:

- The gathering of documentation relating to supplier performance in the following areas:
  - Supplier representative and independent sales representative performance
  - The compliance of supplier products to quality standards
  - The ability and willingness of the supplier to provide production aids to manufacturing and engineering.

Evaluation activities are to:

- Present data for each supplier during the evaluation process
- Grade each criterion for each supplier
- Record supplier grades.

Figure 9-8: Responsibilities for Evaluation Team Member 3—Distribution

NAME OF EMPLOYEE: ______________________________

DEPARTMENT: ______________________________

SUPERVISOR: ______________________________

JOB TITLE: Team Member 3

This is a rotating position. The team member will be required to serve on the evaluation team for approximately ten days in any given evaluation year. Possible candidates for this position are:

- Regional sales manager
- Outside salespersons
- Counter salespersons
- Sales analysts.

POSITION QUALIFICATIONS:

- Five years' management-level experience in marketing, sales, or customer service is the minimal requirement.
- A college degree is preferred.
- This person must be well established in customer relations and know and service customers in our specific market area.
- Direct contact with suppliers and their representatives is required.
- Familiarity with all supplier products and supplier product promotions is vital to this position.
- A good understanding of the grading process and the supplier evaluation and selection program is important.
- It is essential for this person to have the ability to make unbiased decisions based on facts.

OTHER CHARACTERISTICS:

- Decision-making abilities
- An even temperament
- The ability to work with people with varying backgrounds and educations
- Creativity
- Open-mindedness

POSITION FUNCTIONS AND RESPONSIBILITIES:

This position's specific functions include:

- Representing management for the following departments during the evaluation process:
  - Manufacturing
  - Quality control
  - Engineering.

Pre-meeting activities are:

- The gathering of documentation relating to supplier performance in the following areas:
  - Pricing analysis
  - The supplier's performance in emergency situations.

Evaluation activities are to:

- Present data for each supplier during the evaluation grading process
- Grade each criterion for each supplier
- Record supplier grades.

Figure 9-9: Responsibilities for Evaluation Team Member 3—Manufacturing

NAME OF EMPLOYEE: ______________________

DEPARTMENT: ______________________

SUPERVISOR: ______________________

JOB TITLE: Team Member 3

This is a rotating position. The team member will be required to serve on the evaluation team for approximately ten days in any given evaluation year. Possible candidates for this position are:

- Production manager
- Manufacturing superintendent
- Quality control
- Engineering

POSITION QUALIFICATIONS:

- Five years' experience of management-level experience in production operations, quality control, or engineering is the minimal requirement.
- A college degree is preferred.
- This person must be knowledgeable about company products, the manufacturing process, and the relationship outside suppliers have with company products and processes.
- Direct contact with suppliers and their representatives is required.
- Knowledge of supplier manufacturing facilities and procedures is helpful.
- Familiarity with all supplier products and supplier product promotions is vital to this position.
- A good understanding of the grading process and the supplier evaluation and selection program is important.
- It is essential for this person to have the ability to make unbiased decisions based on facts.

OTHER CHARACTERISTICS:

- Decision-making abilities
- An even temperament
- The ability to work with people with varying backgrounds and educations
- Creativity
- Open-mindedness.

POSITION FUNCTIONS AND RESPONSIBILITIES:

This position's specific functions include:

- Representing management for the following departments during the evaluation process:
  - Manufacturing
  - Quality control
  - Engineering

Pre-meeting activities are:

- The gathering of documentation relating to supplier performance in the following areas:
  - Supplier product pricing analysis
  - The supplier's performance in emergency situations.

Evaluation activities are to:

- Present data for each supplier during the evaluation process
- Grade each criterion for each supplier
- Record supplier grades.

Figure 9-10: Responsibilities for Evaluation Team Member 4—Distribution or Manufacturing

NAME OF EMPLOYEE: ______________________________

DEPARTMENT: ______________________________

SUPERVISOR: ______________________________

JOB TITLE: Team Member 4

This is a rotating position. The team member will be required to serve on the evaluation team for approximately ten days in any given evaluation year. Possible candidates for this position are:

- Materials manager
- Distribution manager
- Warehouse manager.

POSITION QUALIFICATIONS:

- Five years' experience in material control, warehousing, or distribution management is the minimal requirement.
- A college degree is preferred.
- This person must have direct contact with suppliers and their representatives.
- Knowledge of supplier manufacturing facilities and procedures is helpful.
- Familiarity with all supplier products is vital to this position.
- A good understanding of the grading process and the Supplier Evaluation and Selection Program is important.
- It is essential for this person to have the ability to make unbiased decisions based on facts.

OTHER CHARACTERISTICS:

- Decision-making abilities
- An even temperament
- The ability to work with people with varying backgrounds and educations is a must
- Creativity
- Open-mindedness.

POSITION FUNCTIONS AND RESPONSIBILITIES:

This position's specific functions include:

- Representing management for the following departments during the evaluation process:
  - Material control
  - Shipping
  - Warehousing
  - Distribution

Pre-meeting activities are:

- The gathering of documentation relating to supplier performance in the following areas:
  - Packaging and labeling
  - Materials handling
  - Back orders/overshipments.

Evaluation activities are to:

- Present data for each supplier during the evaluation process
- Grade each criterion for each supplier
- Record supplier grades.

All these team member functions and the reports by which information is gathered are vital to the success of the overall supplier evaluation process. These reports are explained in detail in Chapter 10.

Evaluation Activities

During the actual grading process, each team member is responsible for grading every supplier in the evaluation program on all of the issues presented in Figure 7-9, the Supplier Performance Measurement Standards. Other responsibilities and duties are to:

- Present his or her specific collection of data on each supplier to the entire evaluation team
- Point out major issues that need to be resolved on supplier performances
- Vote on supplier grades in each parameter presented
- Record supplier grades.

The grading process of an actual supplier is detailed in Chapter 11.

Supervising Grading Sessions and Monitoring Data

As the team leader, it is your responsibility to make sure meeting facilities are adequate and appropriate equipment is provided for visual grading. For example, you can do visual grading by using a chalk board, flip chart, or marker board. By using this method you accomplish two purposes:

1. You can monitor all the data provided for each supplier during the evaluation process.
2. You can highlight any significant changes in a supplier's performance from year to year, making sure causes are properly documented.

This method will be used in Chapter 11 to grade supplier performance.

Using Consultants to Provide Additional Information

There will be occasions during the evaluation meeting when you feel that a supplier cannot be properly evaluated without additional input from specific areas in your company, such as accounting, warehousing, etc. When this happens, you can ask various department and/or product managers to participate in your grading session on a consulting basis only. For example, it is always a good idea to ask the product manager of a specialized product group to assist in the evaluation of the supplier of its product. Product managers will have additional information concerning supplier promotions, incentives, training, advertising, and supplier representation pertaining to their product that is not readily available to you. The product manager's specialized information is important to the overall evaluation of the suppliers. He or she might be a specialist handling a few detailed products or a specialist handling many product lines. They should be called upon as consultants when information is needed on their product lines.

Always be specific about what information you want when you ask someone to participate on a consulting basis. It is important for consultants to understand that you and your fellow team members want factual and documented information.

Consultants participate only when additional information is needed for a particular supplier. After they have provided the information needed, they are excused from the meeting. They are never allowed to vote on any issue during the grading process.

It is your job to make sure the consultant's name and the information presented to the evaluation team are included on the Supplier's Grading Report. In Chapter 11 the use of consultants is highlighted in the actual grading process.

CHAPTER 10

DOCUMENTING AND COLLECTING DATA ON SUPPLIERS

Information for your supplier evaluation and selection process must be factual, documented, and consistent in content. Suppliers will not change based on the way you and your evaluation team members *feel,* but they will implement change when you support your findings with data.

The reputation of your company is at stake, and the credibility of the evaluation process will be challenged by suppliers and representatives who do not understand or question the results of their evaluations. They will ask for meetings with your company president to discuss evaluation results and will want to know what data were collected and how the data were used in the evaluation process. Therefore, it is imperative that you have data with backup to support your performance evaluation process.

Consistency and accuracy begin at the data collection points that are established in all areas of your company affected by supplier performance. All of the information gathered in each department and sales location is measured against the same performance standards for each criterion for every supplier being evaluated.

MAINTAINING SUPPLIER PERFORMANCE MEASUREMENT FILES

Maintaining permanent data files is one of the most important activities in the entire evaluation process. You will want to delegate this responsibility to a person who is familiar with purchasing and has administrative abilities. The natural choice would be a purchasing coordinator. A list of requirements for this person is given in Figure 10-1.

Figure 10-1: Responsibilities for a Purchasing Coordinator—Distribution or Manufacturing

NAME OF EMPLOYEE: ______________________________

DEPARTMENT: ______________________________

SUPERVISOR: ______________________________

JOB TITLE: Purchasing Coordinator

The purchasing coordinator is responsible for helping the purchasing manager establish and maintain computerized and manual backup supplier performance measurement files. Possible candidates are:

- Purchasing coordinator
- Administrative assistant to purchasing
- Executive secretary.

POSITION QUALIFICATIONS:

- One year of experience in purchasing is the minimal requirement.
- One year of experience as a purchasing coordinator, administrative assistant, or executive secretary is the minimal requirement.
- Two years of college are preferred.
- This person must have at least one year of computer experience.
- Familiarity with all supplier products is helpful.
- A good understanding of the grading process and the Supplier Evaluation and Selection Program is preferred.

OTHER CHARACTERISTICS:

- Decision-making abilities
- An even temperament
- The ability to work with people with varying backgrounds and educations.

POSITION FUNCTIONS AND RESPONSIBILITIES:

This position's primary functions include:

- Helping the purchasing manager establish a filing system for data storage
- Establishing computer consolidation reports of data information

- Making sure all data relating to supplier performance are sent in from all data collection points in ample time for consolidation for grading sessions
- Data entry of documentation records
- Maintaining computer files
- Maintaining backup files of original documentation (computer reports, manual reports, etc.)
- Filing backup data in proper supplier folders
- Notifying all evaluation team members of the availability of evaluation data.

Additional functions are:

- Assisting evaluation team members by summarizing information for supplier evaluation
- Assisting the evaluation team leader and team members during the evaluation grading sessions
- Preparing performance letters and sending them to suppliers
- Helping the purchasing manager plan and implement supplier and representative performance awards.

The purchasing coordinator should make and maintain supplier performance measurement files for each supplier to be included in the performance grading session. These files have three purposes:

1. They become the central storage place for all supplier information to be used during the evaluation process.
2. They are used by evaluation team members when they begin to collect data and documentation for the grading process.
3. Completed supplier evaluations, including grades and documentation, are stored in these files for easy access from year to year.

These files contain four types of information:

- Consolidated computer information
- Original data documentation sheets
- Supplier policy statements
- Supplier evaluations, information, and documentation from previous years.

Maintaining Computerized Files

When data are sent to purchasing on a continuing basis, you will want the data consolidated after arrival. The purchasing coordinator can enter the data into a personal computer (PC) using a spreadsheet program or data base program with sorting capabilities. This can be done quickly and gives evaluation team members a lot of flexibility in presenting data for evaluation purposes. For example, all your sales locations will be sending monthly reports on rep calls. Companies with multiple locations will have a monthly rep call report from each location. During the pilot program, reports from 50 locations were maintained easily on a PC. The information from each report was sorted by supplier, by representative, by location, and so on. Every rep's calls could be easily recorded and monitored for all locations.

Using Backup Files

The data and documentation you use during the supplier evaluation process need a permanent storage site. It is vital that you have the actual data (reports, etc.) and documentation (copies of material handling cards, etc.) readily available at evaluation time. You and your evaluation team members will use this information for three purposes:

1. The information will be used during the actual evaluation process for grading supplier performances.
2. Actual data will be required if and when suppliers or their representatives challenge your grading procedures and want additional information about their individual grades.
3. Previous evaluations will be used as benchmarks for future evaluations of suppliers.

You want to be able to back up what you say. Therefore, a permanent, central storage location for all data and documentation is essential.

Using Objective and Subjective Data for Documentation

Objective data. The objective information you use begins with the standards your suppliers have set for themselves in these areas: warranty statements, payment terms, inventory rebalancing, and emergency shipments. Therefore, the purchasing coordinator should include copies of your suppliers' written policy statements in the evaluation files for easy access by Team Member 1.

This information can also be entered and stored in a PC. However, this can be a lengthy job, depending on the number of suppliers you evaluate.

The information will, for the most part, remain the same from year to year. After the first year of the evaluation program, the purchasing coordinator's job will be to update the information on a yearly basis.

Subjective data. The supplier files will contain subjective information and documentation pertaining to supplier performance reports that are gathered from the departments in your company directly affected by supplier performance:

- Purchasing
- Quality control
- Inventory control
- Manufacturing
- Accounting
- Marketing
- Sales
- Warranty (customer service)
- Shipping
- Receiving.

These reports come in two forms: continuous reports that are generated on an ongoing basis and periodic reports that are generated semiannually or yearly. These reports are to be routed to your purchasing department on a regular basis.

Your purchasing coordinator will consolidate the information, then file and store the backup for each report in your supplier performance files until evaluation time. This helps the evaluation team members gather the data and documentation they need for their grading reports. The Evaluation Data Flow Process Chart illustrated in Figure 10-2 illustrates each department affected by data collection, the reports they will be responsible for maintaining, and where each report goes.

Figure 10-2: Data Flow Process Chart

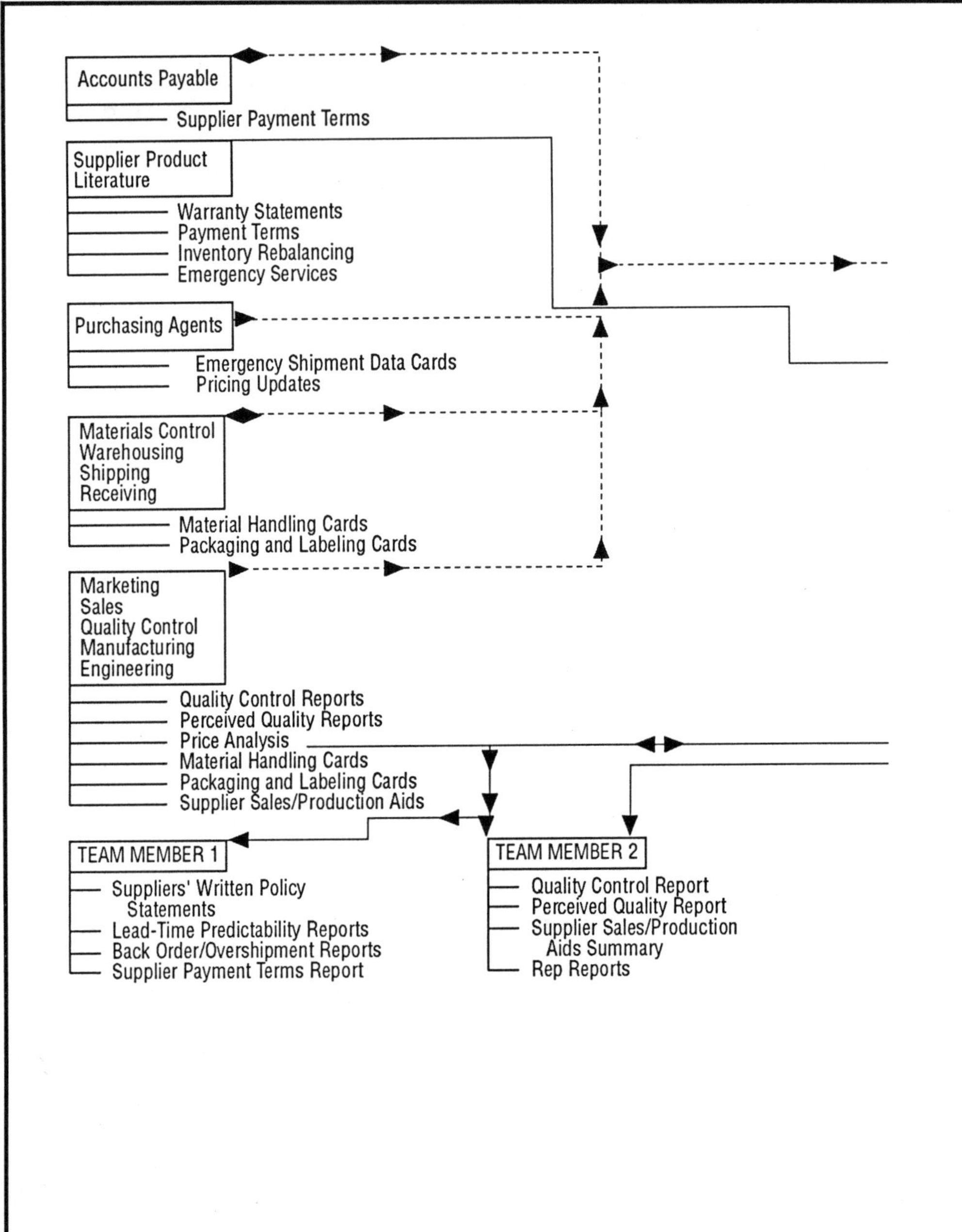

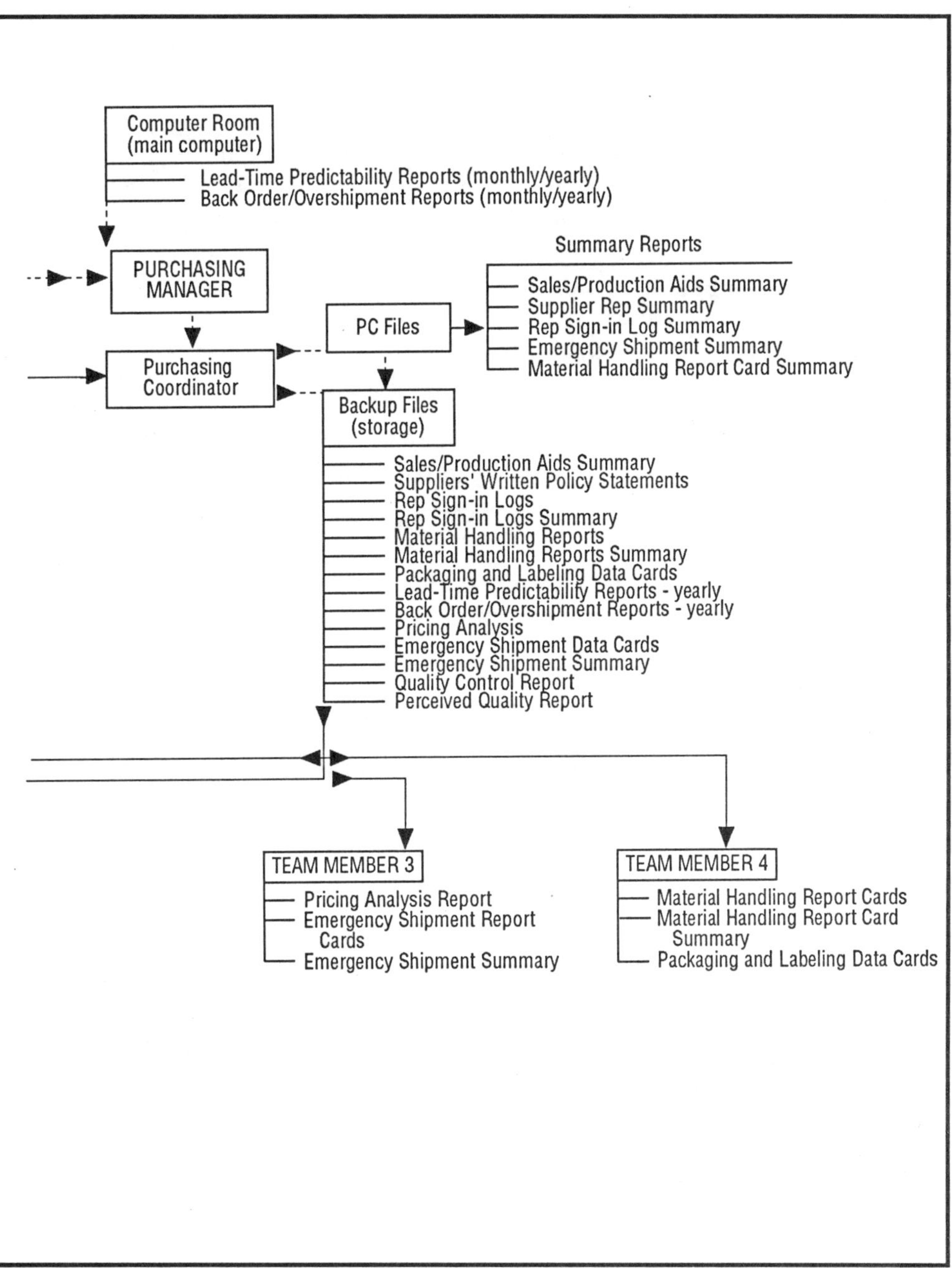
Computer Room
(main computer)
Lead-Time Predictability Reports (monthly/yearly)
Back Order/Overshipment Reports (monthly/yearly)
PURCHASING MANAGER
Purchasing Coordinator
PC Files
Summary Reports
Sales/Production Aids Summary
Supplier Rep Summary
Rep Sign-in Log Summary
Emergency Shipment Summary
Material Handling Report Card Summary
Backup Files
(storage)
Sales/Production Aids Summary
Suppliers' Written Policy Statements
Rep Sign-in Logs
Rep Sign-in Logs Summary
Material Handling Reports
Material Handling Reports Summary
Packaging and Labeling Data Cards
Lead-Time Predictability Reports - yearly
Back Order/Overshipment Reports - yearly
Pricing Analysis
Emergency Shipment Data Cards
Emergency Shipment Summary
Quality Control Report
Perceived Quality Report
TEAM MEMBER 3
Pricing Analysis Report
Emergency Shipment Report Cards
Emergency Shipment Summary
TEAM MEMBER 4
Material Handling Report Cards
Material Handling Report Card Summary
Packaging and Labeling Data Cards

DOCUMENTING AND COLLECTING DATA ON INVENTORY REBALANCING POLICIES

Inventory rebalancing can be documented and graded by using the suppliers' own written policy statements in their product literature. Compare their written standards to their actual performances in inventory rebalancing. By doing so, you will be able to answer the following questions:

- Does the supplier have a published inventory rebalancing (return policy) program?
- Are restocking charges required when material is returned?
- Is offset ordering required with the return of material?
- Does the supplier have a preset dollar amount for returned items?
- Is the supplier's inventory rebalancing program "unconditional"?
- Does material have to be returned during a specific time frame?

Team Member 1 can answer these questions for you during the actual grading process and present the supplier's own written standards of performance as documentation.

DOCUMENTING AND COLLECTING DATA ON WARRANTY POLICIES

Compare your suppliers' written statements regarding warranty to your set warranty standards. By doing so, you will be able to answer the following questions about the suppliers' warranty procedures:

- Does the supplier have a formal warranty policy?
- Is the warranty policy "unconditional"?
- Do defective parts have to be returned to the supplier?
- Does the supplier require authorization before a warranted product can be returned?
- Is verification of the date of purchase required with the return of a warranted product?

- Is repair and return or credit given for defective products based on the customer's request?
- Does the supplier allow over-the-counter replacement for defective products?
- Does the defective product being replaced over-the-counter have to be returned to the supplier?

Once again, these questions can be answered by Team Member 1 during the actual supplier grading process. The supplier's own written warranty statements can be used for documentation in determining the supplier's grade in this area.

DOCUMENTING AND COLLECTING DATA ON QUALITY ISSUES

Data collection and documentation for quality should be established in three departments: quality control (warranty), marketing, and sales. Information about quality will come in quarterly reports furnished by the managers of each of these departments. Your purchasing coordinator will consolidate and store these reports in the supplier performance files until Evaluation Team Member 2 is ready to compile information for the actual supplier grading session.

Monitoring Three Quality Control Issues

Your company's quality control department already has a way of measuring the amount of defective supplier products that are returned each year. You may want to incorporate it into your supplier quality reports. An alternative method might be similar to the sample Quality Control Report shown in Figure 10-3. Such data can be very effective in measuring supplier performance in quality. Three issues you will want to monitor in quality control are:

Length of warranty. This should be based on products with a one-year warranty. When a product is warranted for three-, five-, or even ten-year periods, you can average warranty returns over a two-year period or for the entire warranty period, if your company keeps records that are easily avail-

Figure 10-3: Quality Control Report

Qualitity Control Report

Date: February 24, 1992

P.O.#	Supplier	Part #	Description	Quantity Received	Quantity Rejected	% Rejected	Approved/Rejected		Reason for Rejection
45432	A	53879	Bolts	1,000	10	1.0	X		Faulty workmanship.
T7655	Q	A735	Grille	350	350	100.0		X	Paint is peeling.
46321	R	12536	Screws	5,000	50	1.0	X		Threads damaged.
47333	R	10333	Pins	10,000	150	1.5	X		Diameter too large.

Summary of Quality Control Report

Supplier	Quantity Received	Quantity Rejected	% Rejected
A	1,000	10	1.0
Q	750	15	2.0
R	15,000	200	1.3
Z	1,000	25	2.5

Total quantities received = 5,650
Total quantities rejected = 350

Quality control manager:____________________

This a quarterly report.
Quality control will send this report to the purchasing manager for review.
Team Member 2 will use this report.

able to you. By doing so, you may find that your company is actually a "swap shop" for suppliers with inferior quality products. For example, you may have moderate first-time sales on these products, but you have to carry much larger stocks of the products because of ongoing warranty problems. There is a continual exchange of faulty products for new products. These warranty exchanges do not provide income revenue for your company.

Changes in product quality. The report should also indicate changes in product quality as a result of improved product design, use of better material in the manufacture of products, and so on.

Rejection ratios. The rejection ratio of material to the total amount of supplier products received or sold must be calculated for every supplier marked for performance evaluation. Your list might look like Figure 10-4.

This list indicates the relative position of all of your suppliers' total product sales to returns or failures of defective material. Review these results with your warranty administrator or your quality control supervisor. Companies carrying several different brands of a similar product might want to compare the returns of each company's products in the same manner as above. This will give you the relative position of each supplier and the products each one provides to your company.

Figure 10-4: Calculating Rejection Ratios

CALCULATING REJECTION RATIOS

Grading Period: 1/92–12/92

Supplier	Products	Total product purchased or sold	Total cost of defective returned products	Percent of total purchases/ sales
A	Controls	$ 10,000	$ 100	1.0
B	Raw Materials	150,000	1,350	0.9
C	Nuts and Bolts	5,000	75	1.5
H	Plastic Parts	25,000	125	0.5

Total percent of returns = 150.0

Total number of suppliers = 120.0

Average returns per supplier = 1.25%

The quality control manager should summarize and send these reports to your purchasing department on a quarterly basis. The information will be used together with the data from the marketing and sales groups about your customers' perception of quality.

Determining Measurement for Your Customers' Perception of Product Quality

Information about your customers' perception of product quality can be obtained from your marketing and sales groups. Two issues actually determine this measurement of quality:

1. Customers' perception of quality. Product quality is actually a measure of your customers' perception of quality.
2. Marketing and sales confidence. Product quality is also determined by your company sales force's ease in selling supplier products.

Customers' perception of quality. Your customers have a supplier product preference when they make purchases. Therefore, your data on quality should answer the following questions:

- Do customers ask for the supplier's product by name?
- Will the customer accept an alternate product when the preferred product is not available?
- Do customers regard the supplier's product as being priced too high?

Answers to these questions will determine the quality image of supplier products.

Marketing and sales confidence. Marketing and sales know the products they can sell with confidence because of the product's "quality" image or the supplier's reputation in the marketplace. Therefore, your data on quality should address the following questions:

- Is the supplier's product the industry leader?
- Is the supplier's product a preferred product?
- Can you sell the supplier's product?

The data obtained from answering these questions are the basis for applying evaluation grades for sales aids. You can use a Perceived Quality Report like the one illustrated in Figure 10-5. It should be filled out yearly by your marketing, sales, and location managers and forwarded to the purchasing department for consolidation by the purchasing coordinator. By consolidating the information from all locations, you can eliminate or explain any differences in data. For example, there might be differences between the supplier's and customer's views of product quality. A supplier might have only one product failure during the evaluating year and thus believe product quality is high. On the other hand, the supplier's product might not meet the customer's expectations of durability, serviceability, or priceability.

The information will be stored until Team Member 2 gathers it for the evaluation grading sessions. Then you and the evaluation team can compare it with your standards of quality for supplier grading in this area.

DOCUMENTING AND COLLECTING DATA ON COMPETITIVE PRICING

Data about competitive pricing will come from the purchasing department. As it is your responsibility to see that all supplier pricing is up-to-date, ask marketing and sales to supply you with a Pricing Analysis Report on an annual basis. Figure 10-6 illustrates a sample of what the report might look like.

The manufacturer's purchasing department is responsible for competitive price comparison for production aids. Purchasing staff will want to review products from different suppliers for pricing structures, pricing levels, and value-added features. These price comparisons should be made on an ongoing basis to determine the best value of component parts for the products being manufactured. Each time a value analysis of competitive brands of product is completed, it should be included in the price performance folder of your suppliers as documentation for this parameter.

Your purchasing coordinator will consolidate and store the information until Team Member 3 is ready to collect the data for the evaluation grading sessions.

DOCUMENTING AND COLLECTING DATA ON SALES/PRODUCTION AIDS

The distributor's sales and marketing group is responsible for supplying the data for grading the supplier's performance on sales aids because sales and

Figure 10-5: Perceived Quality Report

Perceived Quality Report

Sales Location: ____________________

Date: ____________________

Customer's Perception of Supplier Products

		Asks for product by name		Is the product an acceptable alternate for the quality leader?		Product Pricing			Marketing & Sales Input	
Supplier	Products	Yes	No	Yes	No	Pricing is too high	Pricing is not a factor	Supplier Product Preference	Can you sell this product?	Industry Leader
A	Controls	X		X			X	C	yes	C
B	Controls		X		X	X		C	no	C
C	Controls	X	Quality	Leader			X	C	yes	C

Sales Manager ____________________

Marketing Manager ____________________

This is a yearly report.
The purchasing coordinator sends this report to marketing and sales three to four weeks prior to the supplier evaluation grading sessions.
Team Member 2 will use this report.

Figure 10-6: Pricing Analysis Report

Supplier Pricing Analysis Report

Date: ____________

Customer's Perception of Supplier Products

Pricing Structure

Supplier	Aggressive Price Leader	Competitive Pricing	Uncompetitive Pricing - high	Availibility of Product Literature	Gives Quantity Discounts	Gives Special Quotations	Price Increases
A			X	X	no	no	yes
B	X			X	yes	yes	no
C			X	Always Late	yes	yes	yes
D		X		X	yes	no	yes

*Purchasing manager: ____________

Sales manager: ____________

The purchasing manager will sign this report because several of the issues affect the performance of the purchasing department.

* This report reflects the pricing structures of each supplier for a 12-month period.
This is a yearly report.
This report is used by Team Member 3.

marketing staff are the beneficiaries of supplier assistance in this parameter. They know firsthand if the supplier's sales aids are effective.

Data collection for technical and manufacturing assistance should be delegated to the engineering and production departments. They will be able to provide information about the technical knowledge of supplier reps and about the technical information and product services provided by suppliers.

This category includes the performance of supplier representatives and independent sales representatives as well as the performance of supplier services.

Monitoring the Performance of Supplier Representatives and Independent Sales Representatives

The evaluation of supplier representatives and independent sales representatives was discussed in Chapter 4. Reps play an important role in supplier representation and assistance to your company. Therefore, you will want to include this evaluation information in your supplier grading sessions. The forms you should include are shown in Figures 4-1, 4-2, and 4-3.

Figure 4-1 is an example of a Rep Sign-in Log. This log becomes part of your data collection and documentation as it monitors the amount and purpose of rep visits to your sales locations. The log is a continuous report that should be sent to you on a monthly basis. The information can be consolidated easily by your purchasing coordinator and stored in the supplier performance files. You might want to use a summary report like the one shown in Figure 10-7.

Figures 4-2 and 4-3 are examples of Rep Performance Evaluation Forms for distribution and manufacturing. These forms should be sent to the marketing and sales managers or engineering and production managers three weeks prior to the supplier grading session. Companies with multiple sales locations should send a form to each sales location to be completed by each location manager. The forms should be due back one week after receipt so that your purchasing coordinator has adequate time to consolidate the information for Team Member 3's use in the performance grading sessions.

Monitoring Supplier Services

Other data for sales aids deal with the services provided by your supplier and are documented by your marketing and sales management. Information on supplier services should help you answer the following questions:

Figure 10-7: Supplier Rep Sign-in Log Summary

Supplier Rep Sign-in Log Summary

Grading Period: Jan. - Dec. 1992

Total Locations: 25

Representative's Name	Supplier	Total # of Sales Calls	# of Locations Visited	Actual Locations Visited	
				Percent	# Designation of Locations
Bruce Thompson	A	21	15	60.0	1,2,3,7,8,10,11,12,13, 14,15,16,17,18,19,
Suzanne Miller	C	20	25	100.0	all locations
Better Rep Agency	Q	75	25	100.0	all locations
Better Rep Agency	T	75	25	100.0	all locations

Purchasing manager: B. Stepp

- Better Rep Agency is an independent agency that representents Supplier Q and T.
- This report is sorted by supplier for easier indentification of representatives.
- The purchasing coordinator compiles this report from daily sign-in logs.
- Team Member 3 will use this report.

- Does the supplier provide national advertising?
- Does the supplier provide local advertising?
- Are effective product promotions made available to marketing and sales?
- Are technical information and drawings always available?
- Does the supplier provide training assistance for proper use of material or services?
- Are cooperative funds made available to your company?
- Are toll-free telephone and/or fax numbers made available for your company's use?

The data obtained from these questions are the basis for evaluation grades for suppliers' sales aids.

A Supplier Sales/Production Aids Summary like the one in Figure 10-8 should go to the manager of your company's sales or the manufacturer's production managers for completion. This should be done three to four weeks prior to the beginning of your evaluation grading sessions.

The form is relatively simple to fill out, and you should expect your company's sales manager or the manufacturer's production manager to return it to you one week after receipt. You also might want to send the report to your marketing manager or the manufacturer's engineering manager for additional comments. By doing so, you document two opinions of the effectiveness of supplier promotions, training seminars, and technical assistance. The marketing manager or the manufacturer's engineering manager should also be able to return the summary to your purchasing coordinator within one week after receipt. This will give Team Member 2 adequate time to gather documentation to be used in the grading sessions.

DOCUMENTING AND COLLECTING DATA ON LEAD-TIME PREDICTABILITY

Suppliers always give delivery dates when orders are placed. Your job is to measure the performance of your suppliers to their own stated or quoted delivery dates. The stated delivery dates should reflect the following information:

- The delivery date should represent the actual time from the date the purchase order is transmitted to the supplier until all the items ordered are received at your location.

Figure 10-8: Supplier Sales/Production Aids Summary

Summary of Supplier Sales/Production Aids

Grading Period: Jan. - Dec. 1992

Instructions: Check the appropriate box and add comments.

Supplier	Provides Information Adv./Tech.	Provides Co-op Funds	Offers Product-Training Seminars for (sales/customers/production)	Provides Toll-free Communication (phone/fax)	Comments
A	X	X		X X	Product promotions are not effective.
B	X			X	Product-training seminars need to be implemented.
C	X	X	X X	X X	Product promotions and training seminars are very effective.
D				X	Productive sales are declining. The supplier does not provide adequate product information.

Marketing manager: J. Hebrick

Sales/production manager: Abraham Hur

- This is a yearly report.
- The purchasing coordinator sends this report to marketing, sales, or production control 3 to 4 weeks prior to the supplier evaluation grading sessions.
- Team Member 2 will use this report.

- The supplier should estimate and include transit time in all lead-time projections.
- If a supplier quotes less than the normal stated lead-time on a purchase order containing nonstock items, the purchase order should reflect the quoted lead time.

You will want to make sure your purchasing personnel understand this information and write the correct lead time on all purchase orders. This is very important because the information becomes part of your measuring stick for lead-time predictability.

A report on lead-time predictability can easily be calculated by using a computer. In fact, it is easy to run a special report of this type. It might look like the one in Figure 10-9.

This quarterly report will be summarized at the end of the evaluation year. Team Member 1 can use the summary report for documentation. If no computer is available, make sure the purchasing coordinator gets a copy of all of the receiving reports from the receiving department at the end of each month. The object is to compare the actual receipt date on the receiving reports to the stated date of receipt on all purchase orders for the entire

Figure 10-9: Lead-Time Predictability Report

LEAD-TIME PREDICTABILITY REPORT

Time Frame: 4/92—6/92

Supplier's Name: ___________

P.O.#	Scheduled Receipt Date of P.O.	Actual Receipt Date	Partial	Complete
36-01234	4/5	4/4		X
36-02763	4/20	4/25		X
•	•	•	•	•
36-02777	5/2	5/1	X	
36-03325	5/15	5/13	X	

Total number of orders placed with the supplier: 10

Total number of on-time orders: 7

Percent of on-time orders: 70%

evaluation year. This information will have to be entered in a PC for storage and final summary. If you are using a report that is being run from a central computer, you can get a final summary report run once a year. It should look exactly like the quarterly report.

The quarterly report is important because you can quickly identify supplier problems in this area. You do not want to wait until the end of the evaluation year to act when a supplier's performance in this area is way below par. It needs immediate attention.

The yearly report will give the evaluation team the information needed for grading each supplier's performance in the lead-time predictability parameter.

DOCUMENTING AND COLLECTING DATA ON BACK ORDERS/OVERSHIPMENTS

The data for back orders and overshipments represent your supplier's ability to complete delivery of goods on time and error free for every item on every purchase order placed during the evaluation period.

Follow the same guidelines given for the lead-time predictability report.

This report will inform your team about suppliers' back orders and overshipments. It might look like Figure 10-10.

You might want to combine this report with the report on lead-time predictability to reduce paper and computer printouts. If so, your combined report might look like Figure 10-11.

If no computer is available, follow the same procedures for lead-time predictability and indicate which receipts were incomplete, that is, back ordered or overshipped. When you summarize the lead-time predictability information, also pick out those that were complete. This report becomes part of your supplier performance file. Team Member 1 can have access to the information and present the final report for the evaluation year during the actual grading session.

DOCUMENTING AND COLLECTING DATA ON PAYMENT TERMS

Data on supplier payment terms come from two sources—supplier literature and your accounting department.

Supplier literature. Suppliers usually have their payment terms written in product literature, which we discussed in Chapter 7. You should

Figure 10-10: Back Order/Overshipment Report

BACK ORDER/OVERSHIPMENT REPORT

Time Frame: 4/92—6/92

Supplier's Name: __________

P.O.#	P.O. Quantity	Quantity Received	Receipt Date	Status Partial	Status Complete
36-01234	50	50	4/4		X
36-02763	25	25	4/25		X
•	•	•	•	•	•
36-02777	75	55	5/1	X	
36-03325	75	66	5/13	X	

Total number of orders placed with the supplier: 10

Total number of partial orders: 3

Percent of completed orders: 70%

---

already have made provision for copies of your supplier's stated policies to be placed in the supplier performance files for measuring inventory, rebalancing policies, and supplier warranties. This product literature will also give you the supplier's stated payment terms. Team Member 1 will be able to present this information to the team during the grading sessions because it is part of the data already collected.

Accounts payable. The accounts payable manager plays an important role in documenting supplier payment terms. This person can answer the following questions for you and your evaluation team members:

- Can your company take advantage of the discounts offered as part of the supplier's payment terms?
- Is your company losing money because of lost supplier discounts and payment terms?
- Is the supplier's accounting department willing to assist in settlement of accounting problems your company has in doing business with them?

In some cases lost discounts occur because an of accounting policy. For example, the accounting department might produce payable checks on a date

Figure 10-11: Combined Lead-Time Predictability and Back Orders/Overshipments Report

LEAD-TIME PREDICTABILITY AND
BACK ORDERS/OVERSHIPMENTS REPORT

Time Frame: 4/92—6/92

Supplier's Name: __________

P.O.#	Scheduled Receipt Date of P.O.	Actual Receipt Date	P.O. Quantity	Quantity Received	Status: Incomplete	Status: Complete
36-01234	4/5	4/4	50	50		X
36-02763	4/20	4/25	25	25		X
36-02777	5/2	5/1	75	55	X	
•	•	•	•	•	•	•

Total number of orders placed with the supplier: 48

Total number of orders received on time: 37

Total number of orders with partial receipts: 12

Percent of completed orders: 75%

Percent of on-time orders: 77%

---

that causes the loss of discounts. However, some suppliers offer special arrangements for the accounts payable manager that allow late discounts to be taken.

You can send a yearly Supplier Payment Terms Report to your accounts payable manager. It might look like the one illustrated in Figure 10-12. The form should be sent four weeks prior to the grading session and be due back within one week so Team Member 1 can have adequate time to study the information for proper presentation during the grading sessions.

DOCUMENTING AND COLLECTING DATA ON PACKAGING AND LABELING

Evaluation of the effectiveness of your supplier's product packaging and labeling is determined by input from the material handling department and your sales and marketing groups.

Figure 10-12: Supplier Payment Terms Report

SUPPLIER PAYMENT TERMS REPORT

Supplier	Payment Terms	Special Conditions
A	1% tenth prox net 30	The supplier is helpful in settling payment problems. Discounts are allowed when resolution of these problems becomes lengthy.
B	2% ten days net 30	
C	net 30 days	
G	1% 30 days net 60	The supplier does not honor payment terms when the customer is at fault.

- This is a yearly report.
- The purchasing coordinator is responsible for setting up the supplier's names and payment terms. This information will, for the most part, remain the same from year to year.
- The accounts payable supervisor is required to add comments under *Special Conditions* and return the report to the purchasing coordinator.
- Team Member 1 will use this report.

Documenting Information from Material Handling

Data for material handling are measured continuously. You should develop cards for material handlers to use when problems occur as a result of inadequate product packaging. Figure 10-13 is an example of a Material Handling Report Card.

Material handlers can quickly fill in the necessary information and turn the card in to their supervisor the same day. These cards are a sure way of pinpointing any product packaging and labeling deficiencies that need immediate attention. For example, inadequate product packaging and labeling can cause bodily injury to an employee or customer. When injury happens, it is imperative that the problem be identified immediately and brought to the attention of the material handling manager and the supplier for corrective measures.

Figure 10-13: Material Handling Report Card

MATERIAL HANDLING REPORT

Date: ____________________

P.O. #: ____________________

Supplier: ____________________

Product: ____________________

Problem: ____

____

____

Material Handler: ____________________________
(signature)

Materials Control Supervisor: ____________________________

(signature)

- This card is used by materials control (warehousing, shipping and receiving) to report problems.
- Copies of these cards are sent to purchasing for review and storage.
- Team Member 4 will use this report.

The materials control supervisor can also use the cards to compile a yearly report for the supplier evaluation team. An example is shown in Figure 10-14. This report and copies of the cards are to be forwarded to the purchasing coordinator. Team Member 4 will use this report during the grading sessions.

Documenting Information from Marketing and Sales

Marketing and sales personnel also provide data on packaging and labeling. The information you want from them will focus on three issues:

1. The overall appearance of product packaging and labeling
2. Whether or not the product packaging and labeling provide point-of-purchase assistance
3. If adequate product information is provided on product packaging and labeling.

Figure 10-14: Material Handling Report Summary

MATERIAL HANDLING REPORT SUMMARY

Instructions: Use this grading scale to grade the overall condition of supplier cartons and labels. Check issues that the supplier addresses in packaging and labeling.

Grading Scale
1 = Poor
2 = Needs Improvement
3 = Average
4 = Above Average
5 = Excellent

Issues	Names of Suppliers: A	B	C	D	E	F	G	H	I	J	K	L	M
MASTER CARTONS													
Sturdy													
Palletized													
Shrink-wrapped													
Bar Coded													
MASTER LABELS													
Easy to read													
Descriptive													
Bar Coded													
Date Coded													
INDIVIDUAL CARTONS													
Sturdy													
Attractive													
Shrink-wrapped													
Bar Coded													

INDIVIDUAL LABELS

Easy to Read

Descriptive

Bar Coded

Date Coded

Marketing/Sales Manager: ______________________________

(signature) (date)

OR

Materials Control Manager: ______________________________

(signature) (date)

- This is a yearly report.
- This report can be used by material control and marketing and sales to report the overall quality and effectiveness of supplier packaging and labeling.
- Team Member 4 will use this report.

This information requires continuous monitoring by marketing and sales personnel. They can do this by using a card system similar to the one used for materials handling problems. Figure 10-15 is an example of a card from marketing, sales, and material control personnel. It also can be used as an aid for making yearly reports for supplier evaluation purposes.

The yearly report and copies of the cards are to be forwarded to the purchasing coordinator for consolidation and stored until Team Member 4 is ready to collect the information for the actual grading sessions.

DOCUMENTING AND COLLECTING DATA ON EMERGENCY SHIPMENTS

The purchasing department is responsible for collecting data and documentation on supplier policies for emergency shipments because purchasing is the focal point when customers need material on an emergency basis.

Figure 10-15: Packaging and Labeling Data Card

PACKAGING & LABELING DATA CARD

SUPPLIER: A　　Packaging Type: Master Carton: ____

Date: ________________　　Individual Carton: ____

P.O. #: ______________　　Label: ____

Product #: ____________

Comments: ____

____

____

Used by:

Material Handler: ______________________________
(signature)

Materials Control Supervisor: ______________________________
(signature)

OR

Marketing/Sales Person: ______________________________
(signature)

Supervisor: ______________________________
(signature)

- This card is used by materials control and marketing or sales to report packaging and labeling inefficiencies.
- Copies of this report are sent to purchasing for summarization and storage.
- Team Member 4 will use this report.

Data for this parameter will come from the supplier's written statements on provisions for emergency needs, a report from purchasing, and reports from any other department that may get involved in expediting emergency shipments, such as marketing, sales, or production. Once again, you should go to the supplier's literature to see what the provisions are for emergency services. Team Member 1 will have the proper information for you and your team members during the grading sessions.

Purchasing should monitor the data on emergency situations on a continuing basis. This can be done by providing an Emergency Shipment Data Card for purchasing personnel to use when they place emergency shipment orders. An example of this card is given in Figure 10-16.

Figure 10-16: Emergency Shipment Data Card

EMERGENCY SHIPMENT DATA CARD

Supplier: ________________ Customer: ________________

P.O. #: ________________ Date of P.O.: ________________

Date Needed: ________________ Date Received: ________________

Product (s): ________________________________

Part #'s: ________________________________

Special Instructions: ________________________________

____

____

Comments: ________________________________

____

____

Purchasing Agent: ________________________________
(Signature) (Date)

Purchasing Manager: ________________________________
(Signature) (Date)

- This report card is used by the purchasing department to monitor emergency shipments.
- Team Member 3 will use this report.

When your marketing and sales or the manufacturer's production personnel become directly involved in expediting emergency shipments for specific customers, you will also want their input on the supplier's performance. They should also be required to fill out an Emergency Shipment Data Summary and route it to you for review. When you are finished with it, it goes to the purchasing coordinator for consolidation and storage.

Team Member 3 will have this information ready for the evaluation team to use at the grading sessions. This person will compile a summary report like the one shown in Figure 10-17.

Data documentation, collection, and storage must be a continuing process. Those responsible for this information have an ongoing task that is critical to the success of an evaluation program. Participants must be well informed of the purpose and importance of these tasks.

Figure 10-17: Emergency Shipment Data Summary

EMERGENCY SHIPMENT DATA SUMMARY

Supplier	P.O. #	Date P.O.	Date Needed	Date Received	Comments
A	73563	3/4/92	3/5/92	3/5/92	Supplier delivered on time direct to job-site.
A	97633	4/14/92	4/16/92	4/17/92	Special items could not be delivered on time. Supplier notified us of delay.

Purchasing Manager: ______________________
(signature) (date)

- This is a yearly report.
- This report is sorted by suppliers.
- Team Member 4 will use this report.

CHAPTER 11

GRADING SUPPLIER PERFORMANCE

Grading supplier performance is a total company effort. It involves input from every level of management in your company plus input from your customers and end users. A review of your company's team will help you understand how the actual grading process works:

Company president. Your company president presents and reinforces the importance of supplier evaluation to your suppliers, company personnel, and evaluation team members.

Department managers. Department managers help with documentation and supplier performance grading and are used on a consulting basis, when necessary, to give additional input on supplier performance.

Team leader. The evaluation team leader is responsible for assigning individual duties to team members and for supervising the supplier performance grading sessions.

Purchasing coordinator. The purchasing coordinator is responsible for establishing and maintaining documentation files and for helping the purchasing manager and the evaluation team in the evaluation process.

Team members. Each team member is responsible for presenting documented information in the areas he or she represents and for supplier performance analyses and grading.

Suppliers. Suppliers are responsible for giving you information about any special conditions that might affect their performance during the evaluation year. For example, a supplier's move to a new and larger manufacturing facility might affect its performance in lead-time predictability.

Customers/end users. The customer's perception of quality as it relates to product quality and pricing affects supplier grades.

There are three keys to successful grading of supplier performances that you will want to review:

1. Confidentiality. All of the information presented during the evaluation meeting is strictly confidential. The issues presented for discussion and individual supplier grades are the business of you, your company president, the evaluation team members, and the supplier being graded. The grades are not open for discussion with other suppliers or company personnel.
2. Factuality. Supplier performance grades are based on facts, not on the personal opinions of various team members.
3. Unity. Unity of purpose is required from you and your team members. Your goal is a fair and successful supplier performance evaluation.

SUPERVISING GRADING SESSIONS AND MONITORING DATA

The team leader is responsible for making sure the meeting facilities are private and that appropriate equipment is provided for visual grading (e.g., a chalk board, flip chart or marker board). This enables you to:

- Monitor all of the data provided for each supplier during the evaluation process.
- Highlight any significant changes in a supplier's performance from year to year, making sure causes are properly documented.

Specific responsibilities are often delegated to the purchasing coordinator to ensure that the evaluation process takes place in an efficient manner. For example, the purchasing coordinator may be responsible for providing the following evaluation aids:

Purchasing files. The purchasing files for each supplier being evaluated must be taken into the meeting room.

Supplier grading reports. A Supplier Grading Report sheet will be used for each supplier being evaluated. They can be kept in three-ring binders for ease in handling and storage. As they will accumulate from year to year, you will be able to monitor supplier performance grades and to see supplier performance improvement from year to year.

Mailing labels. A set of alphabetized mailing labels for supplier and/or independent sales representatives being evaluated should be brought to the meeting room. They can be placed on the Supplier Grading Reports as each supplier is graded, thus eliminating the need to write the names and addresses of these people manually on the reports.

Records. All final performance grades for each parameter for each supplier must be recorded on the Supplier Grading Reports.

Supplier performance measurement standards. Each evaluation team member needs a copy of the Supplier Performance Measurement Standards (Appendix) to use during the evaluation process.

Visual aids. Someone must arrange for the use of a chalk or marker board in the meeting room. The team leader will list the suppliers' names and the parameters being graded on the board. As the grading is a repetitive process, the team leader need only replace the supplier's name and grades when the next supplier on the list is evaluated. This method also allows each team member to see the grading process as it occurs and to make comments and cast votes on each issue presented.

GRADING SUPPLIER A

The Supplier Grading Report (Figure 7-6) will be filled out by the purchasing coordinator as each parameter is graded by the evaluation team. The grading session begins by preparing the visual board. This is done by setting up three columns:

- Name of supplier
- Current grade
- Grades from previous years.

Since this is your first evaluation year, the column for the supplier's grades from the previous year will be blank. During the second year of your program and every year thereafter, you will want to include the previous years' grades for each supplier for comparison purposes.

Grading the Supplier's Performance in Quality

Ask your team members to turn to the evaluation standards section on quality in their copies of the Performance Measurement Standards. Your representatives from the sales and marketing departments are Team Members 2 and 3. Their input will give you information from your customers' viewpoint about Supplier A's perceived quality. For example, Team Member 2 can supply information from the Quality Control Report (Figure 10-3) and the Perceived Quality Report (Figure 10-5) on Supplier A. It might look like this:

- Supplier A's product is not the perceived quality leader of the industry, but it is a very good substitute product.
- The product is well accepted in the marketplace and has a competitive edge because of its perceived added-value quality.
- Marketing and sales personnel are confident in the supplier's product and can sell the product easily.
- Team Member 2 can also give you the product return ratio of 1.0% on Supplier A's product from the Quality Control Report.
- A grade in the 6 to 9 range for quality would be justified.

If Supplier A is being evaluated by a manufacturer, there are two considerations in grading quality:

1. The supplier's grade for quality will be strictly objective, based on the quarterly Quality Control Report that contains the objective grading of supplier performance.
2. When the supplier provides a service or indirect material to the manufacturer, input for grading must come directly from the users of the service or product because quality control is not involved. This will require a total value-to-quality estimate by the user of the material or service, and a subsequent grade will be applied.

Team Member 2 might have additional input about Supplier A's product that could affect the grade for quality. For example, the product might have undergone design improvement during the evaluation year. This would account for the decrease in product returns on the Quality Control Report. A point may be added for design improvement.

When all of the documentation is presented and discussed, the team leader will ask for a vote on Supplier A's product quality based on the grading standards in the Performance Measurement Standards section on quality. For example, team members might agree to give Supplier A a grade of 8 in quality (7 for product dependability and 1 point for design improvement). The grade is written on the visual board. The purchasing coordinator enters it on the Supplier Grading Report for Supplier A and makes a notation in the additional comments section of the report about the improved product quality image because of better product design.

Grading the Supplier's Performance in Sales/Production Aids

The next category is Sales/Production Aids. Team members now turn to the appropriate Performance Grading Standards section.

Team Member 2 can present the information needed for grading this parameter, as he or she represents marketing, sales, customer service, manufacturing, quality control, or engineering. The information will be compiled from the Rep Sign-in Log Summary, which will be summarized to give the total number of calls and sales locations visited for each rep. Information from the Rep Performance Evaluation Forms for either the distributor or manufacturer will determine the quality of sales visits made by each rep being evaluated.

Mr. Bob Smith is the rep for Supplier A, and he made visits to 15 of 25 sales locations. The quality of Bob's visits also needs improvement. His performance in keeping up literature information and conducting training programs was good. He helped central purchasing on several occasions with availability of goods. However, his personal skills, especially with outside customers, is not acceptable. Bob should receive 1 point for the number of visits made and 1 point for the assistance to central purchasing. This informaton should be on the visual board and recorded on the Supplier Grading Report.

As you tally this information, team members can see that the rep visited only 60 percent of your company's sales locations. This is less than 1.4 visits to each of the fifteen locations during a 12-month period. Team members may agree that this rep's performance is poor and vote to give the rep a performance grade of three. The purchasing coordinator should record this information on the Supplier Grading Report.

Team Member 2 can supply information from the Summary of Supplier Sales Aids (Figure 10-7). Discuss and call for a vote on each of the issues that are addressed in the Performance Grading Standards for this parameter.

Team Member 2 verifies that the supplier advertises in national and local media. It makes co-op funds available for local advertising with distributors and customers. The supplier also conducted product promotions during the year. However, they were not announced properly. Information about one of the promotions was not received until the promotion was over and resulted in unhappy customers.

As you and your team members discuss and vote on the grade for each criterion, you will want to record the final grades on your visual board. For example, the visual board might look like Figure 11-1.

After you total the actual points given for sales aids, the purchasing coordinator records it on the Supplier Grading Report. You then prepare the visual board for grading the next parameter.

Figure 11-1: Final Grades for Sales Aids—Distribution

VISUAL BOARD

Parameter: Sales Aids
Supplier A
Representative: Mr. Bob Smith

Possible Points		Actual Points
Representative		
2	21 sales calls	1
1	60 percent of locations covered	0
2	quality of sales calls	1
1	purchasing assistance	1
	Total	3
Supplier A		
1	supplier advertising	1
1	supplier promotions	0
1	training activities	1
1	toll-free numbers	1
Total 10	Total	3
	Grand Total =	6

Grading the Supplier's Production Aids for Manufacturers

Manufacturers will want to grade their suppliers' production aids. Refer back to the standards established for supplier sales aids. Your grading standards will be similar.

The sign-in log might indicate that this rep actually made six calls to purchasing. However, only one visit was made to engineering. The rep made the required number of visits to purchasing, but the visits were not planned or scheduled. Very little product information was provided, and information folders and catalogs were not updated or reviewed. Although the rep made one call to engineering, the visit was not planned or scheduled, and the rep was not knowledgeable about supplier product relationships to our product. The rep would earn one point for the frequency of calls and no points for quality of sales calls. Your visual board for production aids might look like Figure 11-2.

This rep is not performing up to the standards required by the manufacturer. The rep's total grade of three should be listed under sales/production aids on the grading sheet with a notation about the causes of poor performance.

Figure 11-2: Final Grades for Production Aids—Manufacturers

VISUAL BOARD

Parameter: Production Aids—Manufacturing

Supplier B

Representative: Mr. Ted Bear

Possible Points		Actual Points
Frequency of sales calls		
1	six sales calls to this location	1
1	three calls to production/engineering	0
2	quality of sales calls	0
2	availability of training aids	1
2	technical assistance	0
2	toll-free phone and fax numbers	1
10	Total	3

Grading the Supplier's Performance in Product Pricing

The team now turns to the pricing issues in the Performance Grading Standards. Team Member 3, who represents sales or production, can provide information about Supplier A's product pricing. For example, is the supplier's product pricing literature correct, and is it distributed in a timely manner?

Team Member 3 can provide information from the Supplier Pricing Analysis Report. Supplier A might not be competitive in product pricing. For example, the supplier's product pricing might be higher than other suppliers for like products. Based on the first statement of the grading criteria on product pricing grading, team members might vote to give Supplier A a grade of three.

Next, the team looks at the possible additional points available, discusses each issue, and votes.

The team votes on the following information: The supplier does not take the initiative in price competition. However, product pricing literature is correct and is always distributed in a timely and efficient manner. Furthermore, the supplier does not offer volume price breaks and product prices have increased 5 percent during the last 12 months. The supplier's final grading for product pricing might look like Figure 11-3. The purchasing coordinator can transfer this information to the Supplier Grading Report.

Grading the Supplier's Performance in Lead-Time Predictability

Team Member 1 will supply team members information from the computer summary report on Supplier A's lead-time predictability. For example, the report might show Supplier A's on-time ratio for the 12-month grading period as 75 percent. Therefore, the supplier's grade would be 7.5 points for lead-time predictability:

$$75\% \text{ or } .75 \times 10 \text{ points} = 7.5 \text{ points}$$

The grade of 7.5 is added to the Supplier Grading Report by the purchasing coordinator.

Figure 11-3: Final Grades for Product Pricing

VISUAL BOARD

Parameter: Product Pricing
Supplier A

Possible Points		Actual Points
6	Pricing is too high.	3
1	Competitive pricing is not initiated.	0
1	Pricing literature is correct and properly distributed.	1
1	Volume price breaks are not given.	0
1	Prices were increased by 5 percent.	0
10	Total	4

Grading the Supplier's Performance in Back Orders/Overshipments

The supplier's grade for back orders/overshipments comes from the computer summary report on Supplier A's back order/overshipments. Team Member 1 provides this information. For example, the report might indicate that Supplier A delivered a total of 20 orders during the 12-month evaluation period and four of the orders were partial shipments. That is a ratio of 20 percent for back orders and 80 percent for completed orders. According to the grading structure in the Performance Measurement Standards, the supplier should receive a grade of 8 (.80 × 10 possible points).

Team Member 4 can give additional information from the Material Handling Report. For example, some of the supplier's shipments might have caused receiving problems. Perhaps packing slips were not included in three shipments, and items were left off of packing slips in two shipments. This indicates that in addition to the four partial shipments, five of the twenty shipments created problems in receiving. Therefore, the 20 percent ratio becomes a 45 percent ratio, leaving 55 percent of the orders without problems. This changes the final grade from 8 to 5.5 (.55 × 10 possible points).

The purchasing coordinator transfers this grade to the Supplier Grading Report.

Grading the Supplier's Performance in Inventory Rebalancing

Team Member 1 should provide Supplier A's written policy statements from product literature on inventory rebalancing. For example, Supplier A's policy might stipulate that distributors can return any new and unused product any time, as long as they place an order for the same dollar amount with the return. Stated simply, this means that a distributor can swap slow-moving merchandise for items that sell well in the market area.

The supplier might also have a plan for dead or obsolete merchandise. For example, the supplier's policy might state that 10 percent of the cost of the product is allowed for a distress sale if the distributor is willing to match a 10 percent loss of profit. According to the grading structure for inventory rebalancing policies, Supplier A should receive a grade of 5 because there is a written policy statement for inventory rebalancing in product literature. Furthermore, team members might agree to award the supplier additional points because it does not require restocking charges on returned products. Also, the supplier's rep gave assistance in identifying and returning slow-moving items.

Your visual board might look like Figure 11-4 for the final grades in this parameter.

Supplier A's grade is excellent. The inventory rebalancing policy is good, and the supplier performs to the written policy statements. The purchasing coordinator will record this grade on the Supplier Grading Report.

Figure 11-4: Final Grades for Inventory Rebalancing

VISUAL BOARD

Parameter: Inventory Rebalancing

Supplier A

Possible Points		Actual Points
5	A written return policy statement is in the supplier's product literature.	5
2	The supplier does not have a restocking charge.	2
2	Assistance with slow-moving items is provided by the supplier.	2
1	Rebalancing is done once a year.	0
10	Total	9

Grading the Supplier's Performance in Warranty Procedures

Team Member 4 represents material control, warehouse, shipping, and receiving and can provide warranty information for Supplier A. For example, Supplier A's warranty policy stipulates a one-year, limited-parts warranty with return of defective parts. This is an average warranty policy according to the grading standards shown in the Performance Measurement Standards. Therefore, Supplier A would receive a grade of 5 in this parameter.

Team members might also agree to award an additional point to Supplier A's grade because there is a written warranty policy statement in the supplier's product literature. This information should be noted on the visual board as it is presented. For example, the visual board might look like Figure 11-5. After the actual points earned are totaled on the visual board, the purchasing coordinator will transfer the grade to the Supplier Grading Report.

Grading the Supplier's Performance in Payment Terms

Team member 1 can give the payment terms stipulated in Supplier A's product literature. For example, the stated payment terms might be net 30 days. Suppose that during the early part of the evaluation year, the purchas-

Figure 11-5: Final Grades for Warranty

VISUAL BOARD

Parameter: Warranty Policies

Supplier A

	Possible Points		Actual Points
	10	The supplier has an unconditional warranty policy that is stated in sales literature.	0
		The supplier has an average warranty policy based on our standards.	5
		The supplier's warranty policy is stated in product literature.	1
Total	10	Total	6

ing manager and the company president met with Supplier A's upper management and specifically identified the stated payment terms as unacceptable. As a result of this meeting, Supplier A's management made a commitment to increase payment terms to a 2% tenth prox net 30, if the company increased product sales by five percent during the evaluation year.

The team wants to review the Supplier Payment Terms and/or call in the accounts payable manager to document whether or not the supplier actually kept the commitment to change the payment terms. The accounts payable manager documents that Supplier A did give the company the new payment terms for the entire year because product purchases increased by 6.3 percent.

According to the grading standards for payment terms, the supplier should receive a grade of 7 because of the improved discount. The purchasing coordinator will transfer this grade to the Supplier Grading Report.

Grading the Supplier's Performance in Packaging and Labeling

Team Member 4 can supply information on the supplier's master cartons from Material Handling Reports and from the Packaging and Labeling Reports. It is reported that the supplier's master and individual cartons give adequate product protection. They are well marked and give correct information for product identification and handling instructions. Product packaging information from marketing, sales, and customer service indicates that master carton quantities are always consistent.

The packaging and labeling reports might indicate that Supplier A uses bar coding on all master cartons. However, bar coding is not used on individual cartons. The report further states that this is the first year that Supplier A has implemented bar coding of any kind. Team members might vote to give Supplier A a grade of .5 for bar coding based on this information. However, supplier A's products are not palletized for shipment, nor are they shrink-wrapped. Your visual board might look like Figure 11-6. The purchasing coordinator will record the grade of 7.5 on the Supplier Grading Report.

Grading the Supplier's Performance in Emergency Services

Team member 1 can tell the group if Supplier A has an emergency service statement in product literature. For example, Supplier A's emergency statement might require the payment of special handling charges for "same day" emergency shipments and waive minimum quantity requirements.

Team Member 3 can give you information from the Emergency Shipment Reports. For example, the supplier may have a written emergency

Figure 11-6: Final Grades for Packaging and Labeling

VISUAL BOARD

Parameter: Packaging and Labeling
Supplier A

Possible Points		Actual Points
1	Master cartons are well marked.	1
1	Master cartons give adequate product protection.	1
1	Product quantities are consistent.	1
1	Individual cartons give adequate product protection.	1
1	Individual carton quantities are consistent.	1
1	Labels are adequate. (master cartons)	1
1	Labels are adequate. (individual cartons)	1
1	Bar Coding is on master cartons only.	0.5
1	Palletizing is not available.	0
1	Shrink-wrapping is not available.	0
10	Total	7.5

service statement in product literature. Also it provides several different products that are not highly engineered. Charges for emergency services are reasonable and minimum quantities are waived. Emergency services are performed within the stated time frame 93 percent of the time. After reviewing all the information presented, team members vote on each issue in the Performance Grading Standards.

A summary of the supplier's grades for emergency services might look like Figure 11-7. The purchasing coordinator will transfer this information to the Supplier Grading Report.

COMPLETING THE SUPPLIER GRADING REPORT

Now that the Supplier A's grading process is complete, the purchasing coordinator will want to to finish filling in the Supplier Grading Report. This is done by simply multiplying the weight factors (see Figures 7-4 and 7-5) by

Figure 11-7: Final Grades for Emergency Services

VISUAL BOARD

Parameter: Emergency Services
Supplier A

Possible Points		Actual Points
5	The supplier has a written emergency service statement in product literature.	5
2	The supplier complies to the written emergency services statement 93 percent of the time.	1
2	Products are not complex.	1
1	Emergency service policy is effective and charges are reasonable.	1
10	Total	8

the supplier's performance grades. For example, the weight factor for quality is 1.7 and the supplier's grade for quality is 8.

$$1.7 \times 8 = 13.6$$

Therefore, 13.6 is the supplier's total number of points for quality. The purchasing coordinator can continue calculating the graded parameters and enter a parameter grade total in the appropriate place on the form. The total of the parameter grades for Supplier A is 90.25. The supplier's final parameter grade total should also be noted in the grading history for the year being evaluated. This helps keep track of supplier performance improvement from year to year. This is illustrated in Figure 11-8.

This grading procedure is used to evaluate all the suppliers participating in your evaluation process. When the evaluation team has completed the evaluation process for every supplier, your grading sessions will be finished.

Figure 11-8: Completed Supplier Grading Report

SUPPLIER GRADING REPORT

GRADING SCALE

1 = Very Poor
5 = Average
10 = Excellent

SUPPLIER: A

DATE: 2/92

PARAMETERS	WEIGHT FACTOR	(times)	PERFORMANCE GRADE	(equals)	TOTAL POINTS
QUALITY	1.7	X	8.0	=	13.6
SALES/PRODUCTION AIDS	1.6	X	6.0	=	9.6
PRODUCT PRICING	1.5	X	4.0	=	6.0
LEAD-TIME PREDICTABILITY	1.5	X	7.5	=	11.25
BACK ORDERS/OVERSHIPMENTS	1.4	X	5.5	=	7.70
RETURN POLICIES	1.3	X	9.0	=	11.7
WARRANTY PROCEDURES	1.2	X	6.0	=	7.2
TERMS (billing policies)	1.1	X	7.0	=	7.7
PACKAGING and LABELING	1.0	X	7.5	=	7.5
EMERGENCY SERVICE	1.0	X	8.0	=	8.0

PARAMETER GRADE TOTAL 90.25

SUPPLIER REPRESENTATIVE: Mr. Bob Smith

VISITS:
Total Number of Sales Locations: 25
Total number of visits made by rep: 21
Total number of sales locations visited: 16
60 %

COMMENTS: More visits & sales locations are needed. Bob needs to improve product knowledge and customer skills).

ADDITIONAL COMMENTS: Quality - New design award of one point included in perf. grade. Sales Aids - Promotions were not effective. Results were negative. Production Aids - Reps did not exhibit good product knowledge. Did not schedule visits.

GRADING HISTORY	1992	1993	1994	1995	1996
PARAMETER GRADE TOTALS	90.25				
YEARLY RANKINGS					

MAILING INFORMATION:
President or V.P. of Marketing
Supplier's Name
Address
City, State, Zip

CC: Supplier or Independent Sales Rep
Supplier or Independent Company
Address
City, State, Zip
President of Distribution or Manufacturing
Other: ______

CHAPTER 12

USING SUPPLIER EVALUATIONS TO IMPROVE THE SUPPLIER/CUSTOMER/ MANUFACTURER/ DISTRIBUTOR/ END-USER RELATIONSHIPS

Communicating performance evaluation grades to your suppliers, supplier representatives, and independent sales representatives is a very important part of the supplier evaluation. It is the means by which a company continually strengthens its partnering relationships among supplier/customer/manufacturer/distributor and end user. Therefore, your transmittal of information should be timely, concise, and easily understood.

Once the evaluation is complete, the purchasing manager should list participating suppliers according to their performance grades. For example, the list might look like the one in Figure 12-1.

Since performance evaluation is a company-wide effort, there will be company-wide interest in the supplier rankings. If the list is published in an

Figure 12-1: Ranking Order of Suppliers

Total Suppliers = 300
Total Suppliers included in evaluation = 89

Supplier	Rankings	
Supplier S	1	(top supplier of the year)
Supplier Q	2	
Supplier A	3	
•	•	
Supplier D	89	
(continue)		

interoffice memo, remember that the list is confidential until all participating suppliers have been notified of their grades and rankings.

All the members of the evaluation team, including those who supplied additional information on a consulting basis, should be thanked publicly.

Preparing Notification Letters

It is the purchasing manager's job to identify the individual in the supplier's company to receive the grading results. He or she must work closely with the company president and the supplier sales representatives to identify the person in each supplier organization who has the authority to make changes. (Supplier problems identified during performance evaluation will necessitate change.) Final supplier grades and rankings should go directly to this person, and a copy should be sent to the supplier representative or independent sales representative involved.

Notification letters should be sent to your suppliers within ten days after the grading session is finished. Keep your letter simple and easy to understand. By doing so you can avoid embarrassing situations. (A sample letter is given in Figure 12-2.)

During the pilot program, notification letters were sent to each supplier involved in the program. One supplier requested a meeting to review the data used in the grading process.

This supplier had received very low grades in all parameters and a final ranking of 98 out of 100 suppliers evaluated. During the conference meeting, it soon became apparent that the supplier's president had misread the letter and

Figure 12-2: Notification Letter Stating Supplier Grades and Final Rankings

Date: February 18,1993

Hughtony Thompson, President

USA Inc.

1992 Texas Ave.

Anywhere, U.S.A.

Dear Hughtony:

We have recently completed our 1992 Supplier Performance Evaluation Program. We currently do business with 300 suppliers. Eighty-nine of these suppliers are considered to be key suppliers and were included in the evaluation process.

A grading scale ranging from 1 to 10 was used in performance grading:

GRADING SCALE
1 = very poor supplier performance 5 = average supplier performance 10 = excellent supplier performance

All performance grades were determined by a special evaluation team consisting of personnel from sales, purchasing, inventory control, and management.

The following parameters are shown in the order of weighted importance to our company. Your company's scores are as follows:

PARAMETER	GRADE
Quality of Merchandise	7.0
Sales/Production Aids	8.5
Competitive Pricing	9.0
Lead-Time Predictability	7.0
Back Orders/Overshipments	6.1
Return Policies	8.0
Warranty Procedures	8.0
Terms (billing policies)	6.0
Packaging & Labeling	6.0
Emergency Services	8.0

Your company's rank among the 89 suppliers evaluated is 3. (One is the highest ranking possible and 89 is the lowest.) Please feel free to contact me for clarification and/or suggestions.

Best regards,

THE BEST COMPANY

Mica Jones,

President

MJ/jlf

Enclosure

cc: Franklin E. Capps, Supplier Representative
Brandon Stepp, Purchasing Manager

thought a ranking of 98 was 2 points from having a perfect score! Needless to say, this conference turned out to be very awkward for both companies involved.

The supplier's president was soon replaced, and the new president actually used our evaluation guidelines to rebuild the supplier's image. Within three years this supplier became one of our top ten performers!

Also, include a copy of your Supplier Performance Measurement Standards with each letter. This helps your suppliers review the grading process.

Identifying Additional Information for Supplier's Management

Sometimes you might want to send a supplier additional information or special requests with the notification letter. For example, you might want to request supplier assistance in a restocking program. You can design a special report like the one shown in Figure 12-3 listing the slow-moving merchandise for which you would like assistance in final disposition.

These requests get great results from suppliers, but they should not be a continuing stream. They lose their effectiveness and detract from the evaluation program. Here are some reasons why these requests are effective:

- Company presidents can and will make things happen on an exception basis.

Figure 12-3: Supplier Assistance in Stock Rebalancing Form

SLOW-MOVING MERCHANDISE

SUPPLIER: ______________ DATE: ______________

We would like your assistance in the final disposition of the following material:

Item Description	Quantity on Hand	Last Year's Sales	Excess Quantity	Unit Cost	Extended Cost
A	16	1	15	$ 11	$165
B	2	0	2	35	70
C	1	0	1	150	150
•	•	•	•	•	•
Totals	25	1	24		750

Our total sales with your company during the past year = $250,000

Total amount for disposition = $750 = 0.3% of $250,000.

Thank you for your assistance.

Hughtony Thompson, President
The Best Company
1992 Texas Ave.
Anywhere U.S.A.

- Some company presidents do not realize the reluctance of their managers or representatives to help in these situations. Therefore, you might effect a lasting change in the supplier's restocking policy.
- Your supplier's president will actually enjoy giving you personal assistance.

HANDLING SUPPLIER CHALLENGES

Every year some suppliers will ask for clarification of the grading procedures. What is asked for will range from a simple request for more information to a conference between the top executives of both companies. In each instance, it is important that every request and question be fully satisfied.

This is when the data files become invaluable tools. You must be able to answer every question the supplier asks about grades, respond to every statement about performance, and back up your answers with documented information.

Prepare for these meetings in advance by going over all the grading information about the supplier with your company president. Remember, your company's reputation as a quality performer is at stake!

A supplier's president requested a meeting with our company president to review its sales representation. The product line consisted of an engineered product that needed sales representation to provide product information, conduct product-training sessions, and make joint sales calls with our local sales people. They were puzzled by the drop in product sales to our company.

By looking at our detailed Supplier Representative Sign-In Log, it was clear that the supplier's sales representative was reporting many more personal calls to our company than were actually being made. The supplier's president was amazed at the information we were able to provide: dates of visits, locations, people visited, topics covered, etc. Without this backup, our complaints would have been meaningless. The sales representative in question would have been able to pass poor performance off as another company that was not giving the product enough attention.

It is not uncommon for a supplier to request that your regional managers and/or all of your upper management be present during a supplier "challenge." During one such meeting the supplier's president, marketing vice-president, and manufacturing manager came to the meeting and reviewed every point of their evaluation. The president wanted his marketing and manufacturing leaders to hear the explanations first-hand from our sales managers. Why? He wanted to get the information from those closest to the end user. Within two years, this supplier's performance went from one of our poorest performers to one of our best supplier partners.

CASE EXAMPLE

A supplier gave us a list of our criteria along with his own estimation of how his company should have been graded.

Supplier's comments on grading in quality. We are very proud of our skilled workmanship and the top-notch material content of our product. We experienced only one percent return of product during this past year. We feel that we should have received an above-average grade on product quality. Your grade of 5 in the quality parameter is unjustified.

Evaluation team's response to the supplier's grade in quality. During the evaluation year, we experienced a 2-to-3 percent return of your product. However, your warranty procedures are unreasonable and make the return of your product very costly. The cost of freight and your repair and return policy make the return of all your products impractical.

Our customers will not wait to get a repaired product back from you; therefore, we replace your faulty products to satisfy our customers. When we receive repaired products back from you, we cannot sell them as new products, so we lose again because we have to reduce sale prices for used products.

We are not able to obtain a premium price for your product because our market area perceives that your product has an average quality/price ratio. Therefore, we have graded your product to be of average quality.

Supplier's comments on grading for sales assistance. Our company has two sales representatives who cover the territory in which you are located. Their reports indicate that they visit your branch locations on a regular basis. We also provide literature concerning our product. Our product training is the best in our industry. Therefore, we feel the grade of 4 in this parameter is far too low.

Evaluation team's response to supplier's comments on sales assistance. Our records are compiled from the Supplier Representative and Independent Sales Representative Sign-in Logs. By audit, we find that the total number of sales calls made by both your representatives during the entire evaluation year was 43. Further analysis shows that they only visited 17 of 42 sales locations during this same time frame. According to our grading standards, both of your representatives qualify for 1 of the 4 possible points for frequency and coverage of supplier visits.

The quality of sales calls did not receive any points for the following reasons:

- Catalogs were not updated.
- Product fliers were not distributed.
- Representatives did not make joint sales calls.

Product training was not conducted at any of our sales locations, nor was it offered by either of your representatives.

Your points were given as follows:

- 1 point for having a toll-free telephone number

- 1 point for advertising and product literature
- 1 point for the effectiveness of your internal order entry group.

Supplier's response to performance grading for lead-time predictability. Our material control department indicates that we make shipments 90% to 95% complete within our stated lead time. You gave a grade of 6 in this parameter. We expected a grade of 8 or 9.

Evaluation team's response to supplier's performance grade for lead-time predictability. The grade awarded you in this area is a weighted average of all your shipments against an open order until it is 100% complete. By audit, we found the initial fill rate on shipments was between 80% and 85%. The extended shipments to complete these orders varied from two weeks to six weeks beyond your stated lead time.

Our grade is based on quantity delivered divided by quantity ordered, which is extended for the number of days late. Your performance in this area indicates to us that you are unable to estimate your lead time correctly. We will be happy to provide our receipt report, which shows the quantity received and date received by specific purchase order number.

The management of this supplier was astounded by the detail of our replies to its challenges. The supplier was forced to realize that its self-image was not in line with the image of its customers. This supplier began to take an active part in correcting problem areas and became one of our quality partners.

One more time: The frank exchange of factual information between partners will cause change that completely eliminates problem areas.

We as individuals, companies, and as a nation have rested too long on past accomplishments. It is not what we have done, it is what we are doing that counts. Progress and the competitive edge come from striving for excellence in every phase of our businesses. We must work on the inexhaustible edge of creativity—always looking for a better way.

How many times has someone in your company's sales department said, "If we only knew what our customers wanted, we could give them great service." Well, in this case you are the customer, and you are telling your suppliers, loud and clear, exactly what is important to you and your company. You are providing an invaluable service for your suppliers by providing standards of performance through your supplier evaluation and selection process and monitoring their performance.

RECOGNIZING TOP SUPPLIER AND TOP REPRESENTATIVE PERFORMANCE

It is important to recognize your top suppliers and top supplier representative or independent sales representative each year. There are several effective methods for doing this:

Visual awards. A plaque or certificate stating the accomplishment of your top supplier of the year is very effective. You can also list the supplier on a supplier award plaque where everyone can see it. A visual award of this type can also be used for the top supplier representative or independent sales representative.

Certificates of achievement. You might want to have certificates of achievement prepared for your top suppliers and representatives.

Awards dinner. Plan an annual awards dinner and invite your top suppliers and reps to be your guests. You might also want to include their company president on your guest list. By doing so, it helps make the awards more meaningful and valuable to the recipients. This is an ideal way of saying "thank you" and an ideal time to present awards in recognition of outstanding performance.

Internal newsletters. The president of your company can send a newsletter to all company personnel and your suppliers announcing the awards that were earned.

Initiate news releases in the most prominent trade journal in your market area about supplier awards.

You might want to include an extra special "thank you." During the fourth year of our pilot program we decided to say "thank you" in a more tangible way. The suppliers that ranked among our top 10 performers were responsible for supplying the biggest portion of our profits during each evaluation year. A top 10 supplier trip, with all expenses paid by us, was started. The president of each of the top ten supplier companies could take the trip or could designate another person to go instead.

Each year we took 10 suppliers and four of our company's management, including our company president, on the appreciation trip. The trips ranged from going to Las Vegas to float fishing for rainbow trout in northwest Arkansas. Our suppliers looked forward to the trip each year and were proud to be invited. This was our way of saying a sincere "thank you" to a special group of partners who had worked extremely hard to make our business and

Figure 12-4: Letter of Appreciation

E. I. DU PONT DE NEMOURS & COMPANY
INCORPORATED
FREON® PRODUCTS DIVISION
WILMINGTON, DELAWARE 19898

ADDRESS REPLY TO
2001 KIRBY DR., SUITE 812
HOUSTON, TEXAS 77019
TELEPHONE 521-9271
AREA CODE 713

May 5, 1984

Obie Ford
P.O. Box 1636
Houston, Texas 77001

Dear Obie:

Your Supplier Evaluation and Selection Program has been highly regarded by DuPont for several years. The partnerships developed between our companies as a result of this program are very effective, meaningful and profitable for both!

DuPont knows the performance you expect of them as a supplier and their management measures their representatives by the standards you have set. It is refreshing to know what is expected by our customers, and even more satisfying to experience the cooperation and appreciation we get from you and your company in our business transactions.

The personal rewards of being part of your program are numerous. The disciplines I have established as a result of your company's yearly performance evaluations have helped me establish stronger business relationships with companies throughout my sales district.

I appreciate being part of your program. The awards for being part of your top 10 suppliers is an extra plus for achieving performance excellence to your set standards. Thanks for the appreciation trip this year. The fishing and fellowship was outstanding! Striving for performance excellence really does pay!

Yours truly,

Aubrey Fulford

Aubrey Fulford
Senior Marketing Manager
E.I. DuPont DE Nemours & Co.

AF/srm

theirs more profitable. The total expense of these yearly trips was less than 0.1% of the profit generated by participating suppliers.

The final reward is expressed in a letter from Aubrey Fulford, who was Senior Marketing Manager for E.I. du Pont de Nemours & Co., who was among our top ten suppliers during the pilot program. Mr. Fulford's letter (Figure 12-4) is an example of what can happen when two companies commit themselves to achieving performance excellence through successful partnering.

The initial investment made to develop better supplier/customer/manufacturer/distributor/end user relationships through the implementation of a supplier evaluation and selection program has and will continue to result in monumental paybacks—external as well as internal:

- Employees find a new sense of commitment to excellence when they see management's sincerity in making a Supplier Evaluation and Selection Program work.
- Internal tasks become easier as suppliers solve problems that tend to become time hogs.
- Employees take new pride in their organizations as they realize their input is important and plays a major part in effecting change.
- The changes that occur are lasting. The combination of internal and external corrections eliminates problems.
- Innovation surges. More time will be spent in looking for better methods. Instead of having to take care of the same old problems, new ideas will be discovered.
- Sales will increase as sales personnel gain more confidence in suppliers. Sales staff will become more knowledgeable, better trained, and more committed to customer service.
- Profits will increase. The double whammy will take place—reduced expenses and increased sales will have a positive effect on profits for both partners.
- Your company will attract quality suppliers. Everyone wants to work with a winner—a top quality distributor. The reputation built through a Supplier Evaluation and Selection Program will permeate the supplier market that sells the product.
- Customer service will improve. The time now spent on problem solving will be allocated to identifying and providing quality customer services. Customer perception of your company will be a quality image.

Many companies that were once thought to be invincible are now dead—change passed them by. Be innovative. Reach out and meet the challenge for performance excellence through controlled, continuous, constructive change!

APPENDIX

SUPPLIER PERFORMANCE MEASUREMENT STANDARDS

Supplier performance measurement standards are set for 10 criteria. These criteria are ranked in order of importance, weighted in relation to each other, and grading standards set accordingly.

The following grading scale is used:

GRADING SCALE
0—Very Poor 5—Average 10—Excellent

Suppliers can be awarded extra points for added performance or they can have points deducted from their grades when performance is below expectations.

ADDITIONS (+): Additions are additional points a supplier can earn. These points are added to the midpoint value of 5.

DEDUCTIONS(–): Deductions are points subtracted from a supplier's earned points. These points are subtracted from the midpoint value of 5.

Explanations of each criterion with the associated point values are given as follows:

Grading Standards for Product Quality—Distribution
(This is a parameter using subjective measurement.)

	Point Value
The supplier's product is the acknowledged industry leader in quality and price.	10
The supplier's product has a competitive advantage because of customers' perception of its quality. As a result, it can command higher prices in the marketplace.	6–9
Supplier's products are average in quality and price does not add or detract in the supplier's market competitiveness.	5
The supplier's product has below-average quality and pricing and cannot compete in quality and pricing issues.	0–4

Grading Standards for Product Quality—Manufacturing
(This is a parameter using objective measurement.)

The supplier does not have a record of material or service failures. The material or service supplied is always correct.	10
The supplier's material meets or exceeds specifications. However, rejections have occurred during the past year.	

Material Rejection Rate:

< .005%>	9
< .010%>	8
< .0125%>	7
< .015%>	6
< .020%>	5
< .025%>	4
< .03%>	3

Grading Standards for Sales Aids—Distribution
(A parameter using objective measurement.)

Supplier advertising is done on a local and/or national level.	1

Product training sessions are initiated and supported by the supplier.	1
Supplier promotions are easy to administer and effective.	1
Toll-free telephone and fax numbers are made available by the supplier for sales and technical assistance.	1
The supplier rep gives quality assistance to purchasing.	1

Grading Standards for Production Aids—Manufacturing

The rep must make _______ sales calls to the plant location during the year being evaluated to obtain points. This includes visits to production, engineering, material, control, and management.	1
This grade measures the quality and amount of assistance a supplier rep is willing to give to managers.	1
Points are awarded on the basis of training sessions initiated and conducted by the supplier.	2
This evaluates the availability of engineering information from the supplier. The supplier works closely with engineering and material control to insure correct usage of material or services.	2
This grade indicates the availability of toll-free telephone and fax numbers for use by engineering, purchasing, production, and material control.	2

Grading Standards for Supplier and Independent Sales Representatives

This reflects the quality and amount of assistance a supplier's rep is willing to give to distribution's purchasing department and branches.	1
The supplier rep makes at least ____ sales calls to all of distribution's branches.	1–2
How well does the rep perform his duties of product representation?	1–2
Supplier reps have visited 90% of distribution's branches during the past year.	1

Grading Standards for Product Pricing

The supplier is the pricing leader in its industry with the lowest-priced product.	6
The supplier's product price is competitive. Pricing is in line with the pricing of the majority of competitors.	5
The supplier's product is not competitively priced.	0–4

Additions (+)

The supplier initiates price competition and is always the first to adjust pricing to stimulate sales.	+ 1
Product pricing literature is correct and is distributed to purchasing in a timely manner.	+ 1
Volume price breaks are offered by the supplier. Blanket purchase orders are used, and special quotations are furnished.	+ 1
The supplier's product pricing has been consistent during the last twelve months.	+ 1

Deductions (–)

The supplier extends its best pricing through preseason programs.	– 1
When the supplier increases product prices, notices of these increases are always late.	– 1
The supplier cannot or will not supply justification for price increases.	- 1

Grading Standards for Lead-Time Predictability

Grading lead-time predictability is done by calculating the percentage of orders you delivered to us on time using your own stated lead time as a guide for measurement.

Grading Standards for Back Orders/Overshipments

Grading for back orders and overshipments is done by taking the yearly total of orders placed and computing what percent of the total was overshipped or back ordered.

% of Back Orders/Overshipments

0% (every order received from a supplier was shipped complete)	10
10%	9
20%	8
30%	7
40%	6
50%	5
60%	4
70%	3
80%	2
90%	1
100% (every order received from a supplier had shipping problems)	0

Grading Standards for Inventory Rebalancing (Return Policies)

Supplier allows unconditional return of inventory items any time.	10
Inventory can be returned to the supplier with authorization and includes a 15% restocking charge.	5

Additions (+)

Restocking Charge 10%.	+ 1
No restocking charge	+ 2
Authorized return of inventory is allowed with no additional charge.	+ 2
Assists with identification of slow-moving items for return.	+ 2

Grading Standards for Warranty Procedures

Defective products can be replaced over the counter and credit issued to the distributor without having to return warranty items to the supplier.	10
A one-year, limited-parts warranty with defective parts return is an average warranty.	5
The supplier does not have a warranty policy.	0

Additions (+)

The supplier has a stated warranty policy printed in product literature.	+ 1
Defective parts do not have to be returned to the manufacturer.	+ 1
Replacement of defective products is repair and return or credit given, based on the customer's request.	+ 1
Over-the-counter replacement of a defective product is allowed by the supplier.	+ 1
Over-the-counter replacement of a defective product is allowed by the supplier, and the defective product does not have to be returned.	+ 1

Deductions (–)

The supplier's product literature does not contain a written statement of product warranty.	– 1
The supplier refuses to comply with his stated warranty policy.	- 3

Grading Standards for Payment Terms (billing policies)

5% tenth Prox. net 30 or 180 days net	10
4% tenth Prox. net 30 or 150 days net	9
3% tenth Prox. net 30 or 120 days net	8
2% tenth Prox. net 30 or 90 days net	7
1% tenth Prox. net 30 or 60 days net	6
2% ten days net 30	5
1% ten days net 30	4
Net 60 days	3
Net 45 days	2
Net 30 days	1
Less than 30 days net	0

Grading Standards for Packaging/Labeling
Packaging—Master Cartons

Master cartons are well marked and give information for product identification and handling instructions.	1
Master cartons give adequate product protection.	1

Product quantities in each master carton are consistent.	1

Packaging—Individual Cartons

Individual cartons give adequate product protection.	1
Product quantities in individual cartons are consistent.	1

Labeling

Master carton labels identify contents and are easy to read.	1
Individual carton labels identify contents and are easy to read.	1
Bar coding is used on master and individual cartons and labels.	1
Products are palletized by the supplier for shipment.	1
The supplier uses shrink-wrapping for better product protection.	1

Grading Standards for Emergency Services

The supplier always supplies products and correct information when you have to handle an emergency situation for a customer.	10
An emergency service statement is written in the supplier's product literature.	5
The supplier refuses to provide emergency services.	0

Additions (+)

Complexity and Range of Product Offerings:	
Commodity Products	+ 1
Complex Products	+ 2
Effectiveness of the supplier's emergency service policy: (reasonable charges, minimum quantities waived, etc.)	+ 1
Supplier's performance complies to its stated policy:	
95% to 100% performance	+ 2
90% to 95% performance	+ 1

Deductions (–)

The supplier's emergency service charges are unreasonable and discourage the use of emergency services.	– 1
The supplier does not comply to its written emergency service statements and cannot perform to a 90% level of completion of emergency needs.	–1

INDEX

A

B

C

D

QR

S